BELOW
THE HORIZON

MIKE DUGAN

For my mom

Check out the *Below the Horizon* fan page on Facebook for more photos and a schedule of events.

Special thanks to Nicole Musgrave and Chris Finn for their numerous photos…and everything else.

The Med

Panama
Canal

Aden

Bab-el-
Mandeb

Phuket

Maldives

Sri
Lanka

South
China
Sea

Indian
Ocean

Bali

Kupang

Torres Strait

North
Pacific

Coral Sea

Figi

Cairns

New
Caledonia

Tonga

Brisbane

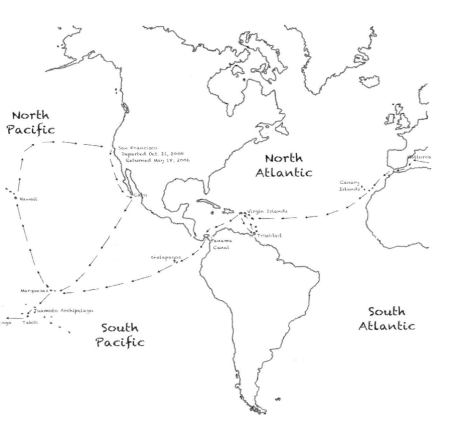

North
Pacific

North
Atlantic

Mallorca

San Francisco
Departed Oct. 21, 2000
Returned May 18, 2006

Canary
Islands

Hawaii

Cabo

Virgin Islands

Trinidad

Panama
Canal

Galapagos

Marquesas

Tuamoto Archipelago

South
Atlantic

nga   Tahiti

South
Pacific

First Passage

I parted the rats' nest of hastily installed wiring entangling the ten-disc changer and slipped in the *Star Wars* sound track as the Golden Gate Bridge passed overhead and we abandoned the protected waters of the San Francisco Bay, surrendering ourselves to the unbound expanse of turbulent blue water and the ancient voices of our salty kinsmen lost in the wind. We left behind all that we knew and submitted our fate to the unknown, to the lair of sperm whales, great white sharks, dolphins, giant squid, massive schools of tuna, pirates, dreamers, hurricanes, tsunamis, and those who wouldn't be yoked to an element that didn't undulate with the energy that coursed through it; to all that was the Pacific and to all that lay beyond.

A grand undertaking necessitated a grand score. I cranked up the volume and as the first notes erupted from the cockpit speakers Matt grinned and tilted his head back assuming a regal posture. I could hear, "Use the force Luke," going through his head as he veered off course. He appreciated theatrics. My girlfriend Amanda was amused but, possessed of a more pragmatic inclination, couldn't keep her head from shaking or her eyes from rolling. The word 'clowns' surely rested on the tip of her tongue.

I'd glanced at the weather report calling for 20 plus knots of wind, but October 21st was our departure date. We'd announced it at the bon voyage party. It was written on the calendar. We were going. The weather report was little more than academic.

We were too awed by our undertaking to be mindful of the actual conditions around us. We were sailing around the world after all; one mile down, only 29,999 to go.

Some joker sailing next to us, standing behind an enormous steering wheel and sporting some fruity looking gloves, had already reefed (shortened) his mainsail. "Clearly trying to overcompensate with that gargantuan wheel," I chastised; reveling in my delusion. "Yeah, but he blows it with those cheesy gloves and that reef in his main… like driving a Ferrari the speed limit," Matt added.

A half mile out of the bay the wind kicked up to 20 plus knots and we decided that reefing the main might not be such a bad idea. We'd never actually preformed the maneuver but I thought I had a pretty good idea of how it should go. It was perfectly simple in theory. Step one: release the main halyard allowing the mainsail to come down to the level of the first reef. A reef is a line of holes in the sail used to secure it to the boom which makes the whole sail essentially smaller. Step one went pretty much as planned, though with considerably more flapping than I'd imagined. After step one nothing went as planned. Attempting to tie the sail to the boom in 25 knot winds, I felt like I'd been charged with the birthing of Rodeo and Wrestling's bastard child. My co-captain Matt and I took turns attempting to break the beast while Amanda looked on skeptically from the cockpit. Amanda seemed calm enough in the brief time I took to consider her existence but she must have been questioning our skills and possibly wishing she was with the 'huge wheel dude.'

2

FIRST PASSAGE

After what seemed like an hour, but was probably more like 15 minutes, Matt and I were able to get the sail sort-of tied to the boom. "Perfect," we chanted, as we did at the end of any task that fell either slightly, or considerably, short of our projected ideal; our frequent salute to Ed Wood, the infamous movie maker celebrated more for his mistakes than his successes.

After we regained our composure, and wondered in silence if it was going to be like that every time, we proceeded to reef the jib. Fortunately it was a much easier task as our beloved sloop Hanuman was equipped with a roller furling system which allowed the jib to be spooled around the forestay (a metal cable extending from the bow to the top of the mast) by simply pulling on one line and releasing another. We'd actually executed the procedure several times prior to leaving so the results of the undertaking, to our relief, went pretty much as anticipated. I extended a cautious yet self-satisfied grin and nod in Amanda's direction which was received with crossed arms and a single raised eyebrow. She ventured a glance back at the protected waters of the Bay and at 'huge wheel dude.' "Looks like he's turning around," she commented wistfully. "Probably got his gloves wet," Matt rebuffed, though with little conviction.

We knew little of balancing the sails to maximize speed and ease of steering so we eventually rolled in the entirety of the jib, only because it was the easier of the two sails to handle, hoping to reduce the boats heeling. We were left with just the sadly reefed main. We still had plenty of speed but the center of effort was much further aft than ideal, making the boat a bitch to steer. At the time I thought difficult steering might just be the norm in such conditions. While conceiving the trip I had pictured myself wrestling the wheel, hurling epithets at Poseidon as he flung wave after wave over me and my stalwart vessel.

BELOW THE HORIZON

As we rounded Point Lobos and headed south we no longer received any protection from land and were exposed to the full extent of the ocean swells. The wind speed also increased another ten knots. Executing an age-old fishermen's technique we eased out the boom in an attempt to spill off as much of the wind as possible. We sailed along white knuckled in that condition for a couple of hours until the wind angle changed a few degrees bringing us from a broad reach to a run; meaning the wind was now coming from directly behind us. It also got another 5 knots stronger. Steering became even more of a struggle. Hanuman accelerated down each passing swell and wanted to round up into the wind when the swell pushed her stern the least bit sideways. It took considerable force on the wheel to get her going down wind again and once she was, all of the pressure on the helm (wheel) would vanish and we had to be very careful not to jibe.

Jibing, when not prepared to do so, can be disastrous. Jibing is when the stern of the boat moves through a following wind, back-winding the sail and forcing the boom and sail across the centerline of the boat to the opposite side. Unless carefully executed, in all but the lightest conditions, this happens with a terrifying crash. The further the boom is out the further it flies across the boat and the more jarringly it snaps into place on the other side. Ours was all the way out. Typically cruising boats rig a preventer line to the boom to prevent such a catastrophe. Unfortunately the so-called preventer line was only a concept floating around in my head.

There was a sinking weightless feeling just before it happened. "FUCK," went through my head as I threw the wheel over hoping to prevent the inevitable jibe. Then "WHAM" as the sail and boom flew overhead crashing to the other side. "Fuuuuuck," I announced audibly and looked up with relief to see the mast and all of the rigging still in place. "Won't let that happen again," I thought. However, in my moment of pre-jibe over compensation, I'd cranked the wheel all the way over to one side leaving myself poorly prepared to take on our new heading. "WHAM!" "Fuck me, not again!"

Matt struggled up from his bunk to see if we were still in one piece, puking as he did so. The period of time between being in the bunk sucking your thumb with your eyes clamped shut wishing to be returned to the womb and being on deck with a view of the horizon can wreak havoc on the unaccustomed bowels.

We decided it would be a good time to actualize the preventer concept. I stayed at the helm as Matt attempted to tie a line from the boom to the toe rail. As he did so I allowed myself to become absorbed in his task which diverted my attention from steering and, "WHAM!" The boom flew across the boat yet again narrowly missing Matt's head but pinning him between the cabin top and the preventer line he was in the midst of rigging. "Sorry... my bad." I thought he was rather congenial about the whole thing considering the poor timing of my fuck-up. We were in survival mode and didn't have energy to spare assigning blame. Plus, we had much more pressing problems on our hands.

This time all of the rigging wasn't in place. The topping lift, a cable extending from the end of the boom to the top of the mast, had parted with the boom and was flailing around like a garden hose in a cartoon. Before trying to get the topping lift under control we decided to take the main down, raise the stay sail (a small, easily managed sail just forward of the mast) and turn on the engine.

The topping lift's sole purpose is to hold the boom up when the main sail is taken down. So, as far as breaking things goes, it could have been much worse. Nevertheless, when we went to take the main down there was nothing holding up the boom so a whole mess of flailing sail and boom came thundering down on deck. We tackled it and lashed it down as best we could. Fortunately Big Red, the engine, fired right up and we were able to keep the bow pointed towards Santa Cruz, our destination.

I didn't take the engine for granted. There were a number of things on the 'to do before we leave list' regarding the engine which we hadn't done. My main concern was that I hadn't gotten around to hooking up the engine gauges so we wouldn't get any warning before it over heated, lost oil pressure, threw a belt, stopped charging the batteries, or ran out of fuel; except for maybe some smoke and a death rattle. Prior to disembarking, we'd only run the engine for a couple of hours at a time. Also, before I purchased the boat, she'd been sitting for many years; possibly decades. Diesel loving bacteria's crap and corpses tend to accumulate in the bottom of diesel tanks that have been sitting in the tranquil confines of a marina for an extended time. The crap and corpses lie dormant at the bottom of the tank until jostled by heavy seas. Heavy seas we were in, and while I had just changed the fuel filters, a tank full of mung could easily clog them.

The topping lift, though partially tangled in the rigging, continued to flail violently. Matt decided to go after it. He crawled forward to the shrouds (the cables running from the side of the boat to the mast head) to where the end of the topping lift was whipping around. He clung to the shrouds and stood upright but was still far from being able to grab the arcing topping lift so he stepped up on the lifeline and extended his free hand skyward, dangling precariously between boat and sea, grasping at the firmament. His finger tips almost grazed the end of the topping lift when it swung downward; almost, but not quite. Even if he could've grabbed it I could see that he wouldn't be able to do anything with it since he was so stretched out and it was tangled beyond hope in the rigging. In the movie version, Matt would have just barely grabbed the wire, possible swung out over the water, detangled it, and secured it smartly to the deck with a little wrist and a lot of flourish. In the real life version it just wasn't happening. We decided the topping lift was just fine where it was. By then it had become so tangled that it wasn't whipping around nearly as much anyhow. "Perfect!" Matt exclaimed crawling back to the cockpit. I nodded in agreement.

I'd become thoroughly drenched by all of the waves crashing over us. I realized I was shivering and went below to put on some rain gear.

Matt and I had spent a year tearing the entire deck off the boat and replacing it. We had no idea the project would take so long. We'd guesstimated we could whip it out in a couple of months. Anxious to be on our way, we figured that with the deck completed and Hanuman water tight, more or less, we were ready to take on the world. We could finish the interior as we went. "Interior inshmerior," we scoffed, jamming all of our crap in the areas where we were going to build some cabinetry in the future.

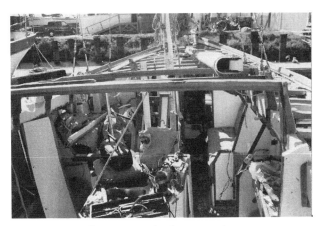

Hanuman under deconstruction

7

Climbing down the ladder, I could barely find a piece of uncovered floor on which to step. Everything had seemed well wedged in when we'd departed but I could see that absolutely nothing remained where we'd put it. It was all sliding from one side of the boat to the other with every passing swell. It wasn't just clothes either. Cookware, knives, all of the charts that were formerly on the chart table, the life raft, a Rubik's Cube, the half full keg of beer left over from the bon voyage party which I'd declined to return to my former place of employment, some tattered porn that an old boat yard salt insisted we couldn't go to sea without, a sack of rice, two generic cans labeled 'pork' we'd gotten from our local St. Vincent De Paul, and a milieu of other formless items were stewing at my feet. Wading forward to the head in search of my rain gear I found the rest of the boat to be just as bad. The hundred or so books we'd put in the area where proper book shelves were to be built had all dove straight on to the floor where they mingled with the screw drivers, hammer, wrenches, pliers, spare engine belts, cotter pins, clevis pins, rusty washers and screws that had spilled from the tool box that was dangling by a rope that was supposed to be holding it in place. I had to kick a few things out of the way to open the door to the head where I extricated my rain gear from the toilet.

I'd planned on having a good look at the chart and plotting our position but after struggling into my rain gear I was ready to hurl and more than content to see the little carrot on the GPS representing Hanuman pointing in the general direction of Santa Cruz. Struggling up the ladder I felt my stomach climb up into my throat and I dove towards the edge of the boat and proceeded to puke…right into the wind. But I couldn't have cared less about the puke dribbling down my chin, or on Matt, and continued heaving until I got to bile. Then I just laid down in the cockpit with my head on a pile of wet lines and let my mind go perfectly blank.

FIRST PASSAGE

Eventually the churning brown sea faded to black as the sun deserted us. It was a clear but moonless night. The stars' silhouetting the coastal range was orienting and almost comforting.

Amanda had gone below hours prior, after witnessing the reefing debacle, and hadn't been seen since. She had a good hibernation instinct and I was glad of it since I was struggling just to take care of myself.

Matt and I started alternating steering shifts, diving into our bunks with most of our rain gear still on when we were relieved. We didn't have any set shifts. We steered until we were completely miserable and then gave two knocks on the cockpit seat above the other's head.

The knock system became the standard that lasted a good three quarters of the way around the world. Two knocks meant, 'make your way leisurely, but not too leisurely, to the cockpit.' Three knocks meant, 'stop fantasizing about food, women, and dry land, and get your ass up here pronto, and be ready to do something.'

At about 2 am the little carrot representing Hanuman started getting close to Santa Cruz and we pointed the bow towards land. Various lights materialized out of the darkness as we approached. We were familiar with basic navigation lights but frustratingly they merged with the land lights behind them. Stoplights can be especially confusing as they go from red to green; the same colors as channel markers. Entering an unfamiliar port at night is a risky, possibly foolish, maneuver. Arrival time hadn't seemed like a major concern when I was blasting the Star Wars sound track. The moon still hadn't risen and it was dark. The deeper we got into the bay the more nervous we became.

The wind still raged but the swells mellowed as we penetrated deeper into the bay. Amanda poked her head up to check the status. She wanted to come into the cockpit and have a look around but the third harness was somewhere in the molten mound of mayhem at the base of the ladder and I was fearful that she might take a tumble overboard. Despite my lack of sailing experience I had spent some time on fishing boats in the Bering Sea and knew the difficulty involved in finding someone in a cold black churning ocean. She hadn't been dead set on coming in the first place. I felt it would be a shame to lose her on the first passage.

Amongst all of the city lights we couldn't find the marina. "I guess we could try following him and hope he knows where he's going," I offered gingerly, pointing toward a nearby work boat. We felt a bit sheepish doing so but we figured he probably wouldn't run into anything. So with a 'here goes nothing' shrug we attempted to casually alter our course, hoping it might it appear as though we were headed that way all along. It quickly became apparent that he wasn't going toward Santa Cruz however, so we abandoned the idea and casually headed back the way we'd been going. As we got closer we were able to discern some lights that appeared to be channel markers and shortly after we spotted sailboat masts.

We closed in on the red and green channel markers until we could make them out clearly. We felt fairly confident in the markers but we could also just make out a beach to the right of the starboard marker which appeared to extend into the channel that we were headed for. The white froth of large breaking waves stood out in the darkness but the night robbed us of our depth perception making it difficult to determine how close they were. Waves appeared to be breaking across what we thought was the channel. I had visions of Hanuman lying on her side, beached, as sea and sand slowly buried her.

We got out the million candle power spot light and did a round of rock paper scissors to see who would steer and who would be on the bow with the light; best two out of three of course. I took the helm, Matt the spotlight, and we went for it; well, not quite. I chickened out the first time. The beach and the breaking waves just seemed so close. I threw the wheel over, doing a 180, and re-evaluated. "'Red right return'...right?" I said, verbalizing one of the most basic rules of navigation. "Right." The channel markers seemed perfectly clear but the breaking waves were hard to ignore. We eventually decided that we had to be looking at the channel so we braced for impact and went for it.

As the water got shallower the swells rose and we were almost surfing between the markers. We later heard stories of people bouncing off of the bottom when the swells were large enough and their draft deep enough. Fortunately, we coasted in without bouncing and the details of the harbor unveiled themselves under the marina lights. We tied up to the first thing we could find. The stillness was incredible. We'd made it.

After the adrenaline wore off, the fatigue and hunger set in. After passing around a cold can of refried beans topped with some Pace Picante sauce we passed out to the gentle squeak of the dock lines.

The morning light opened our eyes to the disaster area Hanuman had become. We had to wade through the knee high pile of crap just to move around down below. On deck wasn't much better. The boom half filled the cockpit with the hastily wadded up main exploding out in all directions. Lines snaked across the deck. The topping lift hung limply from the spreaders. I surveyed the scene with dazed detachment after having only slept for a few hours. I was so content to be tied safely and securely to a dock that I was unconcerned by Hanuman's chaotic condition as long as she was still floating. I surveyed everything through a lens of satisfied indifference. I just wanted to walk carelessly around on land. Normally I have list making tendencies, but despite the situation practically demanding a list, I was opposed to even the thought of it.

By mid day the daze had worn off. Matt, Amanda, and I convened and we drafted a list. Before the list was made however, we adopted a new philosophy. Sailing around the world had gone from a nebulous fantasmic dream to a haunting reality. After the first passage, I could see through the illusion that I'd created into a new paradigm. Sailing around the world was an endeavor of such complexity that trying to sum it up as one thing suddenly seemed absurd. We needed to take smaller bites and chew them well before swallowing. We found ourselves just concentrating on the next passage and the next port. I hadn't been shaken enough to kill the dream but a veil was lifted, opening my eyes to a new reality.

Before leaving San Francisco we'd signed up for the Baja Ha, a cruisers rally that went from San Diego to Cabo San Lucas, Mexico. We'd written out a schedule that had us arriving in San Diego the day before the rally began. "All in favor of forgetting about the rally and taking our sweet time say aye." "Aye…Aye…Aye." "It would have been just hanging out with bunch of old people in crowded anchorages anyhow." "Motion 'sour grapes,' passed."

Down the California Coast

A week in Santa Cruz rolled gently by with a mixture of boat work, wound lickin,' and land lubbin'. Our spirits were bolstered by a local sailor who said, "It was really blowin' out there. You guys came in last night!?" We'd had our asses kicked however, and weren't looking to repeat the experience, so we became intimately familiar with the computer generated voice of the marine weatherman on the VHF radio as we waited for an agreeable forecast.

After checking the most important stuff off of our 'to do before we leave' list and securing a favorable weather window we gingerly uncleated our dock lines and headed south towards Monterey, a comfortable 20ish miles away. The passage was delightfully uneventful. We even dragged a fishing line, though caught nothing.

Matt called the Monterey Bay Harbor Master with VHF radio to reserve a berth and we snaked our way through the harbor to our slip. Maneuvering through the marina put me on edge. Hanuman was big and heavy with no brakes and didn't exactly turn on a dime. It's easy to do a lot of damage in a short period of time and, of course, I didn't have any insurance. There was considerable surge in the marina and the dock heaved with the swell, but after finding our slip we slid in without incident completing our second passage.

Staying in harbors wasn't cheap. We'd been spending twenty bucks a day in Santa Cruz and were going to be spending the same in Monterey. Our budgeting for the trip included a lot of 'livin' off the sea.' I'd managed to rack up about five thousand bucks of dept on my credit card before even leaving. I started the 'round the world voyage' with about six hundred in cash. We hadn't banked on spending so much money on slip fees. The idea was to anchor out and not pay anything. Unfortunately our anchoring experience was limited. Once again, I had a firm grasp on the concept but the one time we'd anchored had been disastrous.

It was our second or third time taking the boat out in the SF Bay and after a full day of drinking, sailing, and weed smoking we decided to anchor just east of Angel Island. We'd seen other boats anchored there and figured it to be a good spot so we dropped the hook, fired up the barbie, unscrewed the 4 litter handle of Carlo Rossi, busted out the bong, and before long passed out amid chicken bones and empty bottles.

Shortly after my eyelids fell and my body went limp in the cockpit I heard someone on a passing boat yell at us to turn on our navigation lights. I scratched my head, "Why would I turn on my navigation lights when I'm at anchor?" I had the anchor light on. Actually it was a deck light, as the anchor light was on the fritz, but it illuminated the boat nicely and, I decided, got the point across well enough. I concluded that everything was copasetic and went back to sleep.

The next time I was awoken it was by a large spot light and a voice on a megaphone. "This is the US Coast Guard who is the captain onboard?" "I guess that's me," I thought. I had a quick look around to evaluate the evidence of our debauchery. Fortunately Amanda possessed a sense of moderation and before going to bed she'd tidied up a bit. I called down to make sure someone had stashed the bong and then responded to the Coast Guard. Probably sensing we might have the unpredictability of a wounded animal they kept their distance and mega phoned over, "has anyone onboard been drinking." Complete denial was out of the question. "Moderately," I responded. Despite the fact that I really had no concept of the word it came across sounding rather believable.

It was about three in the morning and my well conditioned liver and had taken care of most of the alcohol in my system. What was left was over ridden by the adrenaline brought on by the Coast Guard. I seemed to convince them that we were safe to approach so they came alongside Hanuman and informed us that we'd dragged anchor into a shipping lane. I took heart in their optimistic view but wondered if we hadn't actually anchored in the shipping lane or close enough so that when the tide changed we swung into it.

Hanuman was equipped with a hand crack windlass designed to winch up the anchor line. We employed it for the first time. The anchor line we were using was one that had come with the boat. At least we thought it was an anchor line. I quickly realized it was for probably for something else. It was way too thin and not of the right material. I also felt the anchor should've been coming up a lot easier and without creating so much tension in the line. It screamed under the pressure and suddenly looked old, tired, and determined to part. Fortunately the anchor eventually breached the surface and the Coast Guard, after giving us a fix-it ticket for not having a ships bell, was on their way.

I was tempted cut our losses, call it a night, and head home, but we decided to give anchoring another go a bit closer to land. We managed to make it through the night but the following morning was a disaster. The anchor must have grabbed onto something pretty solid. It got to the point where it wouldn't budge. Matt motored forward in an attempt to break it free, a method we'd read about.

Matt and I often had a very different idea of how things should be done. He was more the "go for it and sort out the details along the way," type of a guy. I preferred the, "let's visualize the entirety of the process before we get started," mindset. Our different approaches had often served us well while we were building the boat. He kept me from bogging down over analyzing a project and I keep him from painting himself into a corner. That said, I often got annoyed with his hastiness and lack of foresight. I felt he'd rashly thrown Big Red in gear and gunned it. "Whooooaaaaa," I shouted. "SNAP!" The anchor was gone and we were left with just a frayed polyester line dangling from the bow.

In addition to the memory of our last anchoring experience, the two anchorages we'd encountered thus far lacked the tranquil crystal clear water, where you can see your anchor and chain holding you safely in place 30 feet below, that we'd drooled over in the cruising magazines. The water was murky, brown, and anything but tranquil. The few boats we saw anchored were hobby horsing miserably. I was sick enough at sea and didn't relish the idea of puking at anchor as well. In addition the Harbor Master told us the anchorage was closed due to the rough conditions, making us feel a little better about taking the easy way.

We ended up spending more time in Monterey than we'd hoped to while waiting for a good weather forecast. The numbers reported on the marine forecast had a lot more meaning to us after we'd experienced some of the larger ones. We were content to wait for winds under 15 knots. We got to know the sea lions. I watched my little envelope of money under my mattress get thinner and thinner as we spent the small fortune of 20 bucks a day on slip fees.

Eventually we got the forecast were looking for and pointed the bow south for an overnight passage to Morro Bay. I puked during the night but not as violently as I had before. By late afternoon on the second day out we realized we weren't going to make it by nightfall so we pulled in to San Simeon to avoid another night arrival.

It was the first sunny day we'd experienced in a weeks and we starting to feel pretty good about ourselves and life in general. There weren't any other boats in the bay but there was one large mooring ball. We figured it probably hadn't been put there for us but it was Halloween and we'd planned on leaving Hanuman unattended for the night so we decided to borrow it. I had some friends in San Louis Obispo, knew we'd be 'going big,' and didn't want to worry about the boat. We dressed as castaways, which really didn't require too much modification of what we were wearing, rowed Sputnik, the dinghy, to shore, and hitch hiked into town.

Halloween kicked off a couple of weeks of all out debauchery. The first of November was a sunny day but we had to fight our way back to Hanuman through a thick mental fog. We didn't make it back until the afternoon but I wanted to make the short trip to Morrow Bay that day, concerned that the owner of the mooring might show up.

What was supposed to be a short trip took longer than we imagined so we, once again, entered an unfamiliar harbor in the dark. Since using an unoccupied mooring had worked out so well for us in the previous spot we decided to repeat the procedure. There really wasn't much room to anchor anyhow. We got kicked off in the morning but were able to find transient mooring in front of the yacht club. At 12 bucks a day, on the honor system, it was less than we had been paying in the marinas but still more than we wanted to spend. I still had my honor in tack at the time, however tenuously, so after a couple weeks we racked up a pretty good bill.

Matt decided to fly to the East Coast to visit a girl he'd started dating a couple of months before we'd left. He spent the last of his money doing so. Matt and logic weren't close friends. I was annoyed that he was leaving less than two weeks into the journey we'd spent a year preparing for, especially considering he obviously wouldn't have any money when he returned. Logic aside, I wasn't totally bummed to see him go. I had a lot of friends in the area so it wasn't a bad place to hang out. Amanda and I found a bar that had free food during happy hour so we waited all day to gorge ourselves on Buffalo wings and cocktail franks.

After a week Matt sent an e-mail saying that he had extended his 'vacation' and that we should "feel free to keep heading down the coast" and he would meet up with us. "Thanks!" I thought sarcastically. I decided against moving on. I wasn't quite comfortable handling the boat alone nor was I keen to have Amanda steering the boat by herself at night.

Matt eventually did return and, along with some additional crew, we were off. The guys we'd been hanging out with for the previous couple of weeks, Brandoni, Braden, Chris, and Paul, decided they wanted to come along, so we loaded up the boat with our six surf boards and whatever food and alcohol were left over from the party the night before and the seven of us headed south toward Point Conception.

Beam and cokes were being handed up the companion-way before we even got out of harbor. I declined. The ass kicking I'd been served on the first passage was still warm in my memory and I wasn't ready to compromise any of my faculties while at sea. Plus, I knew the scenario: everybody gets all giddy after a few drinks and proclaims they're going to stay up all night but are all passed out before midnight. Actually, everyone besides me was passed out before ten. A few drinks and the rhythmic rolling of the boat and they were like babies in a cradle. Except that they were all much bigger than babies so there were bodies everywhere. I couldn't even sit comfortably behind the wheel. The cockpit was a mass of flesh and blankets.

After putting in what I thought was more than a reasonable amount of time I called Matt up for his watch. He was reluctant to get out of bed sighting the numerous other potential helmsmen on board. A valid observation, however none of the interlopers had any sailing experience whatsoever which made me reluctant to hand Hanuman over to any of them. Land was close by and there were numerous boats in the vicinity. At night distances can be deceptive and I surely didn't want to wake up to the crunching of fiberglass as Hanuman rammed into some solid object. At least not so close to home. I deemed it more acceptable to go down in some far off port after getting a few miles under my belt. I insisted that Matt steer and he begrudgingly agreed.

Sunrise found me at the helm bleary eyed but happy. In my early sailing days I always found the rising of the sun to be an enormous relief. "Made it through the night!" I often consoled myself during stormy nights with the thought that no matter what happen to me the sun would still rise, if only to shine on my dead and bloated body. I'm not sure why this last thought was consoling, especially with the image of my naked lifeless fish chewed (I pictured tiny fish swimming out of my nose just below my peeled back eyelids) body firmly implanted in my head, but for some reason it was.

The wind dropped to almost nothing but Point Conception rose before us. I considered this a major pinnacle in our journey. We would be leaving the California Current and entering the Santa Barbara Channel. The water would be warmer, the seas calmer, and the women more scantily clad. Rounding the

Point I leaned over to check the water temp: pretty much the same, still cold. It was calm, but then it had been pretty calm on the other side. Amanda was wearing the same clothes as she had the day before.

The crew started coming to, dazed but with a pleasantly contented look on their faces, excited for what the day would bring. Matt decided he wanted to make coffee. He'd been working in a coffee shop before we left and had heisted a large bag of espresso beans on his last day.

We'd yet to transform the galley into an efficient cooking machine. The boat came with a gimbaled two burner stove and oven capable of swinging back and forth to compensate for the rolling motion of the ocean but we hadn't had the time or inclination to get it functioning. Instead I'd unearthed an old two burner Coleman stove from my mom's garage and strapped it on top of the gimbaled one. It didn't swing with the gimbaled stove as I'd hoped, since it was slightly too wide, but it got the job done, more or less. At least it had in port; we hadn't tested it at sea.

We didn't have a coffee grinder so Matt fished out the hammer and started smashing the whole beans on the cutting board. Needless to say beans went flying everywhere. I'd be cursing these beans, and Matt, for years to follow as I pulled them out every crevice Hanuman possessed but Matt could be rather sensitive to criticism and I didn't want to spoil the mood so I held my tongue. After pulverizing the beans he filled one of his socks with the crushed beans, tied a knot in the open end and threw it in the coffee pot. "Perfect." Perfect until it almost slid off the stove with the first gentle roll of the boat. The galley still needed some tweaking but a few Bungee cords placed just so and "voi la…coffee is served."

One reason the crew had swollen so dramatically was Coho Beach; a renowned surfing area with no road access. We dropped anchor mid day in an open bay that finally jived with the image developed while conceiving the trip. I'd reread the chapter on anchoring and was pleasantly surprised when it came off as planned. To confirm, I got out the mask and snorkel, jumped in the water, and inspected the results. The anchor wasn't set as deeply in the gravel as I'd hoped, but looked like it would hold.

The next couple of days were idyllic: surfing, spear fishing, eating and drinking. As pleasant as the anchorage was, however, the surf dropped off on day two and we quickly dusted the alcohol, including what was left of the keg of beer from the bon voyage party, so it was time to move on.

We got a late start on the passage to Santa Barbara and ended up arriving at night, naturally, but were escorted in by a pod of dolphins that left trails of glowing phosphorescence in their wake. The dolphins weren't visible in the darkness, only the illuminated phosphorescence excited around them. A million glowing specks of light shot through the water; conjuring a mirror image of shooting stars above. The moonless darkness made it easy to relax the eyes, blurring boundary between sky and sea, creating the sensation that we were hurtling through the cosmos.

We left behind our extra crew in Santa Barbara, well contented with their journey, and Matt, Amanda, and I continued down the coast stopping in Newport and in San Diego where we readied ourselves for Mexico.

As time passed Matt grew more and more despondent. Amanda and I returned to the boat one evening in San Diego to find him in the cockpit fermenting in his sadness. He barely said anything when we arrived with dinner for him. He just laid there making love to a box of wine and looking at slides of his girlfriend Jesse. I tried to talk to him but he would only respond with grunts. He'd been behaving in such a fashion since Santa Barbara and it had begun to wear on my nerves. "This is pathetic!" I finally said, unable to conceal my disgust with the small negative replies he made whenever I tried to lighten the mood. "We've been slaving to make this trip happen for over a year and all you can do is wallow in self pity. We ate at the Saint Vincent De Paul [a free cafeteria] with all of the homeless people just to save enough money," I continued. In fact we were still eating Saint V's rice and canned pork products we'd hoarded. "I got hit in the balls when I got in the way of that homeless fight. …the balls man!"

Matt wasn't totally pleased with me calling him pathetic but morale did seem to improve afterward. Though it may have been because Jesse said she would be meeting us in Cabo.

Cruising Mexico

After getting our shit together we continued south to Ensenada, Mexico. The out flow of money didn't stop, as we'd hoped. There wasn't space to anchor so we tied up to a rickety old dock. It wasn't much cheaper than in the US, just a whole lot shabbier. There were also fees to check in with the Port Captain, Immigration, and Customs. This was all in addition to the hefty fee we had to pay in San Diego for a Mexican fishing license. Amanda and I were paying all of the fees. This would have been okay with me had Matt simply run out of money on our trip. However, he chose to spend the last of his dough flying to see Jesse and upon his return left me with no choice but to foot the bill for everything.

I could read Matt's mind. In his head he was falling deeply in love. He could easily be more in love with someone he didn't know well or who wasn't around. It's easier to idolize someone who doesn't encumber you with the day to day normality's of living. Matt and Jesse actually seemed to fight a lot in the time I'd spent around them.

Matt probably figured he simply wouldn't spend any money when he got back from visiting Jesse. We'd be in

Mexico before long and living off of the sea. We were also planning on finding work in Cabo, where we would obviously be making a fortune because everybody did in Mexico.

Food wasn't nearly as cheap as we'd hoped in Mexico either. I'd pictured laying down a dollar and being stuffed and drunk by the time it was gone. That just wasn't the case. We heard it was cheaper on the mainland than it was on the Baja Peninsula, where we were. "Perfect!"

We weren't in Ensenada long. It was dry and dusty and we were hoping for greener pastures further south. Things went well for a while as we continued down the coast. Matt seemed to be in a better mood and enjoying the trip. Amanda had been granted full crew status so we split the steering three ways allowing Matt and I more sleep at night. We also rigged up the Auto Helm 3000 auto pilot. The device steered the boat perfectly while sailing in light winds and motoring but as soon as the wind picked up a little, putting more pressure on the helm, the belt that attached the device to the wheel slipped and the control mechanism would start beeping telling us that our recess from steering was over.

The winds were consistently light after rounding Point Conception and we relied on Big Red, the 65 horse power diesel engine, to cover a good portion of our miles. I hadn't pictured doing so much motoring. The trip around the world was conceived while reading about Richard Henry Dana Jr., Captain Cook, and Joshua Slocum. They never had the luxury of an engine. When the wind stopped they waited. Occasionally with no wind and a current against them they actually lost miles. Most of the old sailing vessels were also pigs, designed around large cargo holds, not great sailing ability. The boat that led to Hanuman's design had won the 'Sydney to Hobart,' one of the roughest sailing regattas in the world, three years in a row back in the seventies.

24

We got lazy. Occasionally a breeze would come up while we were motoring and we wouldn't even bother to put up the sails. Too busy relaxing. The gentle rhythmic motion of the boat can have a very subduing effect on ones motivation. "Yeah, I'll get to it in a minute… right after I… see what that frigate bird is up to."

After Ensenada we dropped anchor in San Quintin, an attractive little bay with no town or settlement in sight. No town meant no store, and no store meant no chance to spend money. "Perfect."

We spent three days in San Quintin surfing sloppy waves before moving on. As much as we tried to avoid night approaches they continued to happen. We found ourselves entering Turtle Bay in the dark two hours before the moon rose. It was difficult to estimate how long it would take to get from one place to another because our speed varied so greatly. There were lighthouses on both the north and south headlands of the bay so we hoped coming in at night wouldn't be a problem.

We knew from our chart that the southern light was inland from the actual coast so we hugged the northern light. A bit too closely as is it turned out. We found ourselves tangled in a kelp bed that bordered the northern entrance to the bay. Fortunately we managed to motor through the kelp and find our way into the tranquility of the bay where we dropped the anchor well away from the other boats, all of whom probably wisely used the light of day to safely find ideal spots.

We lingered in Turtle Bay for a week. We met a family that adopted us, had a party in our honor, and gave us food. We helped them build a *palapa* in their front yard but mostly we drank beer and talked about building the *palapa*. They didn't speak any English so it was an ideal opportunity to practice our Spanish. By the time we got around to leaving, which was a few *mananas* after we'd intended, we felt like family.

Being at anchor in Turtle Bay for week put us in touch with our battery charging limitations. We'd purchased one small solar panel before leaving San Francisco which I finally got around to installing in Morro Bay during Matt's hiatus. When the engine was running, which charged the battery, or when we were on a dock where we could plug in, power wasn't a problem. When we were bobbing around at anchor for a week we realized that our one foot square solar panel didn't keep up with our consumption. We liked to have the ten disc changer blastin' whenever we were onboard. On more than one occasion I woke up to find out that we'd passed out with the thing still going. We turned the anchor light on at night as well. I was amazed by how much juice one little bulb could suck up. We also liked to have a few cabin lights on at night so we could see what we were doing.

We could've run the engine for an hour or so a day to charge the batteries but I hated the idea. I didn't like asking any more from Big Red than necessary since I gave him so little. I also felt that nothing ruined a tranquil anchorage like a noisy diesel engine spewing fumes everywhere. We tightened our belts. One hour of music a night, candles and a kerosene lantern for light. It was an easy enough adjustment. The biggest problem was distinguishing between the blue and gray Risk pieces. You can't afford any foolish mistakes when it comes to global domination.

Prying ourselves from Turtle Bay we headed for Magdalena Bay. As usual we arrived at night. Entering the bay itself wasn't too big of a deal. By the time we got there the moon had risen. The bay is enormous however, so entering it was just the beginning. We went north following the bay side of the peninsula which created the bay.

There were two potential places to anchor inside the bay. To get to the first we just had to follow the peninsula for a few miles and anchor in the correct dept of water when the land started curving to the east. The other anchorage was much further into the bay but for some reason we considered it to be more favorable. It, however, required us to navigate through a zigzagging channel. We agreed that it would be probably be prudent to anchor in the first spot upon arrival and proceed to the next in the light the following day.

I went below for a nap with the assurance that Matt would wake me when we got close to the first anchorage. I quickly fell into a deep sleep but awoke suddenly with the feeling something was wrong. Before going up into the cockpit I went to the chart table and plotted our position. I discovered that we were well past the first anchorage and proceeding towards the second. Beyond that we'd entered the zigzagging channel area but were out of the actual channel and in the shallows. Just as I made the discovery I felt a thud against the keel. I flew up the companionway into the cockpit. "Flip a bitch; we're out of the channel!" Miraculously we made it back into the channel without incident. There was no point in heading back to the first anchorage since we were already well into the channel so we decided to see it through.

Our attention was primed. Matt stayed at the helm and I darted between the cockpit and the chart table plotting our position. We both strained our eyes to see the next red or green marker. The markers were lit which could lead one to believe they should be easy to see and to follow but that wasn't the case. While we could see many markers it was hard to tell which marker we were looking at. "Is that the one we're supposed to be headed towards or is it the one on the next leg of the zigzag?" We passed a couple of Mexicans in boat that appeared to be moving one of the channel markers. "Hmmm…wonder what that's all about," I questioned suspiciously. "Nothin' like movin' the ol' channel markers in the middle of the night," Matt reasoned. Eventually we made it through the channel and dropped anchor with a sigh of relief.

I didn't say anything to Matt about his decision to proceed to the second anchorage. He was impossible to talk to after he'd fucked up. He would berate himself for being a fuck up and then slip into a self pitying funk that made him a pain to be around. He'd probably had an image of navigating the channel by himself and then yelling down a very proud, "We're here… let's get that anchor ready!" It was a typical example of his going from A to B without considering the space between. Ultimately I let it go, hoping he'd learned something from the experience, and figuring, "all's well that ends well."

We spent several days in Magdalena Bay and made a hardy attempt to live off the sea. We collected scallops and clams and had a limitless supply of fish. Amanda and I had a competition to see who could catch the most fish in ten casts. I won with eight but she was a close second with seven. I hated torturing the little fish for no reason, we released most of them, but I couldn't seem to stop casting. I think I was making up for the majority of my fishing career where I'd spent 99.9 percent of my time without even a nibble.

Despite keeping busy with all of our pseudo-survival antics Matt still wasn't in the best of spirits and took it out on Amanda when I wasn't around, telling her that she wasn't very independent and couldn't do anything without me. Amanda was in fact quite independent but simply didn't particularly like hanging out alone with Matt since he was often in 'one of his moods.'

We made it into town a few times to check things out. After all, one couldn't gather beer from the bay. Matt got some money wired to him from his parents, improving his spirits. He bought an enormous box of stale holiday cookies and the shoddiest looking mask and snorkel I'd ever seen. It needed a duck tape repair right out of its cheap plastic wrapper. It was like that scene from *Dumb and Dumber* where Dumb sends Dumber into the gas station for "just the essentials" and

Dumber comes back with a huge foam cowboy hat and one of those rubber ball and paddle toys that a five year old enjoys for about ten seconds.

Being financially dependent on me didn't really suit Matt's tastes. Not that it suits anyone's tastes but it was just one more thing that added to his annoyance with life. I wasn't sure what his other problems were but it was clear that they existed. His longing for Jesse was probably chief among them. He frequently made corny toasts to her. Amanda and I played along in hopes of improving his spirits and maintaining his sanity but we had to roll our eyes.

Being stuck on a boat with my girlfriend and me while he wanted to be with Jesse may have been at the heart of his unhappiness. Though he was never excluded he probably felt like a third wheel and resented us for being the other two wheels. Threesomes can easily go south.

We navigated the reverse zigzag with the aid of sunlight. The channel still wasn't one hundred percent obvious but we made it through without any major stress and were on our way to Cabo San Lucas.

We considered Cabo to be the end of the first real leg of the journey and we headed there with significant excitement. Especially Matt, since he'd be reuniting with Jesse in about a week. I took us a few days to get there. Matt and I had some pleasant moments at night in the cockpit under a full moon and things seemed more like old times when we'd been care free drinking buddies dreaming of a grand adventure.

A few miles north of Cabo the water turned a magnificent blue and we decided to jump in and swim around in what we considered to be the middle of the ocean. We'd been motoring and had the engine in neutral but still running while we were in the water. For the first time ever Big Red kind of… hiccupped. He didn't exactly stop running but missed a beat for a second before continuing on as it always had. Suddenly the ocean seemed bigger, deeper, and lonelier. We scrambled back into the boat and continued on our way with a slight feeling of apprehension. We motored on for several hours and the incident faded from our minds.

Seeing Cabo's conspicuous cliffs rise from the horizon overwhelmed us with a sense of accomplishment. However our enthusiasm was quickly curbed when the engine coughed, wheezed, and died. There was moment of silence for our fallen comrade, and for us. We started with the obvious, turning the key; no luck. We didn't have the battery power to waste cranking the engine over repeatedly.

In route from Turtle Bay to Magdalena Bay we realized that the alternator wasn't charging the batteries. I noticed this well after we'd run the house batteries, the batteries that did everything but start the engine, down to nothing. We had to use the starting battery to periodically check our location on the GPS.

We decided to bleed the system. Bleeding the system was the 'go to' remedy for any problems we had with Big Red; much like bleeding in the bygone days of human medicine. Basically it was one of the few things I knew how to do; again, much like the old doctors. Diesel engines can't handle any air in their fuel lines. A little bubble of air that finds its way into the fuel line will shut down the engine.

Miraculously the bleeding worked and we were motoring again, at least for a little while. Big Red whimpered a little and shut down. We were close however, and a little wind came up. We raised the main and did another round of bleeding. Leaches would come later. The engine fired and we were able to get ourselves into the harbor and tied off to a fuel dock. Fortunately it was Christmas Eve and the fuel dock was closed so we had a free place to stay for the night.

Cabo

The engine problems were quickly overshadowed by the excitement of arriving in Cabo. We'd been in rural towns for the previous several weeks and it was dazzling to be in a tourist Mecca. Everything was expensive. Fortunately for Matt it was Christmas Eve and his grandmother had wired him a couple hundred bucks. In his mind we'd have jobs before long on one of the numerous sport fishing boats and have plenty of pesos so there was so need to save any of his Christmas cash.

We decided to go big, at least by our standards. We went out for tacos and beers at a restaurant with actual waiters. I felt a little resentful towards Matt who suddenly had two hundred dollars in his pocket. I'd been paying for just about everything and was pretty much broke myself so I asked him to at least split the 140 dollar Mexican fishing permit I'd paid for in San Diego. He reluctantly agreed, giving me about sixty bucks. I felt uncomfortable asking but it was quickly forgotten after a couple more beers. If Matt and I made questionable sailing companions we, at least, made great drinking buddies. We decided to go looking for some weed.

It didn't take long to find. A couple of kids took us to a slightly older dude who led us to a dilapidated house. He performed the classic over the shoulder glance, pushed aside the piece of cloth where you'd expect a door to be, and led us in.

It was a quaint little drug den with scales, a few serious faced Mexican hombres looking a bit silly in undersized chairs that must have come from a fourth grade classroom, a weathered and hearty looking Mexican women weighing and bagging, and the quintessential dreadlocked ex-pat white dude. We procured a little baggy of weed that, as usual, cost more than I expected. Matt decided he'd get a little cocaine as well, which cost a lot more than I expected, though I wasn't really familiar with the going rate. "It's Christmas," he shrugged, when I showed a little surprise at the price.

The sun set and we proceeded with our merriment. We met a young Mexican couple on break from school and had a few beers with them. We soon learned they were just friends vacationing together. I could see Matt's libido perk up.

Matt was a lover of women. And of the hunt, though he probably never looked at it that way. He really cherished each woman, when he was with her, which probably made his untactic tactic more effective.

The lovemaking started before the female even knew what was happening. He began by getting her on some seemingly innocuous subject of conversation; typically something superficially nonsensical that he could enliven with his own philosophies. He'd read their body language and work his way in physically closer. His face would come as close to hers as discretion and the vibe allowed. He talked softly with his neck canted intently and gravely forward as if he were unraveling a deep mystery. She was forced to lien in to hear what he was saying. Matt gently rubbed his thumb and forefinger together between their lips to enforce his point, subtly emulating two bodies in lust's embrace. He lured her in rhythmically with his voice talking about the essence of some seemingly small facet of life that might hold a larger truth. Her eyes lit light up as she found truth, or at least humor, in something he said. Once he got her head bobbing in sync with his the hook was set and she was gently reeled in.

I don't want to give the impression that Matt was a cunning predator. As I stated, he was smitten with and cherished each women he was with. On Christmas Eve he was cherishing the attractive Mexican vacationer he'd just met. I've forgotten her name but I'm sure he repeated it softly in her ear at the end of every sentence. He loved Spanish and Spanish names. He lived to roll 'R's.' Matt found a girl more attractive if he liked how her name felt rolling off his tongue.

Eventually Amanda got tired and I got the munchies and the two of us headed back to Hanuman to whip up some Top Ramen, leaving Matt to his own devices.

Morning found Matt with a guest in his berth. Amanda woke before me to the sight of Matt's bare ass bobbing up and down and four legs protruding from the foot of his bunk. When I got up to go for a run, and sweat out the poison, he was crawling out of his bunk and tugging up his pants. "It's not like we did anything or anything," he muttered under his breath. I hadn't asked and I missed the old, 'that's life,' shrug that he would have typically used to bring perspective to a seemingly fucked up situation. I knew he'd be beating himself up, and intern Amanda and I, for quite some time to come.

Three days later Jesse arrived. We'd moved out to the harbor and into the anchorage to avoid paying slip fees. Paying for a slip was no longer even an option as we were down to our last few dollars.

Matt dinghied Jesse out to Hanuman on Sputnik, our small Avon inflatable launch powered by a two and a half horse power Tohatsu. He was all smiles. For the next day or two Amanda and I didn't see much of Matt and Jesse. Jesse sprung for a hotel room and they had some alone time. Amanda and I had some as well. It was a refreshing break from Matt.

The four of us decided to spend New Year's Eve camped out on Lover's Beach. Lover's Beach is nature's highlight of the Cabo area. It's pleasantly removed from all of the hoopla of Cabo proper, where the white people get drunk and make asses of themselves. Surrounded by cliffs, it's accessible only by boat or a moderate hike difficult enough to keep most tipsy touristas at bay. It gets fairly crowded during the day when water taxis shuttle people from the harbor but quickly clears out in the late afternoon when the taxis make their last call. We pulled Sputnik well up the beach and had the whole place to ourselves come sunset.

We gathered enough wood to sustain a moderate level of decadence and lighted a fire. Bottles of cheap booze were cracked and the party was started. The night went well from my perspective but the morning told another story. I'd been blissfully unaware of the drama that had unfolded. For starters, Matt had burned his face in the fire trying to light a cigarette and the wound was festering. Whitish yellow puss dripped from his chin. He had the look of death on his face. However, the chin wound was actually the least of his concerns.

Jesse had been suspicious of Matt's fidelity in her absence and asked Amanda if she was aware of any of his exploits. Amanda told her she should ask Matt about it but Jesse insisted she already had and that he had denied any infidelity. Amanda had the image of Matt's ass bobbing up and down as Jesse grilled her and she broke. She'd been disgusted with Matt and felt more kinship toward Jesse.

Matt had been walking a tight rope of sanity for some time and in the intense light of the New Year's morning he found himself in a nosedive at terminal velocity. He paced around the camp picking at the dried puss on his chin repeating himself like a comic who felt the audience hadn't understood the punch line. "I wish I had a gun so I could blow my brains out all over the rocks and make beautiful picture," he exclaimed. I failed to see how that would make a beautiful picture, more of a mess really.

Matt didn't end up killing himself. I assumed he and Jesse worked things out since she didn't leave. Amanda did leave. She'd only really signed on for the trip to Cabo. Matt and I were planning on trying to make some money so the journey was on hold. Amanda didn't share our optimism for making it big in Mexico.

Matt and I eventually decided it was time to buckle down and try and make some money so we donned our most respectable looking clothes and made our way down to the docks with all of the fancy looking sport fishing boats.

We'd been rejected by about ten boats in a row and were feeling somewhat demoralized when we hit the final boat. They told us that not only did they not have any work for us but that we shouldn't even be on the docks asking for work, as Americans could be thrown in jail for working in Mexico. We vowed not to be too put off by our lack of success and to try again soon. "Such undertakings require persistence and a thick skin," I stated assuredly. As it turned out we never 'pounded the docks' again.

Matt and Jesse spent most of their time on land 'doing their thing' while I smoked weed and tried to fix the engine. I enjoyed the Zen like meditation of it and made slow progress. I spent a lot of time reading Marine Diesels Simplified and scraping the skin off of my diesel soaked knuckles. After a couple of weeks of taking things, that weren't broken at all, apart and putting them back together the engine worked. Or so I thought. Once the engine was working again I put the issue to rest. I would later develop a valuable philosophy regarding engines and fixing things in general. "Just because

I've tinkered with something that was previous not working, but that now is, doesn't mean that I've fixed it."

It wasn't long until Matt and I came up with another money making scheme. We weren't the only boat anchored out in front of Cabo and one day when we were scrubbing the algae off of Hanuman's under water surfaces we decided other boats might pay us to do the same for them. We loaded Sputnik up with our scrubbing gear and went boat to boat. The first few boats weren't interested but were a least friendly which was a lot more than we got from the sport fishing boats that looked at us like we were lepers. Eventually we found someone willing to pay for our services. We settled on thirty bucks US. The boat owner was surprised when we didn't go back for our scuba gear. Using scuba gear was the normal practice for scrubbing bottoms but we didn't have any so a mask, snorkel, and fins had to do. His bottom wasn't all that dirty but it still took us a while and by the end of it our lips were blue and we were shivering. The water still wasn't all that warm. In actuality we weren't that far south and it was January.

We dinghied to shore with our hard earned thirty bucks and met up with Jesse. The question became what to do with our loot. Matt seemed to be for spending it as quickly as possible. In fact we were drinking a couple of beers as we discussed what to do with the rest of it. I was for putting half of it into the boat repair/trip fund and spending the rest of it on beer, tacos and such. I think Matt had kind of given up on the trip and had no real interest in any sort of trip fund. Jesse actually agreed with me and thus the trip fund began. Began and ended.

We continued our at anchor quest for employment but didn't get much farther. One couple who'd lost their barbecue over the rail offered us a couple bucks to go looking for it. After repeated dives in thirty feet of water Matt and I spotted it and retrieved it along with its various parts.

While we were diving for the barbie we met some guy who'd lost his anchor. We recovered it for him and were compensated with a couple of warm beers. We liked beer at any temperature but they didn't put us any closer to stoking the coffers for our next journey.

The couple who'd paid fifteen bucks to rescue their BBQ asked if we knew how to splice an anchor rode onto a chain. "Of course, been doin' it all my life." I didn't really say that but something to its effect. In truth I'd done it exactly once when I spliced my own anchor rode and chain. We went back to Hanuman and I reread the chapter on splicing.

Matt, Jesse and I returned to the couple's boat with a lighter and some electrical tape. The woman was happy to see Jesse. The female half of any couple alone on boat with her mate is almost always glad to converse with any other female about something besides ground tackle and sail plans. Jesse also gave us some legitimacy. Matt and I didn't look particularly respectable with our unshaven faces and tattered clothing but if we could keep a female around, unforced, we were probably viewed as less shady than we appeared.

I managed to pull off the splice but it wasn't quite as pretty as those you see in nautical history museums. After plying us with several beers and some delightfully tasty crackers we were asked how much they owed us. I felt bad about charging them. While the splice was perfectly functional it wasn't the sort of thing one pointed to and said, "I want one of those." "The beers and company were more than sufficient," I proclaimed regally. I've never been very good at collecting money. Matt wasn't super stoked on the arrangement and neither was I but the mild euphoria brought on by the beer in our empty stomachs trumped our disappointment at the lack of cash.

While working on the engine I noticed one of the stainless steel cables that connected the steering wheel to the rudder had one small wire in the bundle that had frayed. It wasn't the sort of thing that was going to lead to a loss of steering in the immediate future but neither was it the sort of thing you wanted on your mind while you were crossing oceans. The frayed wire forced a shift in my outlook.

I thought I'd convinced myself that the trip would continue on, money or no money. We could live on beans and rice, and the wind was free. However, with our struggle to make any significant cash and the recognition of the continual cost of maintaining the boat, I had the realization that there would have to be a change in my mental paradigm. Going back to the states to work for awhile suddenly didn't seem like such a far out option. It did, however, blast a hole in my idea of being some sort of privateer, completely reliant on my vessel and the sea for prosperity. Hell, I was struggling just to keep the vessel going.

I found 40 bucks I didn't know I had which brightened my mood considerably and put other problems to the back of my mind. I'd previously been contemplating a meal of small boney scaly reef fish over rice with soy sauce, mustard, pepper, and chili powder but I decided I was ready for an indulgence. It would be foolish to bring the whole forty bucks out with me so I planned to leave twenty of it in the coconut, our trip fund storage container.

Nearly every night in Cabo one bar or another had a ladies night, where chicks drink for free. Matt and Jesse had been taking advantage of these nightly. Eventually we discovered the Jungle Bar. "Tuesday night is men's night, not gay night, at the Jungle Bar. Men drink free from seven to nine," proclaimed a sign in front of the place. I have a weak spot for, "all I can…anything."

We psyched ourselves up for the event all day and hit the beach well before seven. First we went to some other bar that was having a ladies night and Jesse shuttled drinks back to Matt and I as we tried to look inconspicuous in the corner. It was a maneuver we knew we couldn't keep up for long. Matt and I left for the Jungle Bar to make sure we'd have a good spot at the bar when the whistle blew. Jesse would meet us later; she was still getting free drinks at the first place.

As we found our place at the bar we discovered that men didn't actually drink for free. For a price you drank all you could for an hour. We informed the bartender that the sign said free and that it said two hours. He shrugged his shoulders, "it used to be free." We decided against going into the whole false advertising thing.

Despite the fee, which was more than I wanted to pay but not so much that I could back out after getting all worked up, we decided to go for it.

Prior to the ringing of the ship's bell, which indicated the start of the 'all you can drink' hour, I made a trip to the bathroom to empty my bladder to ensure that I had full storage capacity. When I returned Matt looked disgruntled.

A couple of weeks prior Matt had been threatened at knife point. As Matt told it, he'd been taking a shit in a bar bathroom when someone banged on the stall door. Matt grunted to let the person know that he was currently occupying the stall, thinking that they also wanted to shit. The person banged on the door again telling Matt to get out and that he didn't want anyone doing drugs in his bathroom. Matt told the guy that he was just taking a shit and not doing any drugs. When Matt got out of the bathroom the guy pulled out a knife and told him to get the hell out.

As Matt returned to the bathroomless bar where Amanda, Jesse and I were sitting we saw a couple of guys yelling behind him. They didn't follow him but continued to yell after him for awhile shaking their fists in the air. Matt yelled back at them over his shoulder as he walked away rapidly. We could see something out of the ordinary had taken place and listened as Matt told the story.

We sat in silence digesting the troubling tale. Finally Jesse asked, "Were you doing drugs in the bathroom?" "…well yes, but that's not the point," Matt argued. We all agreed that he had left out a fairly critical part of the story. Though we still sympathized with him for having had a knifed pulled on him, we felt a little cheated by the edited version of the story.

As one might imagine Matt wasn't too excited when he saw the knife guy at the Jungle bar. The guy had a kind of crazy look about him. I could definitely imagine him pulling a knife on someone. We soon learned that he owned the Jungle Bar.

I tried to get Matt to forget about him and focus on the task at hand: all we could drink. He rallied rather admirably, I thought, but still occasionally mentioned wanting to kill the guy under his breath.

All too soon the bell rang again and it was over. I was overcome by the feeling I always get after an 'all I can.' That feeling like I should have been able to consume more. "I'm not even really all that drunk," I stated with disgust. I wasn't all that drunk but I was drunk enough to decide that going out for another drink was a pretty good idea.

We made our way to the Love Shack. I realized that I had somehow managed to leave the boat with all of the forty dollars I had just found. Normally, in my slightly inebriated condition, I would have blown through the whole forty. Surprisingly I mustered some prudence and hung on to most of it.

Miraculously, a young couple that Matt and Jesse were talking to decided they wanted to buy us a round. Apparently they were interested in our sailing journey and wanted to hear more. They bought us a few. They were drinkers and were happy to have a group to hang out with but eventually I started feeling like I wanted to move on so the three of us took off.

Matt and Jesse started quarreling about something so, feeling slightly uncomfortable, I snuck off. Matt and I frequently got separated during our reveling so I'm sure he thought nothing of it.

I decided I was done for the night and headed back to the boat. Being the first one back meant that I got to dinghy back to Hanuman. Matt would have to swim out to Hanuman and get the dinghy to pick up Jesse; standard operating procedure. First one back to Sputnik gets home dry.

Jail

Heading back to the dinghy I felt the accumulation of 'men's night' in my bladder and decided it needed relieving. I peeled off the sidewalk into a perfectly inconspicuous patch of vegetation, watered the plants, and was on my way. I walked about ten paces when, out of nowhere, or so it seemed in my comfortably buzzed condition, two Mexicans dressed in green military fatigues grabbed each of my arms. They looked somewhat official though not especially intimidating. I had a good six inches on both of them. I decided I'd make a run for it. Actually, I'm not sure if I consciously chose to run but that's what happened. I didn't get far. As it turned out, I was right in front of the police station. I must have walked by it many times previously but had never noticed it. It was an inconspicuous building; just a cement shack that's thinly white washed walls were slowly being overtaken by the surrounding dirt. A small fading crest containing the words 'La Policia,' was hand painted on the wall next to the doorless entrance.

I was wearing a loose fitting sweatshirt and flip-flops. The *policia* clung tenaciously to my sweatshirt and dragged along behind me for a few steps. The display emptied the police station and before I knew it five guys were trying to wrestle me down. I could see my 'running away' plan had been defeated. Having no interest in a brawl with the entire Cabo police force I threw my arms and the air, "Whoooa, *lo siento, lo siento*…I'm sorry, I'm sorry." They dragged me into the police station. The inside matched the outside; cement and cinder block ornamented with peeling paint. One flickering sixty-watt bulb dangled naked from the center of the ceiling. The room was bare except for a metal desk adorned with a vintage typewriter. The desk was a faded olive green metal unit almost identical to the one the drug dealers had. "They must have been on special," I thought. "Or perhaps they ransacked the same fourth grade classroom." Behind it sat the man who was clearly the chief. He was twice the size of the others and looked incredibly malicious. His shirt sported several shoulder chevrons attesting to his virility. Its buttons strained under the pressure of his well stuffed pot belly. They didn't all match. Clearly some of the former buttons hadn't been up to the task.

I was brought to the center of the room where my pockets were emptied and my wallet, containing 35 bucks, was put on the desk in front of the chief. He leafed through it, fanning its contents on the desk in front of him. He didn't seem satisfied and probed its depths looking for some hidden secrets. Not finding any, he turned his eyes towards me.

He didn't speak English, or refused to if he knew how. His goal wasn't to make me comfortable. I still didn't realize why I'd been dragged in. The previous five minutes of my life had happened so fast and with such intensity that I failed to connect them with the moments prior when I'd been pissing in the bushes. Through a combination Spanish and gesturing I realized I'd been brought in on pissing charges. The fact that I tried to run, apparently, hadn't helped matters. It had, however, helped matters for them, as they perceived it as meaning they could extort more money from me.

I tried to explain to the chief that when the first two guys grabbed me I wasn't aware that they were police and that I thought I was simply running from robbers. When I realized that they were police I stopped running. The explanation required extensive gesturing. I didn't know the word for running so I did a lot of running in place. My story wasn't true, strictly speaking, but it seemed plausible. They hadn't announced their presence. No badges were produced. I wasn't read my Miranda Rights.

Ultimately the chief didn't really care about what I had to say. He wanted more money and wasn't accepting any of my excuses. He waved my ATM card in my face and insisted we go to the bank.

The fact of the matter was that I had almost no money in my account, probably less than twenty dollars. I tried to explain this to him but he wasn't buying it. I began pleading with him. I threw out numerous *por favors*. I even tried to *por favor* some of his peons. I picked out a young one with kind eyes and gave him a pleading "*por favor…amigo.*" He just stared at the floor looking even more frightened than I did. I suspected he was new to extortion business. I looked around at some of the others. One of them seemed to be taking delight in my suffering. He had a pudgy body and smarmy looking smile on his greasy face that made my stomach turn.

We haggled for some time; them for money and I for what seemed like my life. Eventually the chief sneered in disgust, jerked his head to the side, and mumbled something I didn't understand to his peons. I was lead out of the front room and down a dark hall to the right where I was deposited in front of two adjacent jail cells. The peons told me to wait there and returned to the front room, out of my view.

Two pairs of eyes emerged from the smaller of the cells. The faces they were attached to appeared amiable and we conversed about our situations in *Spanglish*. They were in for ten days for selling marijuana. They, now my new best friends, offered me a smoke. I don't normally smoke but accepted the cigarette extended through the bars. I figured what the hell, "when in Rome…" I tried to ascertain my fate. They believed that, on the pissing charges alone, I should be out that night but thought the fact that I'd tried to run didn't bode well. Upon hearing the running part they pursed their lips and shrugged. "Maybe you spend the night."

The greasy faced jailer came down the hall. I set my cig on one of the crossbars of my *amigos* cell. I thought that perhaps I'd be led back to front room for another round of negotiations or maybe even just released. Not the case. He opened the cell door adjacent to my smoking buddies and motioned me in. I was shocked. "*Que pasa?*" He repeated the "you'll be entering the cell and I'll be closing the door" gesture. I entered the cell. He closed the door and walked off.

I peered out through the bars in disbelief. "He doesn't appear to be coming back," I confirmed in my head. I turned around and had a look at my new home. There were no lights but enough light filtered in through the barred glassless window that I could make out the general landscape.

It was a much larger cell than the one my friends occupied. I figured it to be the drunk tank. Against three of the walls was a U-shaped double tier of cement platforms that served as bunks. There were a couple of blanket covered bumps that I presumed to be drunks. They were well passed out and looked harmless. One of the walls had a dark opening that I guessed led to some sort of toilet area. I looked down at my shoeless bleeding feet and was glad I'd just urinated. Of course if I hadn't I wouldn't have been in jail. It could be viewed as 'win win,' in a twisted sense.

Exploring the cell didn't take long. I hopped up on the top tier and paced back and forth on the cement. I knew what caged lions in the zoo felt like. Pacing got old pretty quickly so I went back to the bars and rested my arms and chin on the metal with hope that something would happen. Nothing did. I chatted with my comrades and got the idea that I should be getting my 'one phone call.' I discussed the idea with my brothers in arms. They thought it was worth a try so we yelled out for the jailer. The greasy faced guy slithered around the corner and my friends explained my request to the pudgy snake. To my surprise he left and returned with a portable phone. He handed it to me with a sinister smarmy look on his face I had trouble interpreting but I knew I didn't like. Perhaps he thought I'd be calling someone to come down with some money for him. Perhaps he thought he'd just get a laugh out of watching me trying to call someone. He got the latter. I didn't really know what to do with the phone in my hand. Who was I going to call…my mom? My new friends, who were clearly thrilled to have a distraction, magically produced a phone book and handed it over. "How the hell did they end up with a phone book," I wondered. I flipped through it looking for the American Embassy. No luck. The whole thing was just yellow pages. I landed on the pizza section. "Mmmmmm…. pizza." The greasy faced guy's smile widened as he watched me floundering. Eventually I gave up and returned the phone and the book through the bars.

I went back to pacing. I checked all of the bars on the windows. They were firmly embedded in the cement walls. I set aside the idea of escape and went back to resting my chin on the bars. I felt like a dog waiting for his owner to return.

I heard some noises in the front room. My ears perked up a little and an attractive young Mexican woman in a tight red dress rounded the corner. "That's interesting," I thought. She made her way straight for me and gave me a kiss on the lips.

Greasy Smile grabbed her by the arm and led her away. "Even more interesting."

The event got my friends out of bed. "*No esta una mujer,*" they informed me frantically. "That's not a woman." "*Esta un hombre con el….,*" and they made a cutting motion with their index and middle fingers. "*Aye carumba!*" I made a painfully distorted face and thanked them for the information.

A few moments later they led him/her towards my cell. I backed away from the bars and they opened the door and tossed him/her in with me. He/she had a wily looking grin on his/her face and came towards me slowly yet directly. I jumped up to the upper bunk level. He/she followed. "Come on. Where are you going?" His/her English was annoyingly good. He/she was agile and padded along behind me as I contoured the room on the upper level of bunks. I looked over my shoulder to check his/her pace. As I did so I cracked my head on one of the cement ceiling beams. I went down and he/she was on top of me with one hand on my crotch. I managed to throw him/her off. "What's the matter," he/she lamented. He/she couldn't seem to understand that I wasn't interested. "Don't you want to fuck my pussy?" I eventually managed to convince him/her of the contrary with a few strong 'no's' and he/she backed off.

Deciding I needed a bit of coaxing he/she mellowed and asked me my name. I reluctantly gave it to him/her after which he/she insisted on using it in every sentence, typically in close association with "my pussy." "Miiiiike…don't you want to fuck my pussy? It's so wet." "I'm fine for now thanks."

Greasy Smile had been watching the exchange with unusual perversity and started talking to me. I had no idea what he was saying and looked to my friends in the adjacent cell to give me a rough translation. "He say if you fuck her while he (and they made the universal masturbation gesture) you get out of jail." "Fuckin'-A, you gotta' be kiddin' me!" I thought. I looked over at Greasy and saw him nodding, an even greasier smile spreading across on his face. The smile to seemed overtake the whole of his head. A head that was grotesquely wider than it was tall. "Noooo," I said, emphatically shaking my head violently from side to side and waving my arms back and forth like an umpire giving the 'safe' signal. Greasy just chuckled and walked away but returned moments later and opened my cell door, motioning me out of the cell. I figured I was getting out. "Yee haw." He led me past the front room to the other wing of the jail. He opened the door to another cell and motioned me in. "What? That's no exit," I thought. I looked back over my shoulder and saw that he/she was right behind me. I was being led into the mating cell. He must have hoped that the drunk tank simply lacked the intimacy I required to fornicate with the trans-sexual while he jacked off.

I drew my line in the sand. "Nooo way," I yelled doing an about face. Greasy just smiled and stood aside as I marched back to my own cell and slammed the door behind me.

I was left alone but could hear him/her screaming in the other wing. It didn't sound like true terror screaming however. It had an imposed dramatic sound that made me think that perhaps he/she wasn't totally opposed to whatever was going on. I assumed the 'chin on bars' position and waited to see what would happen next.

I didn't have to wait too long. The screaming died down and he/she came around the corner, lifted his/her skirt, and put a hundred dollar bill on his/her shear red panties over his/her vagina/penis stump. "I pay for you to get out Miiiike." "No thanks," I said, lifting my hand in a limp gesture of dismissal. That was the final image of he/she I was left with.

I gave up hope of getting out that night, climbed to the upper level of bunks, laid down on the cold hard cement, and fell asleep.

I awoke with a strange combination of hopefulness and desperation as the morning light streaming in through the barred windows. I rechecked the structural integrity of the window nearest me, still solid. Having to take a piss I ventured into the bathroom area. There was shit everywhere: in the toilets, in the urinals, on the floor. Inmates had been using newspaper to wipe their asses and that was everywhere as well. The scene was garnished with a swarm of absurdly large flies gorging themselves on all of the shit. Fortunately my foot wounds had scabbed up nicely during the night.

After determining that there was no way out other than the door I came in, I went back to my perch and peered out of the barred glassless window. I could see the bushes where I'd urinated. I could also see the street and some early risers walking down it. I wondered if I could get their attention.

An unfamiliar guard came to the door and called my name. "*Si, si, si, estoy aqui*...I'm here!" I responded, hoping he would be taking me to freedom. He made note on his clipboard and called out the names of the other two guys in my cell with me. They were still passed out and didn't respond but the guard didn't seem to care and made some notes on his board. "What…that's it? Aren't I getting out?" I thought. I stopped the guard as he began to turn around and asked him when I'd be released. "Today maybe," he stated noncommittally. That drained the last of my spirits. "Today maybe?" The 'maybe' didn't sit well with me at all. "Today maybe???"

I decided 'maybe' wasn't good enough. I planted myself at the window and pressed my face up to the bars so I could get a view of the street. The plan was to wait until some white people walked by and ask them to call the American Embassy. The problem was that the street was 30 or so yards away so I'd have to yell quite loudly to get their attention.

Whities weren't coming by all that often but eventually I had an opportunity. "Call the American Embassy, call the

American Embassy," I yelled at a couple of pink and bloated looking retirees. The problem was I couldn't quite bring myself to yell very loudly. It turned out that yelling out of barred window at some passing strangers took some getting used to. I'm not much of a yeller in general. They didn't even turn their heads. I decided that I have would have to dig deeper. I increased the volume for the next set of gringos but still got no response. Eventually I got a few heads to turn but they quickly pointed them back in the direction they were going and pretended not to hear me. "Mother fuckers!" I thought aloud.

I decided to take a break and leaned back defeated against the cement wall when I saw a well dressed Mexican guy approaching my cell. I lifted an eyebrow. "Michael Dugan." "Yes." "I'm from the American Embassy." One of the guards opened the door and I was out of there. He handed me back my wallet, moneyless, and my flip-flips. He told me he had paid the fine and I was supposed to pay him back. The fine was thirty bucks. "I had that much in my wallet," I told him. "Well, you might be able to get the money back but you'd have to fill out a bunch of forms and it would take all day." "No thanks... How did you know I was in jail?" I queried. "I come by every day," he explained in a 'matter of fact' tone.

Amanda had wired me about hundred bucks via Western Union a few days prior but I was hoping not to pick it up to avoid incurring the 30 percent transfer fee they charge. I vanquished that idea. I got my 70 bucks from the Western Union and handed half of it to the embassy guy, whose credentials I was beginning to doubt, thinking that perhaps he was the last round of an extortion racquet, but not really caring, and was free.

I trudged down the beach and swam out to Hanuman. Matt and Jesse were still asleep.

La Paz

After our fruitless attempts to make money in Cabo I decided that going back to the States to work was the only logical solution to my financial challenges. I had the feeling that Matt would be following Jesse whenever she decided to leave, making it imperative for me to find a safe place to keep Hanuman while I still had help. Cabo wasn't an option. The anchorage in front of Cabo is open to any weather coming in from the south and to simply leave ones boat/life at anchor there for three months unattended would've been crazy. La Paz has a very well protected anchorage, hence our decisions to head there.

We'd heard the 150 mile passage up the Sea of Cortez to La Paz could be difficult. We'd witnessed boats limp back into Cabo, defeated, after they'd encountered punishing head winds and short choppy seas which made forward progress painful.

We decided we'd break the passage into three segments. The plan was to leave Cabo pre-sunrise and arrive at the first anchorage prior to sunset. 'Men's night' and jail banished the pre-sunrise idea unless we wanted to wait another day. I was done with Cabo and wanted out. Matt and Jesse felt pretty much the same.

After the hangovers settled and I had a nap we shoved off. We figured we'd sail through the night and arrive in the morning. Big Red fired up nicely and we hoisted the anchor and motored north. There wind was light but we weren't concerned. After the previous night, sailing seemed like a lot of work.

An hour out, Big Red sputtered. There was a heavy silence where one would expect a "fuuuuck" but after the previous night I was feeling "fuuucked" out and, when compared to being in jail, engine failure seemed trivial. Within moments the sputtering repeated and Big Red wheezed and died. Fortunately a slight breeze had just come up. Matt and I silently raised the main and let out the jib. The quiet was nice. The thought of not having a motor all the way to La Paz was not.

The breeze freshened and Hanuman delighted in the heal as our speed became respectable. We didn't think or talk about the motor situation. We just sailed on in a pleasant silence.

Night fell and the wind picked up even more as it started to rain. We reefed in the jib but left the main all the way up. As the night wore on, and the wind picked up yet again, I wanted to reef the main, but it seemed like a lot of work for the middle of the night. I was cocooned in my rain slicker and didn't want to leave. In addition, the new reefing system hadn't been tested and I didn't feel like calling Matt on deck and dickin' around with it.

Mercifully, things never got too out of hand and as the dull gray morning lit our surroundings we found ourselves near our destination. We tacked and headed towards land. Before sailing into the bay we bled the engine in hope of getting a few minutes of run time.

We'd never anchored under sail. Once again, I'd read a lot about it but never actually attempted it. In truth we'd only anchored a handful of times with the motor.

As we entered the bay, and approached our target anchor dropping area, we furled the jib entirely leaving us with just main. We fired up Big Red and got ready to let the anchor go. Before we knew it we were patting ourselves on the back and wishing we had a few beers to celebrate with. We were bone dry however. We didn't even have anything decent too eat and spent the better part of the day fishing for dinner. Fortunately, some friends we'd made in Cabo happened to be anchored close by and, pitying us, made sure that we didn't go thirsty.

Our journey to La Paz put us in touch with Hanuman's sailing capabilities. We hoisted the anchor under sail when we departed for our second leg of the trip and anchored under sail that night completing our first motorless passage.

We sailed into the wind for the entirety of the passage to La Paz which provided us with a lot of practice tacking and gave us a much better feel for what adjustments to the rigging really made Hanuman go. Getting a boat to sail downwind doesn't require much skill but keeping her going well up wind takes attention.

About ten miles from La Paz the wind completely died. We'd been feeling it drop off for the previous five hours, slowing the progress of our final leg to La Paz. Despite our hope for its return, it deserted us. We bobbed, listening to the sails thwack back and forth as Hanuman drifted in circles, until we made the decision to try and milk some life out of Big Red.

She fired up and pushed us along nicely in the smooth seas. It was hard to relax however, knowing she'd surely fail us.

We tried to take our mind off the inevitable sputtering and threw out the fishing line. We caught a small bonito and ate it raw. It wasn't the sashimi fantasy I'd had in mind. Despite heavy spicing I felt like I was chokin' it down.

And then it came, as we knew it would: sputter, sputter, wheeeeze,…silence. We re-bled and re-bled but the effectiveness of the bleeding decreased with every iteration. I got the idea to bleed while the engine was running in hopes of better results. I sat hunched down by the engine with the bleeder screw between my thumb and forefinger, squirting diesel all over myself and the boat, as Matt handled the helm.

A routine formed. At the first note of a sputter I'd fly down the companionway to the engine room, which quickly became known as the emergency room, and try and bring Big Red back to life. We all smiled when she came back from her deathbed. Every piece of cloth, including what I was wearing, within reach got requisitioned as a diesel rag. We eventually coasted into the anchorage area and after getting briefly stuck in the mud, managed to get the anchor down.

After a few days of asking around we found a perfect place for Hanuman: on a bow and stern mooring, right in front of the marina office where Hanuman could be looked after. We also got a good price since one of the mooring balls had floated off, leaving the line attached to the bottom buried in the sand. We just had to get out the mask and snorkel and find it. No problemo, diving for shit was right up our alley. The people who rented us the mooring also took credit cards, specifically mine, making the deal even better.

We cajoled Big Red into action and eased Hanuman into her new home. The next day Matt and Jesse left. Matt didn't help clean or get Hanuman in shape for storage. He just grabbed what he wanted, left what he didn't, and took off. We didn't make any plans for the continuation of the journey. The goodbye was warm and cordial but I was happy to see him go. Matt may not have fully accepted it at the time but we both knew we were at the end of our journey together. Alone on my boat, I felt reunited with a comforting solitude.

Three days later I turned over seat cushions, scraped up the last of my money, and bought a bus ticket to *El Norte*. It was a long ride back to San Rafael, California, but after having to work for every mile at sea the trip was simply relaxing.

Land Lubbin'

A couple of days after leaving La Paz I was back waiting tables at my former place of employment, the brewpub. Fortunately they hadn't yet found out that it was I who stole one of the surfboards off the wall so I didn't have any trouble picking up where I left off.

One drunken night Matt and I got the idea that the hand painted surfboard next to the wood fired pizza oven didn't have any place rotting on the wall and was destined to surf the world with us. Matt and I had no shortage of good times when we were out drinking.

Amanda had stopped at the brewpub to make some money as well. I moved into the back of her truck with her. She hadn't signed on for the next passage into the heart of the Pacific however, so I didn't have any crew lined up.

A friend of a friend had sent me an e-mail before we'd sailed under the Golden Gate asking if I was looking for crew. I had a lot on my plate at the time and didn't get around to responding to him. As my return to La Paz became imminent

I decided to reply to his e-mail; basically asking him what he was up to and if he was interested in a foray into the Pacific. I hadn't really even invited him but the e-mail I received in return stated that he was already on his way down to La Paz and would be waiting for me and getting the boat ready for our departure. I was a bit taken back but decided to roll with it and sent him a list of things to do.

La Paz, Take Two

Three months of hustling tips went by fairly quickly and before I knew it I was on a plane down to Cabo. Amanda eventually broke, and planned to follow a week later.

Lee was waiting for me at the airport. I liked him right away. He'd bought a Pontiac Fiarro in LA, after tiring of hitch-hiking down from Oregon, for six hundred bucks and we jumped in and headed for La Paz.

Lee told me all that he'd fixed over a six pack on the drive up. Most importantly, he'd fixed Big Red. The heart of the problem appeared to be that she was out of fuel and had been sucking up air as the boat rolled from side to side. I couldn't help but laugh. There was no gauge for the tanks so I'd been guessing based on what I thought was a fairly liberal consumption rate of a gallon an hour. The problem didn't lay in my calculation of consumption but rather the overall size of the tank. The guy who sold me the boat, who'd never actually sailed it, said that it had two seventy five gallon tanks. In real-ity they were probably more like sixty gallons.

Lee and I spent a week fixing the other problems, and drinking, before Amanda arrived. Before leaving we did a huge shop-up, filling at least three shopping carts. Lee insisted on twenty bags of tortilla chips. He felt that any meal worth eating should be eaten with tortilla chips. We also got twenty bottles of *agua diente,* which looked and tasted more or less like tequila but cost almost nothing. Lee loved it. I suffered it. Amanda shunned it.

We decided it would be a good idea to have some weed along to round out the tequila so we went on a mission. We found an only moderately shady looking guy who offered us *mota* as we passed by. We gave him the nod. Then we followed him…and followed him…and followed him some more, covering a few miles over hill and ghetto.

Eventually our guy stopped walking. He said the place was "right down there" but that we weren't allowed to go down. 'We give him the money. He comes back with the weed.' Lee, normally pretty easy going about everything, was skeptical about the whole plan and leaning towards backing out. "We've come a long way. Worst case scenario we're out twenty bucks," I reasoned. Lee shrugged, he could be kind of taciturn sometimes, and I gave the dude twenty bucks.

Time went by and Lee was on the verge of an "I told you so," but the guy returned with a folded up newspaper. We were in. He opened the paper and showed us a good quantity of some pretty ratty looking weed. We were pleased. The dude went one way and we went another. Nothing like a good honest business transaction reaffirm ones faith in mankind.

With the boat fully loaded and fueled up we headed back to Cabo. It was getting late in the northern hemisphere non hurricane season and we didn't want to put off the crossing any longer so we decided to make the passage nonstop. It was already May and hurricane season officially began on June first. I wanted to be south of the hurricane spawning grounds, which meant pretty close to the equator, by then.

The First Big Passage

After some last minute shopping in Cabo, the day came. Next stop Fatu Hiva of the Marquesas, 2800 nautical miles away.

I awoke with an uneasy feeling. "Whoa, are we really ready for this," I thought as I contemplated a month at sea. I'd spent 45 days at sea in the Bering Sea on fishing boat but was In no way responsible for getting it from point A to point B.

We hoisted the anchor, motored to the fuel dock, and filled the fuel and water tanks. We also got a few cold beers and more chips. Lee had already dusted five bags. "We should've gotten more," he lamented as we pulled away from the dock.

As we motored out of the channel we raised the main and let out the jib. With the sails set, we decided it a good idea to crack open three *ballenas*, what the large (literally: whale sized) bottles of beer were called. Sun on our face, passage begun, beer in hand, we figured everything peachy. That was until we rounded Lover's Leap, the large rocks on the Cabo headland where Matt had wanted to blow his head off, and the wind was gusting to 25 knots. "Funkin' A." After finding a spot to nestle my *ballena* I reefed in the jib to the size of a handkerchief. Still feeling over canvassed, I decided it was time to take on the main.

During my three month stint on land I'd done further research on the whole reefing thing and had reconfigured the system even further. Of course I had yet to actually test the new system. Amanda took the wheel with instructions to keep the bow into the wind. She had to crank up Big Red to do so. Lee and I did battle with the main.

In a moment of insanity I'm still embarrassed to admit to, I chucked my *ballena* overboard. It was interfering with some of the lines I needed to reef the main and I had a sudden mental image of broken glass littering the cockpit. Despite the potential danger, it was an embarasingly extreme reaction.

At one point I thought the wind might be winning the battle and I threw out a topic for thought. "We could call it a day and give her another go tomorrow when we're a little bit more prepared." The crew was steadfast. "I think we can sort it out," Lee said with a calmness that suggested he was refer-ring to untangling a fishing line. "No guarantee it's going to be any different tomorrow. We might as well get on with it," Amanda chimed in. "Okay," I agreed. I was happy to see the crew keen to continue but a little disappointed not to have another pleasant night at anchor before serving our sentence with Neptune.

Before long, Lee and I had a double reef in the main, my new system having worked almost flawlessly. We put Cabo behind us and pointed the bow towards the equator, easing the jib out for more speed. It was a little hard to steer, as I still hadn't discovered balance, but I decided that it was good enough, possibly even… "perfect!"

Everything seemed to be going well until Lee heard water sloshing around in the bilge. He popped open the floorboard at the base of the entrance ladder. "There wasn't this much water down here before, was there?" Lee asked, looking up at me in the cockpit. Amanda took the wheel and I went down for closer inspection.

I once read that a hole the size of a quarter can sink a 40 foot boat in eight minutes. Water coming into the boat is something to take notice of.

"There's a lot of water down there," Lee stated looking at the brown mass sloshing all over the place. It was still below the floorboards however, not quite giving it that scary edge it would have had had water been sloshing around our ankles. "Yes, but there's still a lot of air above the water," I thought to myself optimistically. "Where's it coming from?" I thought aloud. We hadn't noticed running into anything so it made sense to focus on the holes that already existed in the hull.

Surprisingly, a boat generally has a quite a few holes, with attached valves, in the hull to allow water in, for flushing the toilet and to provide saltwater for cleaning dishes, and to allow water out from the bilge pumps, the toilet, and the anchor chain locker. All told, Hanuman had thirteen such holes. In addition to being an unlucky number, It suddenly seemed like a lot of holes to put in something that was supposed to float.

We conjectured that since the boat was heeling so far over to port that it might be one of the holes normally above the water line. It didn't take us long to figure out that water was siphoning back through the engine bilge pump outlet. I flicked on the switch for the pump. I'd 'fixed' the pump a number of times but it never seemed to work when it was actually needed. Nothing happened. I toggled the switch a few times, still nothing. Amanda squinted down at me from the cockpit, her mouth pierced with quiet, yet concerned, skepticism. Lee looked up at me from the bilge with a "nice job fixin' the pump" grin. "It's not like it's the only pump," I argued. Lee closed the outlet come inlet valve. I climbed up to the cockpit and pumped the Gusher hand bilge that I'd also rebuilt before leaving. Water shot out of its exit valve. I looked at Lee and Amanda, as I nodded slightly, with a look intended to convey, "See… I did manage to fix something."

Before long we heard a slurping noise, like getting to the bottom of an enormous milkshake, and the bilge was clear. Lee sat in a meditative posture peering down into the bilge to see if it would fill again. After what seemed like a reasonable amount of time Lee looked up to the cockpit and gave me the "it seems to be fixed" shrug. I shrugged back and he put the floorboard back into position.

Taking stock in our situation I couldn't help but notice that we'd experienced one drama per hour. Extrapolating: 24 hour in a day, times an estimated 30 day passage came out to 7200 dramas for the whole passage. "Hopefully things will mellow out," I thought.

Things did mellow out and I entered a three day long daze. The wind continued to blow and we sped along. I looked over my shoulder and realized I'd forgotten to get one last glimpse at land. I wouldn't be seeing North America again for quite some time.

On the fourth day out the wind settled, giving us chance to leave the narrow world of steer, sleep, steer, sleep. Despite not puking, I felt acutely seasick for the first three days. The calming of the sea and the lightening of the wind allowed me to break from the routine.

Lee had appointed himself ship's cook. Lee had two claims to fame. Neither of which made him a good cook but one of which made him well suited for life in the galley. "I never get seasick and I never get hangovers," he boasted. Both traits made him well suited for life as a sailor. While his cooking wasn't to die for, just the thought of slaving in the galley made me nauseous. I was happy he'd taken over food preparation.

A couple of days earlier the new steering cable we'd installed in La Paz had stretched out in the rough weather and Lee had gladly crawled under the cockpit and tightened it in the wildly rolling seas; astronaut training as far as I was concerned. I probably could have pulled it off but would have ended up with puke all over myself and a desire to "just end it."

In the calm conditions I was, for the first time, able to pallet what Lee called 'gruel'. Appropriately Lee called every meal he cooked, 'gruel'. It could be characterized not so much by its taste but by the noise it made. In the event that I got my hand on a spoon and troweled it around in the gruel, it sounded like a combination of the noise your tongue makes when peeling it off the roof of your mouth after a night of dehydrating drinking, and walking in mud. Lee didn't encourage the use of utensils. "Chips are for scooping!" was his mantra. If Amanda or I were feeling at bit seasick this gruel, typically a brown beanie paste, possible punctuated by a can of corn or an oily tin of tuna, seemed only slightly more appetizing than licking an ashtray.

Eventually Amanda and I became saturated with gruel to the point where just thinking about it made us dry heave. Thus the 'Broth Rebellion' was born. Against Lee's approval we would sneak into the galley and whip up some Top Ramen, heavy on the broth, light on the noodles. After a couple of weeks of heavy gruel consumption we needed the antithesis of gruel, the anti-gruel venom, to rebalance our systems.

Lee was a little offended by our presents in the galley. "I would have been happy to make some broth for you non-gruel eating pussies," he rebuked. However, we couldn't chance him adding some sort of gruely fodder and destroying the simplicity of the broth. On one occasion he'd done just that, adding way too much of some random very cheap Mexican spice, ruining the broth and preventing us from being able to tolerate any amount of the spice in the future.

As the wind decreased I let out the jib, unreefed the main, and hoisted the stay sail. I spent some time getting all of the sails balanced just right, so that there wasn't much pull on the wheel, and engaged the auto-pilot.

Being freed from the wheel was extremely liberating, like being unshackled. We'd been maintaining a watch system that consisted of two hour of steering followed by four hour of free time. The system was in place 24 hours a day. With the auto-pilot going we still maintained the same watch routine except that while on watch we were just responsible for looking out for ships and making sure Hanuman was on course and her sails weren't flapping. Steering is a full time occupation. Watching for boats isn't. With the auto-pilot (R-2 D-2 as we came to call it, because of the beeping noise it made when annoyed) going we had a lot more time to devote to non-steering activities. A full third of one's day was opened up. Non-steering activities primarily included reading and staring off into space, both highly rewarding pursuits.

After a few days of spotty, variable breezes the wind picked up to a comfortable 15 knots and swung around from the northeast. We'd entered the Trade Winds. With the wind coming from behind we had the problem that the mainsail blocked the current of air from hitting the staysail or the jib. Ideally one has a pole that attaches to the front of the mast and projects in the opposite direction of the boom and holds the jib on the opposite side of the main allowing it unfettered access to the wind. I didn't have one of these poles. When sailing downwind it simply wasn't functional to have both the main and the jib up at the same time. Having only one sail up reduced the total sail area and, in turn, limited our speed. We did have a drifter; a large deep bellied sail similar to a spinnaker. It had a greater sail area than either the jib or the main and with its deep belly could cup the wind efficiently.

We took down all of the other sails, hoisted the drifter, and found ourselves moving along at a respectable speed. The center of effort of the drifter was far forward so it pulled the boat, making steering fairly easy. R-2 liked easy. When steering was more difficult R-2's belt that attached it to the wheel tended to slip causing R-2 to get off course and start beeping angrily.

R-2 had come with the boat but seemed to be missing a part. A part I guessed was probably called the 'belt tensioning device.' We came up with a number of our own 'belt tensioning devices' and added a large rubber band to the drum that attached the drive belt to the wheel, giving the belt more traction. Eventually we fine-tuned it so that hand steering was only necessary when there was no wind at all.

We cruised along nicely under the pull of the drifter for days, without having to touch anything. We hung onto lines attached to the back of the boat and let ourselves be dragged through the water. Amanda wasn't too comfortable with the practice however, and commented, "You guys look a lot like bait, trolling behind the boat like that." Lee and I couldn't help but affirm the resemblance and got out the mask and snorkel and had a look. We didn't see any sharks but were amused to find we'd taken on an entourage of small fish swimming close to the hull. Dragging behind the boat became a daily ritual as long as our speed wasn't over five knots. We quickly found that at speeds over five knots it was hard to hold on and even harder to get back on the boat.

Days rolled by and blended together. It might only be one event that distinguished one day from another. Perhaps Lee's gruel had an especially pungent flavor on one day. Perhaps we caught an especially large Yellow Fin the next.

We attempted to offset the routine. Lee shaved his face like Wolverine and had me blacken it in with a felt tip marker. The next day he made a Greek looking headpiece out of some rope, wrapped his bed sheet around himself, and stood on the cabin top moving from one Herculean pose to the next. "Nice Toga, Zeus," I complemented, with more than a touch of sarcasm. We happened to have a couple of copies of Romeo and Juliet and acted it out over a plastic bottle of *agua diente*. Days rolled by.

The Trade Winds slowly increased as we moved south. When we'd hoisted the drifter it was the first time I'd done so and we rigged it in what was probably a nontraditional manner. As the growing swells passed under us Hanuman rolled from side to side, covering quite a few degrees. The motion of the drifter wasn't synchronized with that of the boat. Its side to side motion was delayed, causing excessive wear and tear on its control lines. I considered taking it down and putting out the jib but our speed had climbed to seven knots and I didn't want to mess with a good thing.

One night I was pulled out of a happy slumber by a crashing noise on deck and Amanda cursing. Lee and I flew up the ladder. The drifter was half on deck and half in the water dragging along next to us. "Shit, …I guess that halyard (the wire that held the drifter up) must have been sawed threw." Lee and I wrestled the sail back on deck and nodded as we eyed the frayed wire.

With the jib set and the drifter stuffed down below, I got ready to crawl back into my buck. I noticed the *indiglow* light up on the cockpit watch out of the corner of my eye. "You're up," Amanda stated, rather unsympathetically. "Damn it." But it was a beautiful night. The moon was out. The boat felt less loose and out of control with the jib up so I figured life could be worse.

The steady winds, that we'd come to assume constant, slowly abated and Hanuman coasted to a halt. The jib hung thwapping against the rigging with each passing swell. We'd arrived in the Doldrums; also known as the Inter-tropical Convergence Zone or ITCZ. Usually found close to the equator, the ITCZ is where the Northeast Trades converge with the Southeast Trades. The wind wasn't quite sure what to do.

There are many passing squalls that produce brief torrents of rain and strong gusts of wind but they are over so quickly that they provide no real mileage. One minute we were heeled over under reefed sails and the next we were dead in water staring up at limp wet canvas. The wind offered the hope of movement but only left us becalmed after its quick passing. "Wind before rain, you'll be sailing a-gain. Rain before wind, get your topsails in." Or something like that. We didn't have any topsails but we did have plenty of time to contemplate old adages while in the Doldrums.

The wind was often absent but the swells rarely were. We took all of the sails down when we were becalmed to prevent the maddening, and wear inducing, flapping of the limp Dacron. Not having the sails for stability, the passing swells caused Hanuman to pitch and roll erratically. The Doldrums can be exasperating not only for the lack of wind but also because you get tossed around like you're in a storm. I smoked a lot of weed and stared at the water, looking for wind ripples, or just watched the wind direction indicator at the top of the mast spin around in circles.

In addition to breaking the drifter halyard we also managed to break the jib halyard. The jib always stayed up because it was on a roller furling system that allowed it to be wrapped around the head stay, one of the wires holding up the mast, when not in use. The furling system had jammed at the top of the mast however, and when we attempted to roll it up we managed to break the halyard. To prevent the jib from falling down we had to keep it rolled around the head stay a few turns. The arrangement made the jib smaller, decreasing our speed.

Eventually we decided that we should have a least one working headsail halyard so I got my climbing harness on and Amanda and Lee winched me up the mast using a the mainsail halyard. I had to hug the mast so that I wouldn't be flung sideways when the boat rolled. At the masthead I attached a new block (pulley) and fed a makeshift halyard through it. The whole procedure took almost an hour during which I felt a lot closer to the sun. Despite feeling like I was baking in a solar oven, the mission was completed and I came down.

We'd duck taped two pieces of line together so that the joint could move smoothly through the block. The idea was to ease the new halyard into place by pulling gently on the temporary line and avoiding putting too much pressure on the taped together joint. For some reason 'gently' slipped Lee's mind (gently wasn't really his way of doing things) and when he went to jump off of the boom, down onto the cabin top, he decided to use the new halyard to support his sub-stantial frame. Under Lee's considerable weight the tape joint parted and we watched the whole halyard go through the block and mound itself on deck, cartoon style.

I vomited my last helping of gruel into the clear blue sea. My head was pounding with what I guessed to be heat exhaustion that I'd developed during my excursion up the mast. I peered into the sea letting the puke drip off my chin, wondering if any fish would come and eat it. They didn't.

After a good helping of water and sometime in the shade it was Lee's turn to go up the mast. At least I'd gotten the block in place, so I felt like my mission wasn't a total waste. The second time around we got the job finished and I was able to reenter my previous mental state. Eyes focused to infinity, lost on the horizon.

We'd been starting the engine every other day to recharge the batteries drained from all the auto pilot usage but I was determined not to resort to using the engine to propel us through the Doldrums. We waited and sailed on what wind came up. Each new breeze made us wonder if we were pick-ing up the Southeast Trades. And then one night as we gazed at the stars and watched the moon rise, a breeze of substance built. I begrudgingly trimmed the sails accordingly, thinking that this breeze too would pass. It didn't. It lifted us up and took us away.

The new wind angle allowed us to fly both the jib and the main. We had record mileage days and flew across the equator barely taking notice. "We crossed the equator about an hour ago." A couple of heads nodded in mild appreciation.

The wind continued to blow, spraying salty waves across the deck and leaving flying fish in their wake. Our increase in speed quickened the passage of time and the last week of the passage sped by.

On our 28th day at sea I had the sunrise shift and in the pale glow of the pre-dawn I could see a black mass on the horizon. As the stars faded and the sun rose, the outline of an island unveiled itself from the darkness. Eventually I decided the time was right, "laaaaannnnd hoooe!" Amanda came up, scanned the horizon silently, nodded her head, and went back to bed. Lee moaned something unintelligible from his bunk about seeing it later. I smiled, contentedly alone in the cockpit with my head back and nose to the air, smelling for land. Arriving in the Marquesas suddenly made sailing around the world tangible. With thousands of miles between Hanuman and the mainland I finally felt the circumnavigation had truly begun.

The Marquesas

The Marquesas are some of the most stunning islands in the Pacific. Geologically young, they haven't lost their height and jaggedness.

As we got closer we could see and smell the luscious tropical green of Fatu Hiva, our destination. We rounded the northern extremity of the island as two Tropic Birds, looking almost cliché with their long tail streamers, flew over head. On the leeward side of the island the wind died and we fired up Big Red; headed for the Bay of Virgins. It had originally been named what translates to, 'The Bay of Penises,' for the phallic looking spires lining the bay. It seems arriving missionaries didn't find the name appropriate, and changed it, presumably to protect the chastity of the natives.

We squeezed into the deep narrow bay and, when we found the right depth, dropped the anchor and put Big Red in reverse to properly set it. Suddenly Big Red made an alarming noise and refused to reverse. I looked around briefly, and the problem hit me.

We'd been trailing an emergency line behind the boat so that in the event someone fell overboard, while on watch alone at night, they might have a chance of self rescue. In our enthusiasm with making landfall we'd forgotten about the line and managed to get it wrapped around the propeller. A very taunt line stretched from an aft cleat down the side of the boat and into the water. "Fuck!"

I dove under water with my knife to inspect the situation. I was astounded at how wrapped up the line had managed to become in such a short time. I hacked away at it with the dull blade. The propeller seemed a little further aft than I'd remembered, but I didn't think much of it. After cutting away the line I jumped back in the boat and decided to have a look at the engine prior to starting her up. Before even looking at the engine I noticed its cover didn't look right. After removing it, things quickly fell into the *no bueno* category. When the line had wrapped around the propeller shaft it pulled the whole engine back several inches snapping the rear engine mounts, leaving the weight of the engine on the front mounts and the propeller shaft itself. "Well…that sucks." It was all I could muster.

Despite the minor disaster, we were still pretty thrilled to be where we were. We jammed a few blocks of wood under the engine, taking some of the pressure off of the shaft. Though we were reluctant to push it, the engine still worked and we pulled up the anchor and moved to a better spot.

Fatu Hiva had little more than a few houses in two villages, each with one small store. Fixing Big Red was out of the question for the time being. The fact that we didn't have the resources for the repair was actually a little relieving. We needed some solid mental separation from the constant attention that the boat demanded during the long passage. We busted out Sputnik and took the beach.

With our feet on the ground we strolled, in a daze, through the village. We received many smiles and *bon jours*. We came across what appeared to be a store and went in to investigate. We didn't have refrigeration on Hanuman so the sight of cold beverages behind glass was enticing. We didn't have any Polynesian Francs but the grocer was happy to exchange our dollars. However, aside from the cold juice and soda, there wasn't a whole lot to buy. It was technically a dry island so cold beers were out of the question. Fortunately bartering was still a prevalent means of exchange and we were able to trade some of Matt's cloths for a chicken.

We spent a week on Fatu Hiva. We hiked across it, jumped off of waterfalls, surfed, snorkeled, and then were off to Hiva Oa. We left at one in the morning, estimating for a noon arrival on the following day.

We wanted to avoid using the engine in its debilitated condition but it was a tight squeeze with the other sail boats anchored around us so we motored out 25 yards before shutting it down and sailing away. Once out of the Fatu Hiva's wind shadow we found the trades and had a swift overnight sail, arriving at Hiva Oa early following morning.

After checking in with officialdom and having a brief look around, we thought it no longer healthy to ignore Big Red's ailment. Lee and I peeled back the engine cover and got down on our knees in a prayer like posture, quietly meditating on the severed engine mounts. Things didn't look good. We weren't dealing with nice clean breaks; more along the lines of a compound fracture. One engine mount looked like it could possibly be welded together but the other had parted right where one of the bolts went through it, tearing away more than snapping.

Our first step was to buy a large red crow bar. It was about three feet long, weighted about 20 pounds, and gave us the leverage we needed to shift Big Red. Using the crow bar and some wrenches we managed to remove both of the mounts. They'd surely never been removed before so I was pleased that they came out without major drama. I considered it a highly successful first stage of the operation.

With mounts in hand, we made our way to the one place on the island that was capable of welding. The welder didn't speak any English, and Lee's French was pretty suspect, but with perseverance we managed to explain what we needed done. I actually thought our plight should be fairly obvious. We clearly had four pieces that needed to be made into two. I initially suspected the welder wanted to make things more complicated, thus increasing the value of his work. However, I eventually surmised that he was concerned, given the regrettable location of one of the breaks, about the strength of a weld.

In any case, he eventually did the work while we looked on hopefully; like a couple of expecting fathers in the waiting room. I felt the weld looked pretty darn good when he was done, and was tempted to exclaim, "…perfect." He said that since he was working in a state welding facility he couldn't technically give us a bill; but he left a long pause at the end of the statement. We were really grateful for his services and glad to pay, but that whole, "just give me whatever you think it was worth," line is always hard to cope with. We handed him what we figured to be a fair sum. He nodded slowly and leaned his head to the side with an expression that said, "This will do, but I would've liked more." I embraced the "this will do" part of his expression, gave a big "*merci bocu*," and we walked off. The "I would like to have more," part of his expression seemed to be ringing in Lee's ears as we walked off, and he ran back and gave the welder a few more francs. Lee was a generous fellow.

We were walking back to the boat, feeling pretty good about our progress, when the port captain pulled over in front of us. He said that there'd been an earthquake off the coast of South America and a tidal wave was expected at around ten that night. He was concerned that the shallow bay where we were anchored might drain completely of water, leaving Hanuman lying in the mud before the wave arrived and clobbered us. "Perfect."

We wanted to leave before sunset, and there wasn't really enough time to install the mounts before then, so we had to go for it with the engine in its precarious condition. At sunset we, and every other boat behind the breakwater, scrambled out the harbor entrance. We spent the night dodging boats as we tacked back and forth in deep water.

Amanda and I must have eaten something bad earlier in the day and we were sick the entire night. I was puking over the rail and she was curled up in a ball with a bad case of gut rot.

Being a huge fan of 'street food,' gut rot became a fairly common occurrence throughout the trip. However, it was never enough to dampen my appetite. It usually just left me feeling, more or less, fine but not entirely able to trust a fart. "OOOwww, that one sounded wet." "It was."

When the sun rose we happily made our way back to the anchorage after a very unpleasant night.

We spent a couple more days on Hiva Oa installing the engine mounts and then sailed over to the nearby island of Tahuata where we found a pristine bay with a deserted beach. We basked in the beauty of the bay for a few days before sailing north to Nuku Hiva. We had the good fortune to arrive when the crew of a mega-yacht sailboat decided they had a budget surplus and threw a huge party, inviting all the boats in the bay.

Lee, feeling he hadn't gotten enough mileage out of his toga outfit, donned it again. I decided I couldn't let him make a fool of himself alone and ripped off my bed sheet. Believing the toga needed accentuation, I added an elaborate headdress fashioned out of tin foil. Amanda decided she'd leave us to our devices and went as herself. As we took the beach and made for the feast we noticed that all of the, typically crusty, sailors had busted out what was probably their best set of clothes. Many of them were even wearing shoes! Lee and I took a moment to reevaluate. I was having some serious doubts about our attire; but it was a long way back to the boat and we could smell the *umu* (under ground pit roasting oven) and we decided to roll with it. I toned down my headdress a little and we entered the party. Amanda distanced herself from us. I didn't blame her.

The mega-yacht crew had spared no expense. In addition to the live local entertainment, the spread was unbelievable. Fifty or sixty people had turned up, and it didn't take more than a few seconds for all of them to crane their heads toward Lee and me. After a few smiles they went back to their drinks. We were actually dressed almost identically to the local entertainment.

Lee and I introduced ourselves to the mega-yacht captain and thanked him for the party. Fortunately he was amused, and not offended, by our attire and grinned as he said, "I thought maybe you got the wrong invitation."

After a couple of drinks I was pretty pleased that we were wearing our togas. They were a hit and added to the life of the party. Originally the captain had intended to just give out two free drinks per person, but decided to open up the bar for a free for all. Lee was on stage playing guitar with the band before the night was over.

Later in the night Lee met a local tattoo artist who was covered from head to toe with tattoos that he'd mostly done himself. Having run out of skin he'd even put tattoos on top of tattoos. Lee decided he had to have one. He gave him just a general idea of what he was interested in before letting him run wild with it. The artist didn't speak English, so I'm not sure how much translated, but he took out his home made 'tattoo gun,' an electric shaver with a sewing needle lashed to it, and went to work. Several hours later Lee had a tattoo that actually looked pretty damn good.

Lee gets a tattoo with a modified electric razor in Nuku Hiva

The Goat Head

Tattoo still bleeding, we pulled anchor and sailed seven miles west to where we planned on hiking to the third highest waterfall on earth. The next morning we took the beach and were greeted by a young Marquesan guy wearing a gigantic necklace made of long brown curved teeth. When Lee took off his shirt the guy saw his fresh tattoo and recognized it as the work of his cousin. After studying the tattoo, and giving it a 'thumbs up,' he asked if we had any cannabis. "No. Do you?" He didn't either. Apparently it was out of season.

Despite our lack of cannabis, he decided to accompany us to the waterfall. A seasoned, and slightly jaded, traveler I'm typically suspicious of anyone who wants to accompany me anywhere; fearing a 'guide fee' at the end of it. He didn't have that aura however and just walked along casually chatting with Lee in broken French/English about tattoos, cannabis, and life's other vital ingredients.

We passed through his village of about 16 people. "Mostly guys," our new friend complained. It was about as idyllic, aside from the lack of women, a little spot as one could imagine; a long narrow fertile looking canyon hemmed in by steep mountain walls blanketed with lush tropical vegetation.

We continued up the canyon through dense jungle, popping out of the vegetation once to be rewarded with a stunning view of the waterfall in the distance. It was the only view of the entirety of the waterfall we got, however. The river took a sharp turn after the waterfall ended and, in the narrow canyon, it was impossible to view the main body of the waterfall. We swam around in the murky water, shared our canned tuna and crackers with our new friend, and headed back down the trail.

On the return voyage our friend left the trail and, along with his two dogs, headed into the foliage. We'd been walking along without him for some time when we heard some intense animal noises emanating from the jungle nearby. We weren't sure what exactly they were coming from, but it was obvious that they were sounds of deep agony. Lee took the small cheese cutting knife from Amanda's backpack and headed across the creek towards the noise. I picked up a girthy stick I thought could pass for a club, and followed.

We didn't have to go far before we found the source of the cry. Ahead of us was a scene that made my jaw drop. A large goat with his front legs on land, struggling to get out of the water, and his hind two in the creek, was being attacked by our friend's two dogs. One dog had him by the throat and was jerking him downward and the other had his teeth into the goat's haunches and was pulling him backwards. The goat was still upright but no longer yelping, seemingly focusing all of his energy on survival. I wasn't giving him very good odds. The dogs appeared intent in the goat's demise.

As I stood there, feeling thankful that I wasn't the goat, Lee entered the fray, knife in hand. I wasn't sure of his intentions, but looked on absorbedly. He trudged into the combat zone, looking rather ogre like, grabbed the goat by the head, and proceeded to saw away at the goat's neck with the knife. "I guess he's on the dog's side," I thought. "Wise choice."

As riveted as I was by what was taking place in front of me, I was pulled out of my trance when I heard Amanda scream. I took off back towards the trail, figuring Lee had things under control. Apparently our friend had caught Amanda, whose attention was strongly focused in our direction, off guard when he dropped another goat down beside her. She'd regained her composure when I arrived.

When our friend saw Lee dragging another goat towards us his eyes lit up like it was Christmas. "Two goat," he repeated over and over as he danced a little jig. He had, I quickly became aware, been hunting goats all along and was thrilled to have gotten two. Lee had picked up on that when he saw the dogs attacking the goat.

Our new friend, and now comrade in arms, borrowed our knife and quickly gutted the goats. He cut the head off his goat, which lacked a good set of horns, and tossed it aside. Then he beheaded the one Lee had finished off and held it in the air, "trophy."

We lugged the carcasses and the head back to our friend's house where he and his brother butchered them. They opened us fresh coconuts to drink. We waited out the rain in their modest house, smiling and nodding in lieu of a common verbal language. When the rain let up they loaded us up with a rack of bananas, several papayas, coconuts, a sack of grapefruits, a sack of limes, half a goat, and the trophy. We could barely carry all of our lute. Amanda wondered what we would do with the goat head.

Removing the goat head at the behest of the Australian customs official

Back in the bay we found some friends, who we'd gotten to know one night when our dinghy almost floated away, had arrived. We had more goat meat that we knew what to do with so we invited them over for a barbeque. With our small marine barbeque attached to the rail, we got things cooking. We didn't bother with any side dishes. "Would you like goat or…goat?" After the ribs and steaks were passed around the chewing began, and continued for the better portion of the night. It was the toughest meat any of us had ever had. It was like chewing rubber. The key was to cut off minute bites, swallow them whole, and hope that stomach acid would do its thing. To top it off we busted out our 'swill.'

Two weeks prior to goat night, Lee, Amanda, and I decided we'd put the empty keg to good use. To it we add the water from twenty coconuts and much of their meat, grapefruits, Kool-Aid, sugar, and a pouch of baker's yeast. In the tropical temperatures the fermentation went quickly and my daily ritual of releasing the pressure from the keg brought a devious smile to my face.

The swill didn't exactly taste first-rate, but it made the goat slide down easier. Regrettably, the swill didn't seem to produce the buzz I was hoping for, but one of our guests reported a mild hangover the next day and Lee did puke from it once, intent on 'feeling something,' so at least it was doing something.

Tuamoto Archipelago

We hit one more Marquesan Island and then headed south toward the Tuamoto Archipelago. The goat head, which I'd tied to the pulpit on the front of the boat, reached an eight out of ten on the reek factor scale. The maggots had really gone to work, leaving a puke colored pool of smegma on the anchor roller.

Worse than the general discomfort of beating to windward was the fact that the cockpit was down wind of the goat head. Even while sailing downwind the occasional flutter of wind was enough to make one wonder, "what's that smell?" Instinctively I would look around the cockpit for some of Lee's putrid mildewing clothes and cautiously advance my nose in their direction only to realize that, while Lee's clothes did reek, they couldn't possibly be responsible for the utterly vulgar waft I'd just encountered. Then the light bulb in my head would flicker and I'd remember, "Ahhh, the goat head…Small price to pay for such a valuable trophy."

The proliferation of flies, presumably brought on by the rotting head, put Amanda in a bad mood one morning. She told me she'd been bitten on the eyelid the previous night and asked if it was swollen. It was. "Once the maggots have eaten all of the flesh off of the head the flies won't be a problem," I assured her.

The Tuamotos weren't spectacular in my mind. Geologically they're much older than the Marquesas and have eroded to the point where all that's left is a ring of sand covered coral that used to surround an island.

Sailing into the ring of coral can be a bit tricky since all of the seawater that goes in or out of the lagoon, due to tides and currents, has to move through the same narrow passes that we used to enter. This often creates strong currents and standing waves. Once inside the lagoon I expected the snorkeling to be stellar but much of the coral was dead and I wasn't all that impressed.

After stopping at of couple of atolls we headed for Tahiti. Tahiti was to be an end point for Lee and Amanda. Lee was headed up to Alaska for the King Crab season. Amanda had purchased a ticket from Tahiti back to the states before meeting me in Mexico. She was adamant about having a ticket home before we left. I think she feared getting stuck on the boat. The whole experience was tolerable as long as she knew there was a definite end point.

We spent a night sailing back and forth in front of Tahiti's capitol, Papeete, waiting for the sun to rise so that we could enter the harbor more safely. After a few days exploring Tahiti, Amanda and Lee flew out on their respective flights. The airline wouldn't let Lee on the plane initially because he smelled bad and his shirt was so dirty. Tahitians have a thing for cleanliness. Lee doesn't. I also made sure he was nice and drunk before I sent him to the airport, which probably didn't help matters.

Lee, I would see again in passing. Despite our intention to continue our relationship, I would never see Amanda again.

Fortunately Brandoni and Braden, who'd sailed down a segment of the California coast with me, hadn't gotten quite enough of Hanuman and flew into Tahiti a week after Lee and Amanda's departure. Lee and Amanda were great companions and crew but I was excited for a changing of the guard, to spice things up. During his last couple of weeks on the boat Lee entered a deep level of lethargy, though he may have described it as meditation. I had an extensive library on Hanuman and Lee had decided there were a number of books he just couldn't leave without reading. I knew Brandoni and Braden would be arriving with several surfboards and a lot of energy.

The Society Islands

Brandoni stepped on a sea urchin as he wadded out to the boat for the first time, thus being initiated into the tropics properly.

Despite a few spines in the foot, the energy level and activity did increase. While hitchhiking back from a day of surfing, one where I broke one of my boards in half, we got a ride from a guy who insisted on taking us to his cabbage farm. He picked us a few mammoth cabbages and led us through the brush to where he had several pot plants growing. A pride filled grin spread across his face. Braden had full head of dread locks so everyone just assumed he was looking for weed, which he was. In addition to giving us the two enormous cabbages, he dropped us off right in front of the boat with six branches from his pot plants.

Before long we pointed the goat head out to sea and started exploring the rest of the Society Islands. Our friends on Golden Emerald, with whom who we'd shared our goat meat, had accidentally put gasoline in their diesel tank and realized that it would not "be okay," the hard way. As such, we found ourselves towing them into and out of anchorages. It was kind of amusing the first time but we tended to sail faster than they did. We would arrive at a new bay, anchor, and then when they arrived we would have to pull up the anchor and go and tow them in. I was happy to help, but fact that their whole 'plan' revolved around us towing them into and out of every anchorage got a little tiresome. They made us dinner a couple of times, but after that it was just, "thanks."

I'd expected the maggots and bacteria to eat the goat head down to the bone, leaving just the skull and horns. The head was actually blocking the running lights. My hope was that once all the flesh was gone, the red light would project out one eye and the green out the other. Things didn't seem to be going that way. One eye was dried shut and the other, looking lacquered, was popping out. The mouth was frozen open in the shape of a scream. The heavy oozing slowed and what was left seemed to just dry out. The smell even mellowed. It wasn't the bone white desert bleached look I imagined, more like road kill, but I came to find its condition even more fitting.

I didn't find myself missing Amanda greatly. With the mental energy I'd been devoting to her freed up, I found a lot more time for introspection. I felt I could be more honest with myself in her absents. The deep feelings that I'd assumed I would eventually feel for her never materialized. She was very attractive, extremely low maintenance, and adored me, but I could never resign myself to a future with her. I recalled when she'd asked me about future plans. I'd taken the question as an offence, surprising even myself by my reaction. I also thought any sort of planning or discussion of life beyond the trip around the world to be sac-religious.

Our tour of the Societies continued in a blur of activity. I smoked a lot of weed. It didn't take us too long to burn through the six branches. Once dried out there wasn't all that much to them. We replenished our supply frequently. Weed was actually kind of expensive but people would often just give it to us or trade something for it. We kept active on the large scale with surfing and exploring, but many of the small things seemed less important in a stony hazed. My teeth were often fuzzy. The munchies were also a factor. We made super long sandwiches with the ever present fresh baguette for lunch and towering pots of pasta for dinner. Nights were typically spent playing Hearts and drinking wine out of one litter cartons, or casks as they were called. Drinking too much and passing out first was a risk. We were pretty heavy into 'chiefing.' I had an assortment of Sharpie permanent markers that were used, without mercy, to defile the exposed flesh of anyone whose eyes were closed.

Bora Bora marked the last of the Society Islands we were to visit. Once stocked up, we were off to The Kingdom of Tonga. Somehow I'd gotten it into my head that Tonga was about 500 miles from Bora Bora, so when I calculated the passage to be 1100 miles, we were caught off guard. Brandoni's girlfriend Sara, along with Dan, a friend of Braden and Brandon, were meeting us in Tonga and would be arriving in two weeks. Suddenly we didn't have tons of time to stop in Niafu as we'd planned. Braden was excited about Niafu. Brandoni was excited to get to Tonga before Sara. I didn't really care too much about going to Niafu and I could certainly see how Brandoni wouldn't want Sara to have to wait; Nuie was out.

The wind slowly petered and left us drifting about ten miles from Bora Bora. We got out the cards and for a game of Hearts. With every game to 100 we gave ourselves new names. There were various penalties for not calling a person by their name. I decided my name would reflect our desire for wind and became 'Wind in His Hair.' Brandoni and Braden followed suite with 'Chief Big Wind' and 'Dancing in the Wind.' The following morning brought the strongest winds I'd experienced.

Braden had the sunrise shift and woke me up with the two knocks above my bunk. I assumed it was simply the beginning of my watch, but craned my head into the cockpit to double check. Braden seemed to be gripping the wheel tightly and have his attention fixed on the sails. He glanced down at me, "it's pretty windy bro." I poked my head above deck to feel the wind's full effect. "Yeah, it is," I confirm. It felt like a squall that would pass quickly, so I hesitated to reef the sails, but the old adage "reef often and reef early" went through my head. I decided reefing wasn't all that much work so I scampered up to the mast in my boxers and rain jacket and reefed the main; a procedure that had become second nature.

One of things that I'd learned in my 5000 thousand miles at sea was that the way to keep the boat balanced was to reef the mainsail before the jib, regardless of the extra effort it required. That moved the center of effort forward, preventing the boat from wanting to round up into the wind, thus making steering more manageable. Furthermore, the stay sail was no longer the first sail I took down, but rather the last. This also kept the boat more balanced, and tighter. I don't think 'tighter' is really a sailing term, but having the majority of the boat's sail area closer to the mast felt tighter; more stable.

What I thought to be "just a squall" turned out to be the beginning of a three day storm. After I reefed the main the wind increased even more, "shit, it's really blowin.'" I brought the main down to the second reefing point, brought the jib in about half way, and started to crawl back in my bunk. "Uh, ... bro," Braden said. "Yeah?" "You're up." "Damn it!"

I geared up and sat down on the wet fiberglass. "At least it's relatively warm," I consoled myself. The wind increased and the waves grew to match. Fortunately we were on a broad reach, so we didn't have to go into the weather. Before long, the waves had built to such a height that we were surfing down them as they passed below us. Braden asked me to pass him down the bucket for puking purposes. Brandoni woken up with a, "what the fuck is going on," look in his eye. We were in the shit.

Eventually my shift came to an end and I called Brandoni up. "Seriously?" He hoped that perhaps these conditions were beyond his rank. "Yup, get yourself geared up." Waves were frequently breaking on top of us by then.

Brandoni made his way into the cockpit, looking rather nauseated and colorless. One had to work the wheel as we surfed down the waves. I demonstrated the steering technique before letting him take over. Once I felt he had the hang of it I stripped down and dove back into my bunk.

I was amazed by how comforting the bunk could be. As long as I just lay there with my eyes closed I was never seasick. In such a state, the mind takes on a wonderful emptiness. There's the subtle happiness of not being in the cockpit, but beyond that there's no ambition of any sort. Not even food or women entered my mind. The main hatch boards were left out and couple of breaking waves managed to wet the foot of my bunk. My mind took in the discomfort of the wetness on my feet and calculated the easiest solution, 'pull feet up.' Problem solved, my mind went empty, and fell back into rhythm with the passing waves.

I was in a mental counter pose to the condition I'd been in during our tour of the Societies, where I was rarely content with the state I was in, and constantly seeking to alter it in some way. I would wake up with the thought, "I wonder when we'll smoke that first joint." The answer was typically, "soon." The high would temporarily put me in a state of acute mental awareness, which I relished. In that state, my attention would turn to the activity that would be undertaken for the day. The state of awareness would typically fade once that activity was underway and before long I was thinking of what I'd be consuming next. I'd spend the rest of the day in pursuit of the mindless pleasure derived from over eating and drinking; a pursuit that would continue, ad nauseum, until I passed out that night.

I may paint the picture of the roller coaster journey of an addict, and in truth I guess, in a way, I was, but the consumption of weed and booze never troubled me so much as the addiction to the mental state of longing. I couldn't find satisfaction in the present without some promise of future gratification. And while I was certainly consuming more than was healthy I rarely woke up with a hangover and ribs showed through my taught brown skin.

Two hours after Brandoni had begun, it was Braden's turn. I told Brandoni to stay there with him until he got the steering down. Brandoni put Braden's steering into the 'good enough' category in short order and wasn't even in his bunk when Braden jibed with the first passing wave. Fortunately I had the preventer in place so that the boom didn't go slamming across the boat, but even with the preventer, jibing was a very jarring experience which Hanuman didn't like. Braden said he'd gotten confused about right and left, and which way to turn the wheel, in all of the excitement.

Using the wheel, one steers the boat just like a car. Turning the wheel to the right caused the boat to go right, and turning it to the left caused it to go left. I felt this was pretty straight forward and wasn't too thrilled about jibing. On the other hand, we were in the shit, and shit happens in the shit, so I tried to muster as much understanding as I could. "When in doubt just round up into the wind," I offered.

Fortunately Braden and Brandoni hadn't been spoiled by the autopilot, and were somewhat accustomed to hand steering. After the incident with the line in the prop and Big Red's subsequent debilitation I decided it was best not to use the engine just to charge the batteries, so R-2 was on the bench.

Lights were off limits, for the most part, as well, so we got by with lanterns and candles in port, and brief light usage at sea.

The wind remained fierce for three days, during which we ate very little. We had a rack of bananas in the cockpit we'd obtained in Bora Bora that seemed to ripen all at once. We snacked on those and any other items that didn't require cooking. Hunger for something substantial would frequently flare up but was quickly quelled by the thought of actually trying to cook something. Eventually the wind let up enough to make cooking bearable and we were able to regroup, scarf down a hot meal, and reassess our priorities.

We'd managed to retain enough weed to roll one joint, but decided we should dedicate it to a special occasion. Catching a fish seemed like a worthy enough event and heads shook in agreement.

"Fish on! Fish on!" I yelled. Braden and Brandoni flew into the cockpit, but their faces showed considerable surprise when they saw the fishing line dragging limply behind the boat. I didn't normally cry wolf and they eyed me suspiciously as I slowly lifted my right hand. Pinched between index finger and thumb was a two inch long flying fish that had stranded itself on deck and died during the night. "It is a fish,… and we did catch it," I argued under their skeptical gazes. They didn't require too much convincing and heads slowly began to nod in unison. "Let's roll it up," shouted Braden, already reaching for the papers.

Tonga

A week after the joint, sunrise revealed the first islands of the Vava'u group of northern Tonga. We snaked our way between islands and past a pod of Humpback whales to the port of Nieafu, where we happily dropped anchor and went to land in search of something to eat besides rice or pasta. Fortunately it was Sunday, so immigration was closed and we didn't have to bother announcing our arrival. Technically, we probably weren't supposed to go ashore before checking in, but we figured we could always play dumb. The old, "we were actually just on our way to check in when someone threw these ice cream cones at us and we were forced to eat them before they melted," routine.

A couple of days prior to reaching Tonga we'd turned on the short wave radio and listened for news of the outside world. We tuned into the middle of what sounded like an exceedingly serious report. We could tell that something significant had happened, we just didn't know what. Slowly the story of September 11 was unraveled. We were taken back by the scale of the attack, but hearing about in the middle of the ocean made it seem as though it was occurring in another world. It didn't really hit home until we got to Tonga and witnessed images of airliners flying into the Trade Towers over and over again on the TV.

Sara and Dan arrived several days later. If I thought there were a lot of surfboards on board prior to their arrival, I was mistaken. I considered just strapping them all on deck, but hated having anything interfering with the actual sailing of the vessel, so they all got crammed below. The forward ten feet of below deck area, referred to as the shed or garage, was devoted purely to storage. Despite sizeable storage space, the garage filled up quickly, and both Braden and Brandoni ended up with surfboards in their bunks. With the addition of the new crew they also ended up with more people in their bunks. Fortunately Sara was petite and could squeeze into Brandoni's quarter birth with him and his surfboard. Braden ended up with Dan and a surfboard for bunkmates.

We spent a couple of weeks in Niafu, the capitol of the Vava'u group, and in the surrounding islands enjoying short easy passages in consistent Trades unhindered by the low lying islands. We explored the island group's unique features including a hidden cave that could only be accessed by diving under water. We bought two live chickens, to the bewilderment of the locals who sold them to us, "you want Tonga chicken?" and killed, plucked, and roasted them on a deserted island.

Once satiated on Nieafu's cheap ice cream, we were done with Tonga and the five of us headed for Fiji. Sara and Dan were seasick and Braden puked as well. It rained constantly.

Braden and Dan had sustained injuries prior to the passage, adding to their discomfort. Before arriving in Tonga, Brandoni and I were lounging in the cockpit enjoying the sunset when we heard Braden scream out in pain from the galley. He was making a pot of tea and had set the kettle on the counter as he reached for cups. As he let go of the kettle, and focused his attention on grabbing the cups, the boat rolled and over went the kettle, spilling tea that had just been boiling, on both of his thighs. From our angle, Brandoni and I couldn't see what had happened, but hearing the kettle hit the floor gave us a pretty good indication. "I guess we're not getting any tea then," we both thought as we said, "you okay?" Braden continued with his, now muffled, cursing and we knew he was. Brandoni and I wondered if he'd make another pot of tea. He didn't.

A few days after arriving in Tonga, Dan was climbing up a small steep embankment when his flip-flops betrayed him. He slid backwards out of them and over a sharp piece of coral slicing open his foot and toe.

We came to refer to Dan and Braden's sleeping area as the cripple den. The front of both of Braden's thighs had blistered and opened. Puss oozed in a steady steam out of his pancake sized wounds. Chaffing against his wounds was, apparently, intolerable so he tucked the front of the legs of his shorts up into his waistband in a fashion resembling the garb of a sumo wrestler. A kind local had noticed his condition and given him a mayonnaise jar full of pure coconut oil to put on his lesions. Braden ladled the oil liberally over his blisters, giving his legs a basted appearance. "I bet some mashed potatoes and stuffing would go well with those thighs…maybe a little gravy."

After slicing his foot, Dan took to the use of a cane he'd fashioned out of a tree branch. The short cane hunched him over like a 100 year old man and gave him the walking pace to match.

There was so much clutter in the forward half of the boat that I rarely went past the chart table. In route to Fiji I thought I'd take a gander in the cripple den and see how things looked. In addition to the area being covered with used wet and bloody bandages, I noticed water trickling down the mast from all of the rain. The vicinity around the base of the mast, Braden and Dan's sleeping quarters, was soaked. Dan had brought a sleeping pad with a bunch of little troughs and ridges. All of the troughs were filled in with water. It looked like a miniature irrigated crop field. I expected little green rows of plants to spring up any day.

Fortunately for the sick and crippled it was a fast passage. We had a record three day run and on the fourth day saw breaking waves through the mist. We made our way through a pass in the reef and dropped anchor in front of Suva, Fiji.

Fiji

The following day I packed up the ship's papers and went to check in. I navigated my way through a disinterested port captain and customs officer, who were liberal with their stamps, before making my way to the immigration officer. The immigration officer was shifty eyed and had a devious way about him but looked too baby faced and doughy to be taken seriously. I presented him with my papers. He only pretended to look at them; had he been holding them up-side-down, he wouldn't have noticed. He told me I had to declare how much money I had on board. Declaring one's ability to be financially independent in a foreign country is not so unusual. The fact that he actually wanted to see the money seemed odd. He insisted I come back the next day with the money so he could count it.

That night I met up with Nick, the captain of the Golden Emerald, who we'd towed around the Societies. He said that the immigration officer had tried to steal money from him.

I went back to the immigration officer the following day with Nick's warning in mind, and, after an hour of waiting, sat down in front of his desk. He looked like the kind of guy who frequently took long lunches. He asked if I'd brought the money. "Yes." "Okay, let me count it," he said licking his fat red lips and pushing a piece of paper towards me. "Here, fill this out." I started counting the money out in front of him. "Give it to me. Give it to me. I have to count it. Fill out that form." And he snatched the money out of my hand. "Don't worry,...fill out that form," he ordered manically, in response to my questioning expression.

I'd counted the money about five times before going into his office. I didn't want there to be any question about how much I had.

I couldn't imagine that he would steal the money right in front of me. I started filling out the form. "Okay, you have 180 dollars," he announced as casually as he could. "What? I just handed you 300 dollars." I had also stated that amount as I was handing him the money. "I only count 180." "No, I just handed you two 100 dollar bills and five twenties," I stated raising my voice. "What? ....here, count it," he exclaimed in an affronted timbre as he threw the money down on the table between us. "I don't need to count it. I know how much I just handed you: 300 dollars." I'd increased my volume a notch and sat erect in my chair staring into his dark eyes. "What? You think I took it?" he yelled as if questioning his ethics was the worst injustice I could perpetrate. "Come look!" he screamed, jumping out of his chair, sending it flying backwards. "Come look!" he opened his arms gesturing for me to inspect the area. "I don't need to look. I handed you 300 dollars," I said in the most commanding voice I could muster, as I rose to my feet. He threw open his desk drawers scattering papers all over the floor. "Look!" he said, pulling open the file cabinet with a force that almost knocked it over. "Look!" he screamed again, "I don't have your money!"

I'd never seen such a display and was beginning to think the guy might be off his rocker. Thief or no thief, one just

106

doesn't behave in such a manner. Even considering possible cultural differences, it seemed like he wasn't playing with a full deck.

Full deck or not, he still had 120 of my dollars. I came around to his side of the desk. I'd been refusing to look in any of the areas he gestured towards. He had taken it, he knew where it was, and I wasn't going to indulge him in any of his nonsense. I maintained eye contact. "Give me my money," I commanded, trying to use Jedi mind control. It didn't work. His lips were quivering with rage and I was hit by a spray of saliva as he continued. "Look, ….look, I don't have your money," he spat, taking a step back and giving the open desk drawer a good shaking, sending few more papers onto the floor.

As he shook the drawer I noticed him moving his leg in a strange manner and looked down at his foot just in time to see him trying to kick a 100 dollar bill under the desk. He followed my gaze down to the floor where he was kicking my money. "Oh look, it must have fallen," he stated casually. "Must have fallen? You were just trying to kick it under the table." He resumed his deeply offended demeanor, puffing out his chest and clinching his jaw muscles. "Where's my other 20 dollars," I demanded. "I don't have it," he repeated as he reached into his pockets and turned them out. "Look." Now I was looking, but I didn't see my twenty bucks. "I know you have my twenty dollars. You were just trying to kick my 100 under the table. Give it to me." I left off the "you idiot," that I really wanted to tack on. He rebuffed his chest, stopped fidgeting, and raised his voice. "I don't have your money."

Fijians are a big people. This guy certainly wasn't their biggest specimen but he had a good 40 pounds on me; that forty pounds was mostly fat, however. I looked into his milky brown eyes and figured I could take him, if it came down to it.

"Give me my 20 bucks!" I demanded once again. He decided to change his tactic. "I don't have your money and if you don't stop asking you won't get your visas." I needed those visas and that stupid piece of paper with a stamp on it. I rolled my eyes, let out a disgusted sigh, and went back to my chair. He closed his desk draw, sat back down in his seat, and resumed paper work in a mannerism that suggested our little interaction had never taken place. "So…where are arriving from again?" "Tonga." "And your crew list?" I slid it across the table. "Any firearms?" "No." He gently stamped our passports and manifesto and handed them back to me. I put them in my folder and put the folder into my backpack snapping it shut.

Secure with the thought that I had my requisite stamps and papers, I decided to resume my campaign to retrieve my 20 bucks. I put my backpack on and stood up. "Where's my twenty bucks?" "You have offended me. Give me back those papers," he demanded with outstretched arm as he rose from his chair. I just stared at him, silently. He sat back down at his desk. "I'm taking away your visas and calling the police, you'll be sent to jail." He obviously wasn't going to call the police, nor was I going to jail, but I'd been to jail, didn't like it, and decided not to call his bluff. In addition, before we left Fiji, I still had to come back and check out with this crackpot. "Don't call the police. I'm sorry I offended you," I let out with a sigh, as my head hung low in front of me. I threw in the towel, feeling defeated, and walked out of the office. "At least I got the 100 bucks back," I thought.

If my goal for Fiji was to see how much beer I could drink, pot I could smoke, food I could eat, and trouble I could get into, I definitely succeeded. Shit was just too cheap. Of course if things cost half what you're accustom to, but you consume three times as much, you're not really saving any money.

Three days after we arrived, the Suva Yacht club put on a dinner. It was ten dollars Fijian, the equivalent of about five US, for all you could eat and drink. That wasn't quite how they billed the party, but that was how we perceived it. Brandoni and I reluctantly forked over the five bucks and the others hoped they might just weasel in once things got started.

Naturally, we starved ourselves all day so that we could get our money's worth that night. And since there was some hinting by the party hosts that there wasn't an unlimited supply of beer and wine, and alcohol is always more effective on an empty stomach, that was how we started.

I awoke in my bunk the following day still drunk. My brain avoided recollection of the previous night's events. "I'm an alcoholic and a drug abuser," I chanted hoarsely several times, which stirred up some conversation about the previous night's revelry. "You and that Dutch chick seemed to be enjoying each other," Brandoni chimed in. I winced as a few unconnected images of myself and the Dutch chick gnashing teeth on the dance floor flooded back into my head. "You remember that Jug (some of my friends referred to me as Jug)?" I could tell Brandoni was grinning as he spoke. "I do now," I replied, and repeated my new mantra. "I'm an alcoholic and a druuuuug abuser."

I licked the new sore on my lip, which I presumed was a result of my sloppy make out session, as my brain worked over the details of my debauchery. I added scoundrel, below alcoholic and drug abuser, to my resume, as I remembered my girlfriend Amanda. We'd agreed upon an exclusive physical relationship during our separation. In addition to defiling my body, I'd defiled our agreement. I speculated that it was only a matter of time before that relationship ended, if it hadn't already.

"Ready to head to land soon?" Brandoni bellowed into my bunk, after whacking the deck above my head a few times, which I initially thought was totally uncalled for, but then wondered if I hadn't done something similar to him the night before. "No, I'm having a boat day. No land for me." The crew was disappointed that they wouldn't be able to show off their handy work. They'd given me a good chiefing when I'd passed out the night before.

I needed a day of reckoning. Plus, I didn't want to run into anyone I'd made an ass of myself in front of the night before. I spent the morning drinking tea in the cockpit and observing the land from a safe distance before taking a nap.

I woke up from the nap thinking that it was a whole new day. I was disappointed when I found out that it was still the day after I'd made an ass of myself. As I lay contemplating my plight, I decided that it wasn't the 'making an ass of myself' part that really bothered me. People spend most of their time thinking about themselves and are rarely concerned with the actions of others that don't directly affect them. In fact, most people are often all too happy to watch someone else play the fool, making them, by comparison, look better. As I smiled, thinking about Braden hitting on some German chick that we later learned was only 15, I realized I was no different.

It was the personal defilement that really bothered me. I had just turned 28, and felt I should no longer be carrying on like I was in college. I felt that if I didn't learn a little restraint I'd have to just resign myself to a life of total dissipation. I contemplated just going for it. I was pretty much there already. I just had to take the final step by simply eliminating guilt and regret from my equation. I decided that perhaps I spent way too much time striving for some sort of purity I rarely actualized. It was all just *maya* anyhow; life's illusion that one destination is superior to another. My chiefing lasted longer than the nebulous thoughts, vaporizing with my dreams after a good night's rest.

We eventually tore ourselves away from Suva, and headed to Yanuca, a small island off the coast of Viti Levu.

There were no other boats in the pristine bay, and we dropped anchor in crystal clear water. We hiked to the small village, presented the chief with a bundle of *kava* root, and asked for permission to hang out. He accepted our *kava*, said we could stay, and offered us some kava juice. We naturally accepted, but were a little disappointed with the buzz, getting only a little mouth numbing. We enjoyed the novelty of the experience.

Yanuca

The following day, invigorated to be free Suva's grasp, we hired a local boat to take us out to Frigates Pass, a famous surfing area. With fame comes notoriety. Yanuca had two of surf camps, most of whose occupants were at Frigate's when we arrived. Having surfed only a hand full of times, I was happy to sacrifice 'the perfect wave' for an unoccupied one. I spent most of the day just trying to stay out of people's way.

Never the less, I celebrated the day's events. We'd run out of weed the previous day, which I'd deemed 'a good thing' since we'd fallen into 'stoned all the time' mode. We had, however, purchased a considerable amount of duty free alcohol before leaving Suva. It was burning a hole in the coffers.

Dan discovered a green worm crawling around in an ear of corn he was husking. The worm somehow made its way into a glass. Everyone silently noted the 'not so small' green worm exploring the glass and wondered what his fate would be. The fact that it was in a vessel of human consumption didn't go unnoticed. I broke the seal on the 57 percent alcohol Bounty Rum and poured a couple ounces of the rich amber fluid on top of the worm. The crew leaned in and watched the worm writhe momentarily before going limp on the bottom of the glass. I was known for not wasting anything, least of all rum, and a nervous smile spread through the cabin. It didn't quite make it to Sara's face, however. She didn't want to show too much interest. She wasn't playing.

Dinner preparation continued as the worm marinated. Braden was inspired while chopping up vegetables and tossed a whole habanero pepper into the glass. "Someone's going to be feeling that one on the flip side tomorrow," I thought.

Eventually the worm screamed for attention and the elixir could no longer be ignored. "How do we decide who gets it," I ventured. "Cards?" Out came a deck. "What's the game? High card takes it?" Heads nodded in appreciation of the simplicity. We decided that we would each put our card on our forehead, face out, so that we could see each other's cards but not our own, adding a smidgen of drama. Braden had a king. I felt pretty safe. And I was. Braden was the 'winner.' He took it down after a brief moment of contemplation and chased it with a full body quiver that sent his dreadlocks flying about the cabin.

Natandola

Dan had arrived with a folder full of surf reports that dictated most of our stops. The next stop was Natandola Beach where, if the weather was right, we hoped to find respectable waves and fewer people. There was definitely less of a crowd, but no waves. It was a rainy, rolly anchorage, and much of the crew had developed a cold, so a lot of flem was added to the mix. Hanuman wasn't a fabulous place to be but we were all getting along for the most part, despite the damp sweaty atmosphere that prevailed. Our salty sweet body odor merged with the boat and we became appendages of a larger being. Fresh water was a luxury only for drinking and cooking. We hadn't showered except for a couple of times in Suva. Matted hair and oily flesh blanketed most of Hanuman's interior. Scabbed, slightly infected, coral kissed knuckles hung from its handrails.

I picked my nose and inspected the yield as I rolled it contemplatively between thumb and index finger. The virus infested crew wasn't overly motivated. The rolly anchorage didn't help matters. "We should take the beach," I offered. A few eyes were pulled out of whatever escapist realm they dwelled in. "C'mon, let's go find a market. Get some fresh veggies. Maybe track down some weed." "Weeeeed," I coaxed. Heads started nodding and the stagnate pool of our existence came to life.

We made our way to a market and snaked through it. Fiji has great open markets; heaps of cheap fresh vegetables. We cased the place for the best looking produce. We were also keeping our ears open for weed. Taxi drivers are always a good bet; possessing that, "I can get you whatever you need" attitude.

I was always too timid to be an effective procurer of weed, but Brandoni had a gift. We'd all gotten separated in the maze of a market but I made eye contact with Brandoni a few stalls away. He gave me the nod and I joined him.

We followed a conspicuous looking fellow down the main street. He looked like a drug dealer. If he was conspicuous, we were just plain stand-outish. Brandoni was wearing a bright yellow rain slicker and I had on a bright orange one.

We followed our man up some stairs to a typical looking family dwelling, and entered. Dad was playing a game on the computer. Son was playing with a fire truck in the corner. Mom came out of the kitchen whipping her hands on a dishtowel. She sized up the situation without expression, left the room, and returned with a rolled up newspaper. She opened it in front of us and… "whooooa, that's a lot of weed." Brandoni and I looked at each other with the same wide eyed expression… "whooooa, that's a lot of weed." Dad mentioned a price. It was quite cheap, but it seemed like way more weed than needed. We explained that half that amount would be just fine. The mom and dad look at each other blankly and shook their heads. It was all or nothing. We shrugged and Brandoni negotiated a price. We handed over the cash. We all nodded and Brandoni jammed the newspaper down his pants.

As soon as we got down to the street in our florescent rain slickers it seemed like everyone was looking at us. It reminded me one of one of those slow motion scenes in the movies just before the guy who just sold us the weed jumps out with a gun and a badge. I had a flash back of my Mexican jail experience. We weren't even technically supposed to be in the country anymore. I'd checked us out to New Caledonia in Suva, not wanting to repeat the experience in some other Fijian port.

Providentially, it was neither the movies nor Mexico and before we knew it we were back on Hanuman joking about the whole thing and rolling up a Cheech and Chong style joint, using four pieces of rolling paper; a four sheeter.

After three days of waiting for waves and weather, and enduring a crappy anchorage, we decided we'd had enough and headed for the next place.

In Momi Bay we met up with some Kiwi friends we'd made back in Suva. Rod and Wendy had sailed a 100 year old wooden boat up from New Zealand. A drunken Irish guy and a couple of Canadians, who were paying to be on board, accompanied them. "Hmmm," I thought. Suddenly my crew started to seem like a bunch of ingrates. Rod and Wendy were a couple, but Sara had spent some girl time with Wendy and she'd said that they were splitting up when they got to Australia. Again, "hmmmm."

The first thing I noticed about Wendy was how she handled their dinghy. They had a pretty kick-ass set up: brand new 15 horse sitting on the back of an enormous red Zodiac. We, the five crew members of Hanuman, rolled with a two point five horse Tohatsu held together with duck tape in a four man inflatable that had to be pumped up before every use and required someone to be permanently bailing. "Don't step on the floor if you can avoid it, your feet might go through.

No,… seriously." I'd patched it up many times, but all of the fixes were ephemeral. Sputnik got a lot of use.

I loved watching Wendy start their dinghy. It was a polished Zen-like motion. Choke out with left hand, move left hand back to tiller/throttle, one pull on the starter cord with the right, a puff of blue smoke, goose the throttle, snap back the choke, throw her in gear and she's off on a plain; beauty in motion. Wendy had a sturdy build. The contrast between her muscular arm pulling the starter cord and her soft bra-less breasts, swaying with the motion under her pink tank-top, captivated me. It actually captivated all of the male crew on board Hanuman. Brandoni's and Sara's relationship foundered a little. It appeared that Brandoni lost some of his tenderness for Sara in a flurry of testosterone. He longed for the hunt.

One tranquil morning I had a vision, drug induced of course, where I saw the entirety of Wendy and my relationship. We met up Australia, when she was no longer with Rod. I was of course, or perhaps not 'of course,' was not seeing Amanda any longer. We hit it off and next thing I knew she was living on the boat with me. We started planning our future sailing together, and I was happy not to have to seek crew, but there was something not quite right; something missing from the relationship. Perhaps it was a vacant look I caught in her eyes. We didn't have the communication I was hoping for and before long the relationship dissolved and I found myself saying, "Whew, glad that's over."

Musket Cove

Rod and Wendy convinced us that we'd be missing out if we didn't go to Musket Cove. It wasn't really on the itinerary, but itineraries are made to be broken and, after they'd talked the place up so fervently, we decided, "what the hell."

Dan's time had come to an end. He got his final Sputnik ride to land and was left to make his way to the airport.

We arrived in Musket cove on Halloween. While Rod and Wendy were talking up Musket Cove, we were talking up Halloween. They'd never heard of it but thought it sounded, "Brilliant!"

They arrived in Musket Cove at about exactly the same time we did but were already in costume with beers in hand. They came as the 'Wherethefukarewe' tribe. They'd found a few bolts of cheap cloth, fashioned some tribal attire out of it, and added face and body paint to top it off.

Feeling under dressed, our crew went to work. It was more a matter of scrounging around for something, than 'picking out' a costume. There was only so much to work with. Aluminum foil was always a good place to start. I eventually decided on Captain Morgan, but thought the idea needed an edge, so I went as 'Captain Morgan struck by lightning.' The costume involved a burnt bandana, a good quantity of aluminum foil, and a great deal of rum. Brandoni went as a flasher: basically in his rain slicker with stuffed sock tied to his groin with 'your name here' written on the side of it. He attempted to rig an articulation string, but gave up and just let it hang. Braden went as an Australian tourist. Sara went as me.

I'd been wearing the same cloths since she'd met me a couple of months prior. She donned my shorts, (though she probably wore underwear) Marin Brewing Company T-shirt, sweat incrusted visor, and even penned in a beard with one of our chiefing pens. She looked just like me.

After a few drinks with Rob, Wendy, and their crew, we took the beach and discovered the $2.50 bar, where beers where $2.50 Fijian or about $1.25 US. Not as cheap as I would've hoped, but affordable. The highlight of the bar however, was the row of self-service barbeques. Also provided were wood, newspaper, and spatulas. A small store sold cheap meat. We barbequed every night.

There were several resorts on the island, all of which were sailor friendly, allowing us to spend most of our days lounging in one of their six pools. Wendy and I spent a lot of time together talking, which progressed to flirting. The Canadian couple, Wendy, and I found ourselves separated from the others in one of the pools. Melody, the Canadian girl, suggested we have a chicken fight. "Uh-oh," I thought. I hesitantly agreed. Wendy got on my shoulders and Melody got on Gary's. With Wendy's vagina wrapped around my neck, we proceeded to do battle with the Canadians. It was an intimate experience. One that I remembered thinking I wouldn't be too wild about a girlfriend of mine sharing with some shameless philanderer like myself. I technically still had a girlfriend, but Amanda had become more of an abstract thought than an actual person. I was far too wrapped up in my own interests to overly concern myself with the feelings of others. I allowed myself to become a victim of inertia, and slid down the slippery slope before me, barely noticing the scenery; barely aware that any other direction existed. My busy schedule of barbequing, drinking, and lounging by the pool, insulated me from introspection.

Fortunately the chicken fight ended without a watery love scene and I kept a thin facade of honorable intentions intact. As the sun fell and my buzz rose, our flirting became less and less discrete. We seemed to take it a little further each night. There was way more touching than could be considered casual. We spit water on each other in the pool. It may have seemed innocent through a drunken blurred prospective, however it was anything but.

Brandoni and Sara had decided that they weren't going to be sailing past Fiji. Brandoni had run through most of his funds at the $2.50 bar, and other such places, and was living mostly off Sara. Sara was probably feeling their relationship slip away. The boat was a tough place to work through such things, especially since Brandoni probably wasn't too keen on 'working through' anything. And she had been on the boat for awhile and was probably thinking her life back in California was missing her. By the time one was wearing my clothes they'd pretty much had the experience. Anything beyond that and you were making a life of it. I was disappointed in Brandoni for leaving, especially since I was counting on him for the passage to Australia, but knew he had to do what he had to do.

One aspect of my existence on Hanuman that I despised was the fact that I had to rely on other people. I was a little taken back when Brandoni, Dan, and Sara announced that they'd all be leaving in Fiji. I didn't really expect Dan and Sara to stay past Fiji, but I had expected Brandoni to. "What about you Braden?" I asked after I received the other's news. "I'm with ya' bro." I loved him at that moment.

I admired Braden's stick-with-it-ness. He'd decided he wanted to sail all the way to Australia and wasn't going to change his mind because funds were a little low, he was having women problems, or he had a hangover. He had a firm grasp on his goals.

After a week of lounging and barbequing, and lounging some more, our time in Musket Cove was coming to an end. Brandoni and Sara would be taking a ferry to Veti Levu and flying back to the States. Braden and I were headed for New Caledonia. It was our last night in Musket Cove and the end of a major segment of the journey. We didn't usually have to look too hard for a reason to party, on this night we were obligated.

We met up with the 'Wherethefukarewe's,' who were still in costume from Halloween a week prior, and began drinking with vigor.

The evening came to a head when we reached the last resort. It was a natural stopping point; there was a bar, music, a pool with a water slide, and not much beyond it. We were all drunk when we arrived but that didn't prevent us from continuing to drink.

Wendy and my flirting had reached new heights. Between figuring I was leaving the next day, so what the hell, and being drunk, discretion went out the door. I saw Rod milling around the pool where Wendy and I were swimming and could tell something was coming. Despite deserving it, I wasn't in the mood for confrontation, and took refuge underwater; perhaps not so much to hide, but to retreat to a quiet peaceful place, if only momentarily. Holding my breath underwater has always put me in a calm tranquil state not easily emulated on land. Unfortunately the hunger for oxygen eventually trumped my happy trance and I had to come up for air.

Rod stopped pacing around and gave us a, "what's going on?" I decided to spare him the, "what do you mean," and went right into an apology. I felt bad. I liked Rod, and, despite my actions, didn't want to cause him any unhappiness. I said that I'd be leaving the next day, hoping that would make everything all right.

The following events are a bit of a blur and came quite unexpectedly. Rod faded with disgust into the background and Wendy asked if she could sail with me to Australia. I told her that I had a girlfriend, but in the same breath asked if she was sure. She said she knew and she was.

Next thing I knew, everything had vanished and we were walking back to the dinghy alone, unleashing the desire that had been masquerading as casual flirtation.

It must have been the witching hour because dramas were playing out all across the beach. Apparently Sara, who was involved in an extended production with Brandoni, had unloaded on Braden. Brandoni, annoyed with Braden for, what he perceived as interfering, got into a scuffle with Braden.

The Canadians, Gary and Melody, were also having it out. Apparently Melody wasn't all too satisfied with the give and take portion of their relationship and the alcohol reminded her of Gary's past infidelities. She was on a rampage and wanted blood.

Gladly I wasn't around for either of the performances and my mind had momentarily blocked out the outside world as Wendy and I frolicked. Though I did have a few, "what the hell am I doing," pangs before the alcohol kicked back in.

We ended up back on formerly Rod and Wendy's, now Rod's, boat. Wendy had to gather her belongings. Things started out surprisingly congenially. I drank the beer that Rod handed me and we chatted amiably as Wendy stuffed her meager belongings into a couple of garbage bags. "Sweet, we could use a couple of garbage bags," I remember thinking. The sea brings out one's basest pragmatism.

The atmosphere changed as Rod started talking about how hard it was to give Wendy an orgasm. He sarcastically wished me better luck. Rod exhaled a few more understandably rude comments to quicken our departure and sped it with, "people can leave when they start to feel uncomfortable." We were halfway in the dinghy at that point and didn't waste any time motoring away. It was like a typical trailer park scene, only at sea.

Braden and Brandoni had passed out and I gave them a quick chiefing, more out of obligation than actual desire. They weren't in the deepest sleep however, so I wasn't able to accomplish a great deal. One also had to be careful around Brandoni when chiefing. He would occasionally fire out an unaimed fist, just to test the waters.

Wendy and I rehashed the evening in the cockpit with Sara for awhile, before crashing on the foredeck.

The harsh morning sun, which didn't take too long to find us, chased us down below into my bunk. Not long after, I heard a dinghy approach and Rod ask Braden to talk to Sara. I was curious as to what Rod could possibly want with Sara but had no burning desire to find out. I later discover that Sara and Rod had been doing some serious chatting the night before and, either Sara had asked Rod if she could sail to Australia with him or he'd asked her. I would guess the later, but what takes place in the dark folds of a drunken night can never truly be unraveled.

Sara, mostly sober, eyeing Wendy's garbage bags, came to her senses. She would be on the ferry that afternoon. At that moment I was sure she couldn't wait to be on plane flying back to a saner world.

We made one last trip to land to drop off Brandoni and Sara and spent the rest of our Fijian dollars before pulling anchor. Wendy shed a tear as we pulled out of the anchorage, "I'll miss that dinghy."

New Caledonia

Braden, Wendy, and I sailed through the pass in the reef in pleasant sunny conditions and were on our way to New Caledonia. The passage was ideal. We didn't set any speed records, but the wind never abandoned us, rain was minimal, and we caught plenty of fish. Braden belabored his favorite adjective, 'awesome,' a disproportionately large number of times.

We arrived at the pass in New Caledonia's barrier reef, second in size only to Australia's Great Barrier Reef, in the dark and spent the night on the outside battling 40 knot winds, not wanting to navigate the reef in the dark. When the sun rose the wind dropped to nothing and we motored through Dumbea Passage and 15 miles of lagoon to Noumea.

We received a free night's stay at the marina and a free drink from the bar upon arrival. Checking in went smoothly. The officials came to the boat, so we didn't have to spend two days tracking down their offices. The French were official and expedient. I was spared the bullshit I suffered in Fiji. Fortunately they didn't scrutinize our paper work. I'd just scribbled Wendy's name onto the bottom of our official Fijian crew list. I also noticed during the passage that we hadn't received departure visas from Fiji when we'd left. Luckily the officials didn't pore over our passports either. As long as your boat is registered and you have a passport, the French don't seem to sweat the details. "Actually, wouldn't be a bad place to go if I'd just stolen a boat," I pondered.

We spent a mellow week in Noumea before deciding to make way for Australia. Australia was to be a regrouping point where I planned to make some money. I was eager for some stationary time and looked forward to getting there.

We pulled anchor, sailed for about three hours, and were within a mile of the pass, when the wind completely died. We found ourselves within 200 yards of a couple dozen moorings off just off of Admiralty Island. We didn't relish the idea of motoring or bobbing around all night so we decided we'd just grab a mooring, have a restful night, and sail off in the morning.

I grabbed my snorkel and decided to have a look around. The fish were huge. In a frenzy of excitement I called for my spear and had it caulked, with my sights on a large fish, when it occurred to me that the fish seemed unusually tame. It dawned on me that we were probably in a marine park. I decided against the slaughtering and instead cracked open a box of wine. The French craft a mean box of wine.

The sun had set, we'd downed a couple of boxes of wine, and eaten an excellent curry, when the wind piped up. I didn't sweat it until I recalled the veracity of the wind on our arrival night. The wind built to about 20 knots and the 12 mile fetch to New Caledonia allowed short sleep waves of two to three feet to build. We were in shallow water on a short mooring chain which poorly accommodated the wave motion; preventing Hanuman from riding over them. Instead, the bow jerked down sharply with each passing wave, putting severe stress on our mooring line.

I added an additional line to the mooring ball and figured, "perfect," before returning to my cask of wine. I came back on deck 15 minutes later to take a piss and have a look at the lines. As I walked forward I felt an unholy crunch vibrate under foot. "Shit!" I saw two frayed lines hanging off the front of the boat. I felt another crunch; even more solid sounding than the first.

I dashed below and touched the two wires together that started Big Red. The key ignition had corroded to dust several months prior. I wasn't greeted by the normal roar of the beast. All I got was a rather pathetic clicking noise. I quickly reevaluated my normal starting procedure. Everything seemed to be in order so I again, 'thought start,' the second to last line on the engine start protocol, and joined the black and yellow wires. A little blue spark danced between the copper, but only resulted in more clicking.

I took Big Red out of the equation. He was dead to me. It was time for plan B. I flew back on deck to develop a plan B.

The crunching of fiberglass on coral was now constant. We'd been fully blown onto the reef. The sensation was horrid. The rigging shook with each collision of boat and rock. Hanuman screamed in pain. We were still upright however, which meant that the coral was hitting the bottom of the keel, and not the side of the hull. There was a great deal of fiberglass and lead to grind though at the bottom of the keel. The key was not to get pushed any further onto the reef. We had to stabilize our position. I jumped in the water with a line and swam it over to a nearby mooring while Wendy and Braden attached the other end to the bow and put as much tension on it as they could.

Wendy suggested we set the stern anchor to stabilize the back of the boat. I jumped in with the anchor. Its weight kept me on the bottom, slightly less than six feet from the surface, so I was able to walk the anchor 15 yards out from the boat.

Being under water in the dark provided a surreal reprieve from the madness above. The prolific phosphorescence supplied countless tiny points of light and made me feel like an astronaut on a space walk.

I didn't get too far from the boat on one breath but managed to wedge the anchor into a crevasse. We secured the anchor chain to a large winch in the cockpit and it seemed to hold.

Now that we weren't getting any further onto the reef it was time to try and get off of it. We put the bow line that was attached to the mooring on a winch and started cranking; no effect. Exasperatingly, the line attached to the mooring exited the bow at a 90 degree angle. We were essentially trying to drag ourselves sideways.

After a huddle, we decided to use the anchor and try and drag ourselves forward. We exhumed Sputnik and the outboard and got them ready for action.

In the heat of the moment I told Wendy I loved her. I'm not sure what prompted it, or how it came out, but I was just so charged by all of the action that I simply blurted it out.

We loaded Sputnik up with the anchor and chain, dinghied 25 yards ahead, dumped the anchor, and started cracking in the chain with the windlass. The anchor slowly made its way back to the boat without grabbing the bottom. We decided to try again; there was no plan C. The second time, we got the anchor a little further from the boat, cranked on the winch, and it grabbed. Tension increased on the anchor chain and we started to inch forward.

There was elation in the realization that we were making progress. "I might not lose the boat after all," I thought. Our forward motion continued and we eased out the stern line to allow us to advance. Eventually the crunching stopped and we were floating free. It was a magical feeling. I had trouble believing I'd taken it for granted for so long.

We used our mooring line to pull ourselves to a secure location where we attached about a dozen lines just as the wind died to nothing and it turned into a beautiful night. I took one last swig of wine and passed out, totally spent.

We awoke to a colossal mess on deck. While Braden was ogling two mating lobsters I had a look at the damage. The keel was pretty scraped up, but overall seemed to be in fair shape. The rudder was a different story. A crack ran along the entirety of the seam at its bottom.

We decided to return to Noumea and reevaluate. Unfortunately the engine was still on the fritz and we didn't want to rely on the sails in the maze of reefs. Some tourist boats filed into the anchorage and we tried in vain to procure a tow back to Noumea. A mega-yacht also arrived and Wendy and I sputtered over in Sputnik, to see if their engineer could give us some advice. She couldn't, but she did have a book that she was happy to lend.

The book actually recommended banging on the starter with a hammer, something I was contemplating doing anyhow. According to the book there was a widget in the starter that could get itself slightly out of sync, causing the whole thing not to work. I busted out Thor, the hammer, and whacked at it gingerly before bringing the heat and banging the shit out of it. I looked at Wendy and Braden, we all shrugged, and I touched the start wires together after thinking 'start;' more pathetic clicking.

I reopened the book and read past the 'whack it' paragraph. It said I could bypass the solenoid by bridging the positive and negative poles with a screwdriver. I got out my biggest screwdriver, extended it gingerly toward the solenoid, braced myself, and connected the poles. Sparks flew and Big Red roared to life.

We made our way back to Noumea and spent a week deciding whether to haul the boat out of the water and do a proper fix or just jury rig something to get us to Australia. Ultimately hauling out was expensive and required insurance, which I didn't have.

Rod found his way to Noumea with a gorgeous Dutch blond who'd joined his crew, and his bunk. I didn't feel so bad about the circumstances, and things weren't as awkward as one might think, at least not for Rod or me. He was quite pleased with himself actually.

I eventually gave up on the idea of hauling the boat out and opted to fill the crack with underwater epoxy and clamp it in place with a couple of C-clamps.

After a huge Thanksgiving dinner, hosted by an American boat in the marina, we set off for Australia. We arrived in Scarborough, Australia after ten days of difficult sailing, rudder still intact.

Australia

In route to Australia I fished out a pad of paper and listed what I felt Hanuman should have preceding the plunge into Asia. My plan, prior to the calculations, was to try and find some under the table work in Australia for six months during the hurricane season. After my calculations, however, I had difficulty imagining I'd be able to make as much money in Australia as I felt I needed for maintenance and upgrades. Not to mention saving enough to continue sailing. The next work stop after Australia would be a long ways off. I'd be in developing nations for a year. I decided that flying back to the states for work might be the most efficient course of action. After some discussion, Wendy and I decided that she would go to the States also; with hope that she could find some under the table work.

The second passage with Wendy hadn't been as blissful as the first. I had the first pangs of, "what the hell did I get myself into?" I tried not to dwell on the feelings however, and proceeded forward as we'd planned.

Once in Australia, most of my energy was put into finding a place to haul Hanuman out of the water and store her while we were in the States. My relationship with Wendy took a back seat. By the time I decided that the whole plan might not be such a good idea, we'd already purchased our non-refundable plane tickets to San Francisco International.

We eventually discovered the cheapest possible place to keep Hanuman. It was up the Caboulture River, not far from where we were. The river was only navigable at high tide, making it a tricky passage, but we arrived without incident and found ourselves hauled out, in a world far different than the Pacific Ocean we were used to.

A week later we were on jet to the US. It was Wendy's first time. She was a timid little lamb. I joked that she wasn't ready for the world's last superpower. She thought I was serious. Somewhere high over the Pacific we'd sailed across, the girl who'd mesmerized me by starting an outboard, was lost.

I felt sincerely bad for putting Wendy in such a situation. So far from all she knew, I shouldn't have been surprised that such a different person emerged. Our relationship, born of the sea and based primarily on how she pulled a rope, dissolved under the pedestrian pressures of land life; at least in my eyes. Wendy's visa expired after three months; subsequently she flew back to Australia, a single woman.

I stayed at my mom's in Davis, California for another two months, substitute teaching by day and waiting tables by night.

Australia Part II

Five months after leaving Hanuman I was back in the boat yard with two boxes full of new, or new to me, gear, and a pocket full of cash. I felt butterflies in my stomach as the cab pulled up to the boat. It was like meeting up with lover after a prolonged separation. "Will she look the same?" "Will she still like me?"

I was pleased to see she was still there and relieved she wasn't lying on her side or missing any critical parts. "At least nothing catastrophic happened in my absence," I thought, as I climbed gingerly up the steal boatyard ladder and had a look on deck. The cockpit drains were clogged with leaves and a good four inches of water had accumulated over the cockpit floor, housing a small ecosystem. Mosquito larva gyrated madly. Water bugs mated furiously. I looked for fish, possibly a new species, before unclogging the drains, but found none.

The deck was covered with little brown specks of rust that had blown over from the guy next to me who was building a steel boat. I looked over and cursed the rusting hulk. That aside, all seemed well and I was, for the most part, relieved by Hanuman's condition. A lot can happen in five months.

I spent the next month doggedly working on the boat, finishing some of what hadn't gotten done before we left San Francisco, and fixing what had broken after.

Joe arrived a month after I did. I'd run into Joe, who was a friend of a friend, during my working stint in Davis, and talked up the sailing life to the point where any other of life's possible preoccupations seemed trivial. Joe spent a week varnishing the rails and fishing in the Caboolture River, while I finished up various other projects.

With about half of what I'd planned on accomplishing completed, it was time to go back in the water. Hanuman was loaded up in the cradle and wheeled to the water. We had to wait for the tide to come in so we had a couple hours of hang time. I decided to make sure the engine would turn over before we got in the water. Joe held a hose up to the raw water intake and I turned the key; one solid "click." "Damn it." I thought I'd fixed the problem with the starter, but given the clicking noise, decided to resort to the screw-driver method. It was a different sort of clicking noise than I'd dealt with in New Caledonia, but I shrugged off the dis-crepancy and hoped for the best. I thought, "Start," joined the poles on the solenoid with the big screwdriver and… "CLICK." "Fuck!" Only hours before we were planning on going in the water I'd realized the engine wasn't working. I consulted my book. I now owned the book that I'd bor-rowed from the mega-yacht back in New Caledonia. It indi-cated that the engine might be seized, a terrible scenario. I put a large pipe wrench on the flywheel lug nut and tried to turn it… nothing. The engine was indeed frozen. "Double fuck!" Joe and I both got on the wrench and put our backs into it, no dice.

We went over to our friend Adrian's boat, for advice. He poured us some coffee. "Want some whiskey in that?" he offered. "Yeah…I guess I'd better."

We hashed out a plan, by the second whiskey, to use his dinghy to pull Hanuman over to a small dock where we could sort out the problem at our leisure. It wasn't a long term solution, but at least we'd be moving forward, and avoid the possibility of having to pay to have Hanuman re-moved.

I felt the dream of getting back to sea slipping away. Sorting the engine out was a potentially costly affair. I also didn't have all the time in the world with regards to the non-hurricane seasons in the various areas I was planning on passing through. I envisioned blowing all of the money I'd made on getting the engine fixed and having to return home to work again, without having gone anywhere. The thought was devastating.

Joe was also getting antsy. Monty's Marina, on the Caboolture River, wasn't exactly his idea of a vacation, or an adventure, and I could tell he was already making a back-up plan to get on a bus, if things didn't work out with Hanuman.

I decided that I wouldn't pay anyone to fix my engine. If my fate was to spend weeks taking Big Red apart and learning how to fix it, then I would accept it. "Perhaps in the long run I'll get more out of learning about my diesel than I would sailing along the coast," I thought, trying to be optimistic.

We got Hanuman onto a dock with minor drama, but no damage, at around 10:30 at night. The high tides were at night, so our departure, if we were lucky enough to have one anytime in the near future, would also have to be at night.

I got started trying to fix the engine right away. I could see the whole process taking awhile and, getting a slight panicky feeling, wanted to get started. By then I'd collected advice from the boat yard crowd. The consensus was that I needed to pull out the injectors and dump a diesel and oil mixture on top of the pistons. The hope was that the mixture would loosen the rust that had formed in the cylinders, allowing the pistons to move.

With effort, I got the injectors out and gave Big Red his medicine. After that, there was nothing to do but wait. I sat back and surveyed the scene. The place was a disaster. I'd rendered everything ship shape only hours before, only to destroy it. I detested a cluttered boat.

The following day, Joe and I got back on the pipe wrench. We grunted and sweated but there was still no movement, though we did manage to loosen the lug nut when we turned it counter clockwise.

While we struggled fruitlessly, Adrian enlisted a local boat guru known as 'Peter Perfect' to come to our aid. He was known for completing a project to perfection, but also for charging "the queen's ransom."

He strolled onto Hanuman as I sat staring at the broken engine. "I heard you're having some problems with your engine." He was a large gentleman and the ladder moaned as he descended into the cabin. Despite his bulk, his movements were precise and careful as he appraised the situation. Aside from not working, he said the engine appeared to be in "fairly good nick." It seemed like little consolation given the situation, but I was looking for positives, and took it as a good sign. "Thanks," I responded, knowing he probably hadn't been attributing the engine's "good nick" to me. He said we should put more tonic in the engine and that he'd come back the next day with a bigger wrench.

I was nervous that there might be some time when he asked for money, but decided I would address that situation when it arose. I was happy to have a 'man of knowledge' in my corner. My spirits lifted and hope returned.

Peter returned the following day, as promised. I was again sitting on the floor, staring at the engine. He had a huge wrench. It offered even more hope. "Now we're talking leverage," I thought.

Without wasting time, he got the wrench on the lug nut and put his considerable weight into it… no movement. My spirits waned slightly. He said that, due to the position of the pistons, it is often easier to move it in one direction over the other. In the opposite direction, he proceeded to loosen the nut, just as Joe and I had.

He stared at the engine for a moment, in deliberation, and asked for a flashlight. I was able to hand him the flashlight quickly, which made me feel good about myself; like slightly less of a hack who couldn't fix his own engine.

Slowly and deliberately he got his head down to the front of the engine and moved the flashlight around, having a look. Satisfied, he stood up, twisted the mini-mag to the off position and handed it back to me. With his huge hands he lifted the gargantuan wrench and tried to position it on a metal flange between the lug nut and the alternator pulley. I saw what he was trying to do. "The wrench is never going to be able to grab on to that small round flange," I thought. But I'd underestimated the power of the grand pipe wrench. Its' considerable teeth bit into the flange as Peter applied some muscle. There was no movement however. I could tell he felt good about the setup though, and he asked Joe and me to help.

We joined him on the wrench and clung to it like it was our salvation; which in my mind, it pretty much was. We jockeyed for leverage. White knuckled, and with muscles screaming, we squeezed sweat from every pore. If the wrench slipped off the flange, something was going to break. Finally, as I thought my teeth would be crushed by the clenching of my jaw, there was movement. We eased our grips on the wrench. My face was alight with joy. "It moved," I released hesitantly from my relaxing jaw. I felt the look on Peter's face wasn't acknowledging the grandeur of the situation. "We're saved… right?" I directed at Peter. His normally stoic face curled into a smile as he observed my youthful exuberance. "Yes," he replied with a chuckle. Joe's head nodded up and down in happy affirmation.

Once the engine was moving it was just a matter of working it back and forth until we'd scoured off all the rust that had accumulated on the insides of the cylinders. It took Joe and me all day, but the euphoria of knowing that we were on the home stretch of the job made it an easy task. By the end of the day we had the engine back together and it was just a matter of turning the key. I decided that I'd save it for the following day. I didn't want to challenge the prevailing euphoric mood.

Big Red didn't let us down, and fired right up, spewing some delightful black smoke out the exhaust pipe. "We're back in business." We reorganized the boat and it was just a matter of waiting for the high tide at 11:30 that night.

Peter never made any mention of payment, but he had saved our asses and I felt indebted. "How much do we owe you," I asked. He gave me a sidelong glance with a grin, mumbled something about how it was obvious we didn't have any money, and finished with, "just make sure you change that injector oil." I bought him a large bottle Bundaberg Rum that he accepted with a genuine smile, and never saw him again.

The River

Joe and I shoved off with the tide at 11:00 pm on a moonless night. I was at the helm and Joe stood on the side deck with the million candle power spotlight, cutting the darkness. Navigating the first part of the river wasn't too challenging and, aside from a few dicey moments in the fog where we couldn't locate the edge of the river, we didn't have any problems.

As we made our way further downstream however, the river fanned out and became braided. The single channel became many, but only one was deep enough. The correct channel was marked with red and green buoys, which are usually pretty straight forward. Here, there weren't all that many of them. It was as dark as the inside of a cow and, after passing a channel marker, we found ourselves proceeding on blind faith until Joe could locate the next with the spotlight.

It had been a long time since we'd seen the last marker, too long. I eyed the depth sounder as the orange line indicting our depth, blurred with the orange line indicating zero. I felt our progress come to a halt as we sunk into the mud. "Shit, we're in the mud!" I announced.

Joe continued scanning the horizon for the next channel marker and eventually found it. I gunned the engine in reverse, trying to get us back into the channel. The mud was forgiving and we slowly eased backward. The progress was comforting but the smoke bellowing from the engine compartment was not. "Fuckin' A, what now?" I thought. I couldn't deal with the smoke at the moment. I just wanted to get off the bottom.

We managed to find our way into the channel and quickly dropped the anchor. Once secure, we shut down Big Red. "Damn, I just want to be back in the fuckin' ocean." I went below to investigate and was enveloped by the sweet smell of anti-freeze. I lifted the engine compartment and steam poured out. Coolant was boiling out of the coolant reservoir.

I'd just installed a new sea water pump in the engine cooling system. Upon closer inspection I noticed the pump's coupling to the engine was no longer coupled. The engine was originally designed as a tractor engine and I felt some of the marine conversion components were poorly designed; the coupling was a prime example. When the coupling had uncoupled seawater was no longer pumped through the heat exchanger that cooled the anti-freeze. With Big Red throttled to get us out of the mud, the anti-freeze quickly heated to a boil and steamed its way out of the engine.

I used some bits of rubber and wood, and a small C-clamp that had held the rudder together, to fashion a new coupling, and realigned and re-coupled the pump. It looked… "perfect," but we'd missed our tide window so we were stuck there for another ten hours. I was hoping the heat hadn't melted the piston rings to the cylinders, again seizing the engine.

Joe and I called it a night and crawled into our respective bunks. We were so exhausted that we barely noticed all of the tools flying across the cabin as the tide went out and Hanuman came to rest on her side, in the mud.

Morning found us floating again. It was time to try the engine. She turned over and fired right up, relieving us greatly. I inspected the coupling, which appeared to be functioning within tolerances. When the tide allowed, we were off. Before we knew it, salt air filled our nostrils and Hanuman was back in the Pacific. We hoisted the sails and shut down the engine, embracing the peace of the Pacific; free at last!

The Queensland Coast

Joe and I sailed north for a day and half in favorable conditions until the wind dropped and we were left to tease what progress we could out of the shifty land breezes. Exacerbating our slow pace, we were asked to sail around a World War II movie that was being filmed. Apparently Hanuman didn't fit in with their set.

Eventually we found the wind and started making some respectable headway. The wind strengthened, and before long our situation was less than comfortable. As the sun set I decided it was time to reef. The main reefed down nicely, but the jib roller furling unit jammed and wouldn't retract more than two turns.

It had been five months since I'd been at sea and I was suddenly feeling queasy. To top it off, the wind shifted around and we found ourselves beating to weather. It was Joe's first time sailing and he gave me an "is this normal" look.

The wind continued to build and a layer of threatening clouds blanketed the previously cerulean sky. With the jib unable to furl, the boat wasn't well balanced and steering became a struggle. To make matters worse it started raining and the seas grew angry. After taking a couple waves in the face, I got out my rain gear and donned it over my wet clothes. One of the snaps on the jacket busted off as I tried to buffer myself against the wetness. "Mother fucker," I mumbled, suddenly feeling that being back in the boat yard didn't sound all that bad. It was winter in the Southern Hemisphere, and neither the air nor the water was all that warm.

We were in the shit. The wind howled. Waves hammered the cockpit. Steering was a bitch. I felt like puking. Minutes passed like hours as I checked the cockpit Timex, wishing my watch be over. Eventually I saw a double zero in the minute slots and gave Joe the double knock. His head slowing craned into view. I squinted through the water laden air into his vanquished gaze. "Uhh…," he began. I had a bad feeling about the subjugated look in his eye and an even worse one about the tone of his, "Uhh." "I think this is above my level. I'm just barely managing in the bunk," Joe continued in the monotone of a zombie. He was seasick and found the thought of trying to steer the boat beyond his capacity. I was disappointed, but it was in fact Joe's first time sailing. I could definitely see where he was coming from, and respected his position, but I was wet and cold and awfully excited at the prospect of diving into the womb of my bunk. "Alright," I said, avoiding eye contact. "Oh, and it sounds like there's kind-of a lot of water swishing around down here," he finished, before diving back into his bunk. In fact, there was enough water to throw some of the floorboards into the air when the boat lurched dramatically to the side.

The electric pump under the engine naturally wasn't working. The other electric pump in the deep bilge worked nicely for a little while until it became clogged. It came down to the hand pump in the cockpit, which thankfully performed admirably. As long as it wasn't an emergency I was too nauseous to explore where the water was entering. Fortunately it was a manageable inflow so I just pumped it out every hour or so. The hand bilge, however, only pumped out the aft bilge, leaving a substantial amount of water sloshing around in the forward portion of the boat. It wasn't enough to be dangerous, but it was certainly unnerving. Seeing the floorboards popping up atop of a geyser of water had an unsettling effect. Hanuman and I hadn't been to sea in half a year and we were both feeling it.

My perspective on life was filtered through exhaustion and nausea. I watched without emotion as we rolled over wave after wave; my bloodless left hand glued to the wheel, holding the angle, my right assisting when wind and wave endeavored to overpower my left. My shoulders tensed and head bowed instinctively after hearing the hallow thud on the hull announcing water bound for the cockpit. My eyes mindlessly followed the water draining off my raingear after each douching.

The storm continued for two days, though diminished enough on the second day for Joe to feel comfortable resuming his steer duties.

The second night of the storm it rained even harder, but thankfully the wind wasn't as strong and Hanuman practically steered herself as she reacclimated to her element. I was thankful for the GPS in the near zero visibility. Beyond the poor visibility, there was a strange combination of haze and light that played tricks on my eyes. I jibed once in a panic, thinking I was seeing a reef only feet away.

The gray dawn of morning found us in sight of Lady Elliot Island, our destination. When the sun was high enough to give us a decent picture of the surrounding atoll, we found the narrow pass in the reef, entered the lagoon, and dropped anchor. We were definitely relieved to have completed our first passage, but we hadn't exactly arrived in the paradise we expected and felt we deserved. It was still windy as hell.

At high tide the waves made it over the protective reef, making the anchorage rolly and uncomfortable. The water was freezing, and the only land was a scrubby looking patch of park which didn't even seem to justify getting out the dinghy. We never made it to land. We jumped in the water just long enough to confirm that it was too cold to enjoy. We spent several days on the boat fixing what had broke and waiting for the weather to pass.

Eventually the wind eased a little and our boredom grew a lot so we hoisted the anchor. As we were leaving the lagoon we smacked into a large coral outcropping. Joe was on the bow, guiding us through reef infested lagoon using hand signals, but got distracted while tidying up the anchor chain and didn't see a huge coral head until it was right in front of us. I saw a panicked hand signal to starboard, and within a second felt a bang that halted the boat, shook the rigging, sent me over the wheel, and almost put Joe in the drink. Fortunately we bounced off it instead of grounding ourselves. Joe took the wheel as I dove in the water to inspect the damage. I was pleased to find that despite the impact Hanuman only suffered a relatively small gash on the lower keel.

"Let's stay focused up there this time," I shouted forward to Joe, stating the obvious, as we resumed our transit.

We were rewarded with mellow sailing as we continued north. Joe found his sea legs, came to enjoy the motion of the ocean, and took up cooking. He said he'd never really gotten into cooking in a normal land kitchen, but thought the added challenge of everything trying to get away from him made it more interesting. He was stating as much as he went flying across the cabin with a pot of rice in one hand. Wham! "Oops," he chirped. I could tell he'd broken something and hoped it was minor. "One hand for yourself, one hand for the ship," I reminded. And added, "You won't be able to cook me dinner if you're injured." "…and more importantly: no breaking the boat." To his credit, he hadn't spilled any of the rice.

We stopped in a couple of deserted anchorages on our northward progression but quickly decided that we'd spent enough time soaking up nature and wanted to find somewhere to soak up beer and girls, preferably in large quantities. Airlie Beach was the spot. It was a well known backpacker hangout so we put aside picturesque beaches and set our sights on more carnal desires. Wendy also happened to be living and working in Airlie.

Airlie Beach was a turning point in our journey. It marked the end of the trial and the beginning of the reward. We'd found our way into the Trade Winds; strong and steady, and always from astern. We were able to move along at a good clip without even using the main. Another major addition was the used Aries Wind Vane unit I'd purchased in California during my work stint. I bolted the thing to the back of the boat in Caboolture, but didn't fully assemble it until we got to Airlie.

The Aries was one of the greatest inventions of all time. Basically a very simple device, it used the direction of the wind and the power of the passing water to steer the boat. Despite being basically simple it could be a little tricky to get set up and working properly, but after some trial and error Joe and I got it working fabulously. Over the next few years it would become my favorite crewmember. In the right conditions it could steer unassisted for days. It required no power, no food, and no fresh water. It never drank the last beer. It never bitched or complained. It never left the boat.

"I was about to say 'it's alive' but I'm going to give it some more time to see what it can really do," Joe commented after our initial engagement of the Aries. He ended up inadvertently confirming it as sentient not too long after, when he stated, "I was just about to help it, when I thought, 'It has to learn.'"

We found Wendy not long after arriving in Airlie. She'd adapted well to her new environment, gotten a job she loved, working on boats, and made a plethora of friends. I was happy to see her contented with her new life, having felt guilty about dragging her away from her old one, only to cast her aside after I tired of her.

After a week of shenanigans, Joe and I continued north, stopping at a few islands off the Queensland coast. We picked up some backpackers who were looking for a little adventure, and eventually arrived in Cairns.

Joe decided that he wouldn't be continuing beyond Cairns. I was a little disappointed, and surprised, by his decision to leave earlier than originally planned, but I had a suspicion that he'd made some sort of desperate pact with Neptune while we were bashing through the shit and was probably obligated to get out of His ocean before Hanuman left the coast. I'd been hoping he'd stick around until Bali. We got along well, he had his sea legs on, and aside from leaving the peels on the onions, (in this instance I think he took my 'nothing gets wasted' mantra a little far) was a decent cook.

Joe was going through one of the mental transformations that people tended to experience after a stint on Hanuman. Often their thought process led them to the conclusion that they needed to go back home and re-orient their lives.

While stuffing our faces with meat pies, after a solid night of drinking, I let Joe know how I really felt about his idea of going home. "You don't have any pressing issues back home. Certainly nothing as potentially as cool as sailing through the Torres Strait and into Indonesia," I argued. I didn't feel Joe had really gotten the full Hanuman experience. Thus far we'd just sailed along the coast. We hadn't made any real passages. We hadn't been to any truly exotic locales. A thousand 'out there' experiences still awaited him.

I did my best to outline just how things would go for him when he returned home and went on the road trip he was already planning. It ended with him relaying the saga of his sailing adventure to someone who would ultimately ask, "So,… why did you end up leaving the boat?" To which Joe's only honest response would be, "I'm not really sure." Joe would later tell me things played out just as I had predicted.

Joe had actually purchased his airline ticket in Airlie Beach, probably with Neptune and the punishing weather we'd endured still fresh on his mind. By the time we reached Cairns I think he may have already been having doubts about leaving, but he had his ticket, and had mentally committed to the idea of leaving.

With Joe departing, we naturally had to up the intensity of our profligacy. A week of partying culminated on August 30th, second annual beard day. Our favorite bar was hosting a competitive open-mic night. Joe was pretty proficient on the guitar and Aaron, a Canadian backpacker who'd sailed to Cairns with us, played drums in an actual band; albeit of the garage variety. We decided to enter the competition. Having no musical skills whatsoever, I was nominated to sing; substituting inebriation for talent. We had no plan. Aaron basically just wanted to bang on the drums and Joe was anxious to get his hands on the electric guitar, compete with 'wa-wa' pedal. I let them do their thing for awhile before jumping in with some lyrics I made up on the fly. I wrapped my hand around the microphone, hoping that it would muffle my toneless voice and lack of coherent lyrics. Aaron and Joe ended up sounding pretty good. I was terrible. Fortunately our 'song' didn't last long and before I knew it I was safely back behind my beer.

Joe found his way to the airport and I was left alone to contemplate my situation. A week of partying had left me with a cold. I took a few days to just chill out before burdening myself with plans for the future.

After regrouping, I decided I should start looking for crew. Part of me had a desire to take off solo but the old 'bad idea alarm' sounded the more seriously I contemplated the plan. I put up a few fliers, stating I was looking for crew. Crew had always fallen into my lap and I wasn't thrilled to be soliciting strangers.

I received an e-mail from, and met up with, a young couple who were keen on sailing to Bali. However, they'd just come from crewing on a boat that was paying for all of their expenses. I had no intention of paying for anyone to sail with me. In fact, I'd been flirting with the idea of charging people, not with intention of making any money, but in hopes of covering some of my expenses.

I argued that a shared food and fuel bill wouldn't amount to much. They seemed like they'd make good sailing companions and I was hoping to have them along. They decided they could swing the food and fuel but were worried about being stuck in Bali without any way of leaving; a reasonable concern. They said they'd think about it and get back to me.

The situation ended up resolving itself when Mathieu, a Frenchmen and the male half of the couple, was caught breaking parole. He'd been serving out his parole in the French territory of New Caledonia when the opportunity to sail to Australia came up. He decided he wouldn't be missed. Apparently he had. He received a call from a friend in New Caledonia that his parole officer had been looking for him. He had to get back into the country without being noticed or face 18 months in jail. I never found out his fate; either way, I was crewless.

I was surprised to find myself slightly relieved when I received the news that my potential crew wasn't coming. The idea of sailing solo had been rolling around in my head even before I bought the boat. I wasn't seeking a whole new theme for the journey but part of me was curious to see what it would be like. I also wanted to change my relationship with crew in general. I no longer wanted to have to rely on having to find people to continue my journey. I didn't want to be at the mercy of someone else's whims. I felt I would come to appreciate crew more if I wasn't relying on them; if they were around simply because I wanted their company and insight into life. Not because I needed someone to maintain a heading for 12 hours out of the day.

I was also looking for something less definable. I sensed there were secrets below the horizon revealed only to those who went alone.

I spent a week readying Hanuman and myself for our journey. We both required a fair measure of preparation. We wouldn't be encountering many of the amenities of a westernized nation until we reached the Mediterranean; about 9,000 miles away!

I filled a couple of shopping carts full of rice, pasta, tomato sauce, onions, potatoes, and two minute noodles, and pushed them back to the boat. Water and diesel were topped off. I got a bunch of jugs of kerosene and methelated spirits for the new stove. I purchased a new battery for my wristwatch and a couple of five-liter boxes of wine, for medicinal purposes of course, and the newly born I-Hanuman being was stocked. The feeling of a well stocked boat always put me in high spirits. Just add wind, and the world was mine.

I received an e-mail from someone responding to the crew notice I'd put up and decided I should give him a call. Even though I was pretty much mentally set on going solo, I still wasn't fully sold on the idea. Somehow I felt I shouldn't be going alone unless I really couldn't find anyone. I called the number but was told that the guy who'd e-mailed me had gone north to Darwin. "Phew," I thought, "close call."

Solo to Kupang

Eventually preparations reached a crescendo; it was time. With wind and tide in my favor I hoisted the anchor and put to sea, bound for Kupang, Indonesia, 1800 nautical miles and two oceans away. It was the second longest passage I'd attempted thus far. In addition to the mileage, the Torres Strait, a 140 mile long reef strew passage between Australia and Papua New Guinea, made the undertaking a questionable first solo undertaking. I'd told my mom that the ex-convict couple was going with me. I didn't see the need to make her worry any more than she already was.

The first obstacle was the Great Barrier Reef. A protected inside passage exists between the mainland and the reef, but I decided to sail north to the Torres Strait outside of the reef, where I'd have some breathing room without the constant worry of hitting reef while I was sleeping. I wanted to make my way through Trinity Pass and into the open sea before dark.

I spent the first day tacking towards the pass in light airs and readying myself for the open ocean. I rigged a safety line behind the boat that I could grab onto in the event that I fell in the water. I also attached a trip line to the Aries that would disengage it from the wheel if I pulled on the safety line. Once the Aries was disengaged Hanuman would, ideally, round up into the wind and stop, making it easier for me to pull myself back on board. I also wore a safety harness that tethered me to the boat. I felt it important to equate falling off the boat with falling off a skyscraper. I forced myself to imagine bobbing in the water as I watched Hanuman sail towards the horizon without me, to force the importance of staying on board to sink in. Injury was also something I wanted to avoid. Any injury that hindered my ability to handle the boat could go from minor to life threatening terribly quickly.

I got naked and paraded around the cockpit, just because I could, but soon decided that a sunburned crotch was no way to start a passage.

With daylight hours numbered, I fired up Big Red, not wanting to get caught inside the reef at night, and managed to slide through the pass just before sunset. The wind filled in just as the sun dipped below the horizon. It was freeing to be in the open ocean with some room to stretch out. I felt connected to all possible destinations in the world. I shut down the engine and pointed the bow north.

I decided to start off using R-2, the electric auto-pilot. It was extremely reliable and I didn't want to add too many new variables to my first night alone. After taking in the stars on the moonless night, I ventured into my bunk for some sleep. There were no ships on the horizon so I set my alarm for twenty minutes and closed my eyes. I felt relaxed and at ease and managed to turn a good 15 of those minutes into sleep.

The alarm beeped and I crawled up on deck, happy to find everything doing its job without complaint. There was no light, save that of the stars. Hanuman raced through the night like a comet, leaving a trail of glowing phosphorescence in her wake. No ships on the horizon, still on course, I returned to my bunk.

R-2 woke me not long after returning to bed, with the troubling noise he expelled when his belt was slipping. The wind had increased in front of a small squall, putting more pressure on the helm and forcing R-2 to work harder. I eased the jib sheet out six inches, R-2 got himself back on course, and I returned to my bunk.

The squall passed, dropping a gentle pattering of rain on deck. I smiled, happy not to be on deck getting wet, and dozed back off to sleep.

I felt a great sense of accomplishment when the sun rose and all was still well. I turned off R-2 and engaged the Aries. It picked up where R-2 left off flawlessly.

Strong and consistent winds ushered us north for four days. We raced the dolphins as we surfed down long rolling waves. The Aries steered, requiring minimal assistance, and we ticked off miles with ease. I didn't read or write, cooked very simple meals, and found myself well rested despite the short sleep intervals. I spent most of my time just sitting in the cockpit swaying with the waves. My eyes followed a hypnotic cycle, moving from the Aries, to the sails, to the wind indicator at the top of the mast, and then back to rest on the horizon. I didn't even think all that much. I just swayed, enjoying the wind flow through my oily hair and kiss my salty shoulders.

The wind lulled on day five, but a week after leaving Cairns I'd covered the 700 plus miles to the Torres Strait.

I'd purchased some instant coffee in Cairns, anticipating times when sleep might not be a possibility. I decided to experiment with it the night before I got to the Strait, heaping a couple of spoonfuls of the course powder into my mug, as I'd thought I'd recalled my father doing years before. I soon discovered why he had such a hairy chest. The spoon was really more like a ladle and the resulting mixture more like a syrup.

I was game however, and the first cup went down rather well, producing a favorable effect. There was still some hot water left and since 'nothing gets wasted,' I decided I'd have another cup; just one shovel full of coffee this time. I downed it in short order, as I tend to do with any beverage placed in front of me. Then it hit me; and all at once. I felt like someone had given me an injection of strychnine, or at least how I'd imagined that feeling. My muscles contracted involuntarily. I felt I was on the verge of a seizure, and spasmed in the cockpit until the feeling passed. I never touched the stuff again.

I entered the Torres Strait in the late afternoon. I would've preferred to get started in the morning and have a full day of sunlight to sink my teeth into the strait, but perfection wasn't my fortune. I hadn't gotten much sleep the previous night, due to the instant coffee epileptic incident, and was feeling a bit groggy. The channel weaves its way through reefs and islands and is somewhat crowded with large ships. I knew that sleeping would be out of the question as long as I was in the Strait. Another dark night fell on Hanuman and me.

I made my first tack, changing our heading from west to south, as I tried to stay on the edge of the channel and out of the way of the large ships. In the milky blackness I found our new heading disorienting. The wind was adequate, but we didn't seem to be making any headway. A strong current often runs through the Strait from east to west, which was generally the way we were headed, but after my tack I figured we must have been trying to sail against it.

As I tried to determine what was happening and what I needed to do, I noticed a large ship bearing down on us. I started off only seeing his green port (right) side running light. Before long I could see both his green and red running lights, indicating that I was looking directly at his bow and he was heading right for me. However, given my direction and speed, I felt I should pass before him prior to a collision. I waited for my view to change from red and green to just red, indicating I'd passed before him. It wasn't happening. The lights just got larger and the hulking blackness of the massive ship began to block out the stars on the horizon. I willed us forward but we were still in its sights. I could see welds on the metal hull lit by the running lights. Huge cranes on deck hovered above like gallows. I decided it was time to fire up Big Red. She roared a cloud of white smoke as I threw her in gear and gunned it. We accelerated forward and the prow of the steel beast silently slid by.

The incident woke me up, but the adrenaline soon faded and I found myself having to do a lot of head shaking to avert nodding off. Keeping my eyes focused required a herculean effort. I decided it was time to bust open the pack of No Doze I'd acquired in Cairns. I was nervous after the previous nights encounter with the instant coffee, but decided extreme measures were in order, so I popped a pill. 15 minutes later I found myself perking right up. I wasn't tired at all and experienced no jittery side effects. "That's some pure shit," I thought.

On the southern leg of the Strait, our course, and the wind, shifted slightly, putting us at the limit of Hanuman's windward capabilities. There was no room for tacking and I worried that if the wind shifted anymore we'd have to downce the sails and motor to windward; making for slow and laborious progress on the southern leg. Fortunately the conditions favored us and we were able to beat into the stiff wind while making over seven knots, a more than respectable pace.

I popped another No Doze as the moon rose and we followed the channel to the west.

Less than 24 hours after I'd entered the Torres Strait, I spilled into the Arafura Sea, much relieved to have made it unscathed. All I had to do after that was sail the 1100 nautical miles to Kupang. I set the Aries, unconcerned with the accuracy of our course; just happy there wasn't anything to hit, and crawled into my bunk and passed out.

The first few days in the new ocean brought a lively wind. Our pace was fast and I naively extrapolated our arrival time based on our current speed. "I'll be dropping anchor in Kupang in a week," I said to myself, in an almost congratulatory tone.

That was not to be. The winds gradually diminished until I decided that I was no longer on the Arafura Sea, but rather Lake Arafura. The water glassed off to a degree I'd never experienced in the open ocean, broken only by the frequent jumping of fish. "I think that was a trout."

The island like consistency of Hanuman's position made her an irresistible hangout for any creature in the vicinity. I tossed some onion peels in the water. With their light weight and sail like shape I assumed they would drift away. They didn't. Hanuman became surrounded by all of the refuse I jettisoned over board.

A sea turtle came by for an inspection. He had four barnacles hanging off his shell. I named him Barnacle Bob. He hung around for half a day frequently banging his shell against the hull. I wondered if the asymmetrical location of his barnacles affected his ability to swim. I had time to ponder such things.

I jumped in the water with mask and snorkel to have a look around. A number of curious fish came around to nibble the skin on my toes, but quickly realized their mistake and returned to pecking at the onion peels. There were some dolphins in the distance that I'd hoped would come and play with me, but they didn't venture close enough to be seen underwater.

Eventually, enough of a breeze came up to at least allow me to point Hanuman in the right direction and we were able to pull away from the onion peels. The wind filled back in, albeit with only moderate strength and poor consistency, for the next week and I was able to make some small but comfortable mileage and do a lot of reading.

Day after repetitive day at sea allowed me copious time for contemplation and reflection. It was easy to gravitate towards life's bigger questions, like "what should I make for dinner," but also found myself recollecting Annie's question.

Annie was a woman offering free yoga at Geoff's youth hostel on Magnetic Island back in Australia. Being a sucker for anything free, I went there every day. She was clearly someone who'd spent time meditating on many of life's answerless questions. I invited her over to one of our nightly barbeques at the free electric grills by the beach. After enough beers were consumed to pacify our societal residence towards personal questions, Annie decided she'd try and penetrate my swarthy exterior. "What's your deal? Why do you always feel the need to take things to such extremes?" Her tone was light hearted, but the question sober and personal; it went outside the comical banter that had pervaded the conversation thus far. Her query silenced all of the side conversations. Everyone sensed that the mood had changed. Like prey sniffing a predator on the wind, many sidled off to the next picnic table to avoid becoming future victims of group scrutiny. I was slightly taken back with the question, but interested in engaging in the conversation. I crossed my arms as I contemplated my response. She smiled and released a pinky finger from the beer she was holding to point out the defensive posture I was already displaying.

Through previous conversations and time together, she'd gathered that I had a tendency to push things past their comfortable resting point. She asked why I always had to take things to such an extreme level. She challenged that I could never be satisfied with things as they were, and that I ought to be more appreciative of what was going on in the present moment.

None of this was really news to me, but it's one thing to have knowledge and another to act on it. She continued to expound on parallel philosophies while I finished most of her ideas for her. She found this a little frustrating. Not that I was finishing her sentences, but that I knew all this, yet in my stubbornness refused to actualize it.

After bludgeoning the topic of living in the present, she moved on to fear, and ultimately the fear of death. She said that she was conceived as a twin, but her brother died prior to birth and his umbilical cord had wrapped around her neck, suffocating her during the birthing process for about 20 minutes. She was born weighing only 2.3 pounds and not expected to live. She said that, through her aunt, she was able to recall the experience.

I found the notion of being able to recall ones experience in the womb a bit sketchy. I wondered if she remembered it, or if through her aunt, she'd created the memory. The subtleties of the difference weren't really important, and I didn't want to get bogged down on the disconnection between metaphor and reality, but I often found it bothersome when people took metaphor for reality; one of my problems with religion. The essence of a story doesn't have to change based on whether it's a metaphor or reality, but there is a difference.

Annie said that through her recollection of the near death experience, she was able to overcome her fear of death. She explained that she conceptualized death as just another unknown frontier that doesn't have to be the end.

The wind lightened as sun melted into another Arafuran sunset. As I traveled west the air got damp and heavy, dulling the horizon during the waning hours of the day. My hair felt greasy and my skin was moist and sticky, but the milky haze was a pleasant respite from the dry heat of the day.

I soaked in the tranquility and contemplated what Annie had been saying. I wondered if one had to have a near death experience to lose ones fear of death. I questioned why she had to convince herself that death wasn't really the end in order to obstruct her fear of it. What if it was the end? Could she not except that all things end, and still live without fear? Could I?

As daylight faded I began my favorite daily ritual. I put on a pot of water for tea, got out the short wave radio, and scanned the band to see what programs would be lining up with my antenna. The ABC (Australian Broadcasting Channel) had been the most consistent of late, but I would also pick up the Voice of Iran ('The Islamic Republic of Iran's Public Broadcasting Channel,') the VOA (Voice of America,) Dutch International, The German Something or Other, Radio Netherlands, Radio Yugoslavia, and various others. I actually managed to stay much better informed of world affairs at sea than I did on land.

The Voice of Iran was broadcasting a show titled, 'Worldwide Hatred of America's War Mongering Tactics,' a fairly common topic on many stations. I began to see why traveling Canadians were so emphatic about plastering their flag on every item they owned. I often wondered if they were really so proud of being Canadian, or rather of not being American.

During a long draft of green tea my mind strayed from the distant voice channeling through the short wave, back to death. As the sun fell, I mused that every setting of the sun was a little death. The end of another day destined to dissolve beyond memory. I wondered if perhaps our own deaths could be analyzed from a more metaphorical perspective.

I recalled one of Seinfeld's monologs where he stated that people's number two fear is death and their number one fear is public speaking. By Seinfeld's logic, it stood to reason that if a person was going to a funeral they'd rather be in the casket than giving the eulogy.

It seemed to me that the only fear that existed was of death, and that every other fear was just a manifestation of that fear. At first, Seinfeld's logic would seem to contradict this; until one considers, not physical death, but rather death of the ego. The fear of public speaking comes down to the fear of saying something stupid and having the audience think we are less of a person because of it. If we are judging ourselves by what others see in us, and we perceive that we have lessened ourselves in their eyes, then we have indeed become a lesser person based on the value system that we've created. In essence, it becomes the death of who we are. All of the precepts that we create to define ourselves, and our worth, can destroy us when we feel we've lost the admiration of those, including ourselves, whose opinion we've, consciously or otherwise, assigned importance.

Perhaps I didn't need to have a near death experience to lose my fear of death, but to in fact die. To lose my attachment to my perception of who I was. To free my actions from pride and simply take care in them. Care that once taken, is released.

More days passed with inconsistent winds. I shattered my previous record low daily mileage of 24, set in the doldrums, with a whopping 15. In case the old record didn't get the message, I did 22 miles the following day. Five similar days ran in succession and I got the feeling I was getting nowhere.

Despite what could have been a maddening period, I found myself content. I had plenty of food and water. I knew the wind would come up eventually. I was enthralled in 'War and Peace,' which allowed me to travel out of my own existence and into that of another. I was also only a couple hundred miles away from Kupang and knew that all I needed was a two good days of good wind to get me there. My only real concern was that my mom would start to worry if I didn't check in soon.

The water between Australia and Indonesia is heavily patrolled for illegal immigrants by Australian Customs. I frequently conversed with them on the VHF radio as they flew overhead. They started off asking the basics about vessel name, homeport, port of departure, and destination. Before long the conversation digressed to, "is that still you down there Hanuman?" "Yup." Eventually they stopped calling me all together. I didn't miss the dialog. I was in my own world and found their inquires a distraction from my solitude.

My chief concern was the fact that I'd run out of the 'good cookies,' a prime component of my nightly ritual of drinking tea and listening to the short wave radio. All I had left were some dubious looking cream filled numbers. Everything about them was wrong. They were a rainbow of florescent colors and looked less like something to eat and more like something one would use to decorate a Christmas tree. They smelled of chemicals. I muscled down a few of them before setting them aside for more desperate times.

26 days after leaving Cairns, with a strange combination of utter elation and nostalgic recollection of the passage, I dropped anchor in front of Kupang, West Timor, Indonesia.

Kupang

After tidying up the boat, and a brief moment of reflection on what I'd just accomplished, I launched Sputnik and took the Beach. A frail looking Indonesian man who appeared to be about 100 helped me drag Sputnik up the gray pebbly beach. With some hand gesturing and a toothless grin, he indicated that the dinghy would be safe with him. There were a few other dinghies in his care with various scraps of clothing, presumably the old man's, placed over their outboards ostensibly to protect them from the suns intense rays, but more likely to indicate that he should be paid for his services. Judging from the condition of his tattered tarp and plastic bag domicile on the rocky shore, I figured he couldn't be charging much.

It was Saturday, and my cruising guide said that the Harbor Master and so forth should be open, so I decided it prudent to check in. I wandered around for awhile, hoping that I might just happen upon the Harbor Master, but Kupang is a large town, in fact the capitol of West Timor, and I soon gave up on the futile task, realizing the odds of stumbling upon the four places I needed to go were unlikely at best. As I said, in my experience taxi drivers can usually get you everything you need.

The driver had a grasp of the fundamentals of English and new where the Harbor Master was located. I asked how much it would cost to get there. I had no idea what the exchange rate was or how much the 70,000 rupees he was charging amounted to, but it's always nice to arrange a price ahead of time. He also knew a guy who could exchange US dollars. "Perfect!"

On our way to the Harbor Master I chatted him up a little. He'd learned English while living in Darwin, Australia. He said, with a grin, that he had to leave because his girlfriend's daughter "fell in love with him." Despite a slight revulsion, I couldn't help but return his grin.

We arrived at the Harbor Master following a pleasant drive. After working for every nautical mile from Cairns, I fully enjoyed a few 'free' miles in the taxi. I rolled the window down and sunk deeply into the padded seat. My elbow rested on the door, a warm breeze ruffling my salty beard, and I felt an imperturbable sense of peace and relaxation I'd never experienced.

I entered the office and went straight to the guy with the most rubber stamps on his desk, thinking I'd skip all the bullshit with the underlings and go right to the head honcho. He was pecking away at an archaic typewriter one finger at time and didn't look up for an extended period. I waited patiently. There was a large window behind him and I gazed contentedly out at the ocean I'd just crossed. He eventually looked up, only to indicate that he didn't speak any English. I later gathered that when you hire an agent to walk you through the process, officialdom gets a cut. Thus he was deliberately stubborn. Fortunately my black market guy was on hand to do some minor translating. I shoved a bunch of papers in front of the Harbor Master who begrudgingly acknowledged them but said that he wanted more copies and that I could just come back when I was ready to check out. "Fine by me," I thought. Once I'd exchanged money with the black market guy my taxi drove me back to Kupang proper and let me loose on the town.

I wandered around with satisfied aimlessness. I felt an afternoon breeze tickle my neck and chuckled at myself as I looked skyward for the masthead wind direction indicator, as I had thousands of times in the previous 26 days. It, of course, hadn't followed me from the boat.

Hunger set in and I found a little restaurant where I had dinner and a coke for less than a buck.

The following day I resumed my exploration of the city. Fortunately it was Sunday, so I didn't have to worry about continuing the checking in process. I happened to turn down a narrow alley lined with kiosk type shops. In front of one were two locals sitting around drinking what was clearly some variety of alcoholic beverage. One of the drinkers was shirtless and had one guy massaging his feet and another massaging his hand and arm; the hand without a drink in it. This was Ama. I smiled thinking, "this guy knows how to live." He motioned me over with his beer laden hand and before I knew it an upturned bucket appeared for me to sit on. I'd been enjoying my walk and was a little leery of getting caught up in whatever they had going on, but decided to indulge in their hospitality. As I eased onto the bucket, two milk crates were placed in front of me to serve as a table. Ama reached up to the kiosk he was planted in front of and started haphaz-ardly pulling things from it and placing them before of me; a small bottle of water, some sort of deep fried treats... He didn't speak any English but motioned me to indulge. I did, happily.

No words were exchanged but we all smiled and nodded congenially. A plate with some odd-looking small green fruit type things was place on the 'table.' A little mound of salt was added to the plate. Tooyus, a lean taunt looking guy with playful Asiatic eyes and a few sun blurred tattoos, was the third pillar of our drinking triangle. He pulled a toothbrush from the kiosk and used the end of it to mash fresh chili peppers into the salt. He then used a bit of blue tarp hanging off the kiosk to wipe off the toothbrush and put it back on the display rack, "good as new."

They demonstrated how the fruit was eaten; pressing it into the salt and chili paste, and motioned for me to partake. Once I'd tried a few, and imparted my enjoyment, they indicated that this was drinking food, and I was given a shot of some low proof whiskey type stuff.

We exchanged names and hung out in a relaxed manner as I continued to devour anything they set before me. This seemed to please them. They smiled and nodded every time I ate something.

One might expect that I'd be itching for some conversation after 26 days alone at sea, but I thoroughly enjoyed just chillin' on the bucket in the company of others without the burden of talking. I quickly realized that the kiosk served more as a clubhouse than as an actual place of business.

After a few more rounds of the whiskey type drink Ama busted out a cell phone. He dialed, pointed to it, said "English," and handed it to me. "Hello," I ventured. I was greeted by a young female voice. "Hello, how are you?" she replied. I was intrigued. "Fine thank you, how are you?" I responded. "Fine thank you, how are you?" she said. I hesitated. "Fine thank you, how are you?" "Fine thank you, how are you?" she repeated. After it was well established that we were both fine I thought I'd try and mix it up. "How old are you?" "Fine thank you how are you?" I tried a few other lines but continued to receive the same response. I eventually just handed the phone back to Ama, smiling and nodding, "English," I repeated.

We finished off the green fruity things and the whisky and before I knew it I was on the back of Ama's motor scooter tacking and jibing through Kupang's narrow dirt allies. I had no idea where we were headed but I was thoroughly enjoying the ride and a little disappointed when it ended.

We arrived at a modest well kept house of cement and cinderblock. Ama motioned me in and I had a seat on a couch in the living room where two young boys were playing Super Mario Brothers on their Nintendo. Ama was in one of the back rooms and from what I gathered from the tone of the conversation, was trying to convince the girl who I'd talked to on the phone to come out and chat with me.

She eventually emerged, blushing, with her hands in front of her face. Before long she relaxed and we engaged in a rudimentary conversation. I found out that she was Ama's niece, Ronni. Her mom, Ama's sister, brought me out a piece of cake type stuff that I gobbled down with my usual exuberance.

I'd brought a pocket sized notebook that I started using to compile an Indonesian dictionary with Ronni's help. We alternately watched Jackie Chan and conversed until food was served.

Ama and I sat at the kitchen table and scarfed down some rice, vegetables, and a meatbally soup. All of which was delicious. Everything I'd been cooking on the boat had started to taste the same, so any variation was a treat.

With Ronni's help we pieced together each other's stories and after learning about my trip, Ama and the others decided they wanted to see the boat. Tomorrow didn't work. Neither did the next day. After some pondering, 'now' was arrived upon as the best time. Not being a huge fan of future commitments 'now' or, "this minute" as they said, was fine with me. Ama conjured a van and we were off.

I pumped up Sputnik and we brought her down to the water. The wave action was significant. When the van had arrived, Ama, Ronni, Ronni's two brothers, Tooyus, and I all piled in, but I didn't really think that everyone intended on coming out to the boat. As it turned out, they did.

The first wave came over the bow, half filling the four man dinghy with water before anyone was even in it. I was contemplating a retreat back up the beach to drain the dinghy when Ronnie dove/fell in. She ended up soaking the majority of her clothing, and we had momentum, so there didn't seem any point in starting over, especially since everyone else was already wet as well. The rest of the group climbed in on top of Ronni. I gave one good shove to get us past the breakers and we were off. After a couple of pulls the 2.5 horse fired up and sputtered angrily, everyone looked back at it. I patted it gently with my hand, "she just needs a little love." They understood. Tooyus bailed continuously as we made our way out to Hanuman.

Hanuman was hobby horsing significantly in the passing swells, but everyone managed to get on board without falling in. I made tea and passed out some crackers. It was the best I could do. Tooyus and Ama were jazzed and wanted to head out to a nearby island, but Ronni and her brothers quickly became seasick, so we headed back to land. Landing Sputnik went much smoother than launching. 500 rupees for the toothless man, about six cents, and we were in the van heading back to Ama's.

We settled in behind Ama's house in an area that was an auto shop of sorts. As beer and whiskey magically appeared, I got the feeling that the shop saw a lot more drinking than mechanicing.

More beer, whiskey, and a five course meal prepared by Ama's wife Siti, materialized. The buzz I had going made me more comfortable using the Indonesian, or Ba'asa, I was learning but it didn't do anything for my memory. So, while my dictionary on paper was expanding, my speaking capabilities digressed to *mabuk* (drink,) *tamba lagie* (another or fill-her-up,) and *chukup,* which, though rarely used, means enough.

Various neighbors and extended family filtered through our soirée, one of whom spoke English reasonably well. I made some inquiries about religion and learned there was a broad mix. Ronni's mother was Muslim and her dad was Hindu. Ronni was being raised Hindu and her brothers were being raised Muslim; a fairly common arrangement. "Tolerance," they all seemed to know in English. No one seemed to be of the orthodox variety I noted, looking over at Ama, a Muslim, holding a cigarette in one hand and a beer in the other.

Eventually the night wound down and Ama, and a few of the others including Tooyus (now passed out in the back of the van with an ink mustache drawn on his upper lip; I'd decided to usher chiefing into Kupang upon finding a Sharpie marker in my back pack), dropped me off back on the beach with the promise that I return the next day so that they could drive me to the immigration office.

I arrived not too early the next day and while waiting for Ama to hunt down a van, was served coffee and cake by Siti, Ama's wife. Tooyus showed up, or woke up from wherever he happened to have passed out, with a bottle of whiskey in his hand. I'd learned that he was a fisherman, explaining his drinking tendencies. He thrust the bottle my way. "No, I can't start drinking now; it wouldn't be in my favor to show up at immigration smelling like booze." Of course I couldn't say any of that in Indonesian, and as he thrust the bottle my way a second time, with a look of confusion on his face, I accepted it with a strained smile. I figured one couldn't hurt.

The immigration girl was wholly cute. She said she needed a crew list. "No crew, just me," I responded. She said she needed a list none the less. I tore some paper out of a spiral notebook and scribbled out a crew list, in triplicate, and handed them to her. We flirted. She gave me a bunch of stamps, no charge.

I decided I'd go back to the Harbor Master and get that whole rigmarole out of the way. I spent a good portion of everyday in Kupang hunting down one stamp or the other. As soon as I was done checking in, I started checking out. I didn't mind. I enjoyed walking and having a mission.

The Harbor Master was on the other side of town, and Ama hadn't been able to hunt down a van, so I started trekking. I arrived drenched in sweat, as I did everywhere, and laid my papers on the same desk as I had before.

The desk was occupied by a much friendlier gentleman than it had been previously. He grinned broadly as he looked down at the papers I'd fanned out in front of him. He picked up one, looking as though he'd never seen anything like it before, and slowly rotated it to face him. He studied if for a long moment. "Mick-ale Doo-gain." "Yup, that's me." After that he chuckled and started tugging on my beard. "Yea, that's real." He gestured to an associate, pointed at me, and said, "Jesus." I decided to take it as a compliment, "thank you." After thoroughly amusing himself, but doing nothing with my paperwork, he passed me off to a guy with more stamps on his desk. The new guy wanted more copies of the papers I'd just gotten from immigration. He said he could get me an agent. "No thanks, see you tomorrow."

After a good deal more sweating I arrived back at Ama's, planted myself in the shop, and waited for some activity to begin. It did; coffee, beer, whiskey. Siti fried up a whole school of guppy sized fish and added them to a table already filled with mango slices and other drinking munchies. The little fish were delicious. Like popcorn, only better.

After a couple of hours at Ama's I accompanied Tooyus back to his place where I met a whole new group of people. They asked if I was hungry. Tooyus had told me he was bringing me over to feed me, so I thought it might be rude to refuse, despite being quite satiated from the snacks at Ama's. Most of Tooyus' friends and family were sitting outside but I was led by one of Tooyus' relatives into the house, where they sat me down alone in front of a small table and served me dinner. It was a little awkward to be eating all by myself with people just watching me but I got over it and enjoyed my meal.

After eating, a number of single girls were marched in front of me, seemingly to see if they met my approval. I just smiled. They thought I looked like a terrorist. I preferred the Jesus analogy, but they were smiling when said it, so I didn't really mind.

After things wound down at Tooyus' place, we headed back to Ama's and found him making a fire out of coconut husks. He put a makeshift grill on the fire and placed a bunch of fish individually wrapped fish in banana leaves on the grill to cook. We drank while the fish cooked.

Before long he pulled the fish off the fire and we all dug in. After consuming the body, I set my fish head on the plate, thinking I was done. Tooyus and Ama pointed to the head lying on my plate and gesticulated in a manner that indicated that the head was in fact the best part. I felt like I'd just discarded the heart of an artichoke.

The fish weren't very big to begin with, and I wasn't seeing a whole lot of meat on the head. "Suck out the eyeballs?" I questioned. They didn't know what I said but they nodded. I sucked. They weren't as rubbery as I was expecting.

I soon saw how they were eating their fish heads. They put the whole thing in their mouths, chewed for awhile and spit out a mess of crushed bones. I wasn't all that hungry to begin with and decided I'd save the head chewing for the next time.

The following day I continue my never ending quest for stamps and returned to the immigration office to check out;

I'd decided to leave the next day. Unfortunately I didn't get the same girl as I had when I checked in, but things still went smoothly, and I was on my way with no charge.

Just as I thought I was out the door, the cute girl from the day before came running after me and told me I had to return the following day before I left. She was smiling broadly, and I was flattered that she wanted to see me again, but I was tired of the sweaty trek up to the office, so I told her that the guy I'd just talked to had said that it would be alright if I didn't. He hadn't actually said that, but I really didn't feel like going back. She nodded meekly. I felt bad.

Immigration done, I headed back to the Harbor Master for the third time. He warmed to me once he heard my newly acquired command of the Indonesian language, and sent me on my way in short order with no charge.

I brought a spare atlas I had around and gave it to Ama's family. They were very happy to receive it. While they maintained a very comfortable, and apparently relatively carefree, lifestyle where they never seemed to be in lack of food, cigarettes, whiskey, or clean clothing (although Tooyus didn't change his clothes the entire time I was there, but then again neither did I), they lived a fairly Spartan existence in terms of possessions. Their house consisted of a simple indoor/outdoor kitchen with an aging propane burner, a sparsely furnished living room with very few knick-knacks (although they did have a television), off of which was one room for the kids and one for Ama and Siti. The walls were constructed of a mortar, stone and wire mixture which crumbled at the tops and didn't quite reach the corrugated metal roof. Despite the modest construction, everything was kept very clean and orderly, presumably by Siti.

Between something to do with vans, and the shop in his back yard, I guessed Ama was a sort of businessman who didn't actually have to do all that much physically, and lived mostly as a man of leisure. His house wasn't quite as nice as his sister's, Ronni's mom. I had the feeling that Ama may have placed greater value on his leisure activities than his home. I watched Siti cooking. She was attired in very clean and new looking Western garb. Her appearance contrasted with the dirt floored, crumbling concrete area in which she was cooking. I wondered what she valued. I tried to ponder it without projecting a lifetime lived in an entirely different culture. If she had any dissatisfaction with her life she hid it well and always found an easy smile. When she found out I was leaving the following day she seemed quite distressed and insisted we go sightseeing or *jalan jalan*.

Jalan jalan soon became my favorite Indonesian word. It translates to 'sightseeing' but it can also mean so much more. As a westerner in a 'developing' nation it is common to get hassled a little, or a lot, by the locals. People often want to sell you something. They want you to hire their taxi or stay at their inn. Or they simply want to lead you to a shop where you can buy something that they'll receive a commission from. Compared to other countries I'd visited there were comparably fewer of these people in Indonesia, though they still existed. That was until I discovered *jalan jalan*. At that point they ceased to exist at all. Whenever I got the "What are you doing?" "Where are you going?" I would simply say "*jalan jalan*" and they would smile, wave, and wish me well.

On one occasion two guys were asking me the usual "What can I get for you? yada yada yada," and I busted out with my "*jalan jalan*." One of the guys continued to ask me what I wanted, aka, what he could get for me, and the other one shoved him, "He's *jalan jalaning*, don't bother him."

Ama commandeered a van, and Ama, Siti, their four kids, Tooyus, and I were off on a *jalan jalan*. It was dark by that time, so there wasn't all that much to *jalan*, but we stopped for beer and snacks and it didn't really matter. We *jalan jalaned* for many hours before they dropped me back off on the beach late at night, or early in the morning, with the promise that I'd stop back the next day before I left.

Drinking with Ama and Tooyus in Kupang after 26 day solo passage

Tooyus was waiting with a bottle of whiskey in the morning. "Not before I sail," I gestured, pretending to crash the boat. Tooyus gave me the eyes of a reprimanded puppy dog, melting my resolve. Of course one couldn't hurt. Tooyus wanted to come with me but I'd already checked out with only myself on the paper work. I gave him the 'one wrist over the other' gesture, which seems to be the universal sign for going to jail. He'd spent a couple of years in an Australian jail for working illegally. He understood, and poured some more whiskey into my Dixie cup.

As I sat sipping whiskey with Tooyus, the wind began to build and I got the feeling that if I didn't leave soon I'd be there for the rest of my life. My hope was to have the anchor up before the wind built, but Siti was preparing a large farewell meal so there was no leaving.

With the meal eaten, we loaded up the van with half the neighborhood. Siti gave me a hand woven sarong and a bag of goodies consisting of six packs of two minute noodles, two bags of fruit, a bottle of hot sauce, a bottle of sweet soy sauce, a mango, a small bag of fried guppies, a beer, and a bag of molasses sugar disc things.

We didn't head directly for the beach. The first stop was the kiosk where I'd met Ama and Tooyus. The owner, Tomas, pulled down nearly all of the coffee packets and shoved them in a bag. I wasn't allowed to pay. The next stop was the open vegetable/fruit/live animal market where Tooyus jumped out of the car and started running around picking things up and pointing to them until I shook my head. I ended up with a sack of tomatoes, a sack of chili peppers (way more than could be safely consumed by one person hoping to maintain rectal integrity), bell peppers, and a bag of sea salt. Again I wasn't allowed to pay for anything. At that point I had more than I could carry and we headed to the beach.

With the van parked, we walked to the dinghy. People took notice of our hoard converging on the beach and followed just in case I was some sort of celebrity, which I was beginning to feel like. Everyone seemed to think I looked like someone.

With the dinghy pumped (by Tooyus, at his insistence), my adopted family rolled up their pant legs and shoved me into the choppy sea. I fired up the 2.5 and as I gave a final wave over my shoulder. I thought I heard, "was that Chuck Norris?"

Cruising Indonesia

It was afternoon by the time I got out to the boat and the wind had built to a gusty 20 knots, as if fearing it might be ignored. The wind and swell made pulling anchor a chore, but it got done and I was on my way. However I only managed to get seven miles before the wind abruptly ceased.

The passage to Flores Island was slow and uneventful save one detail. The second night out fell windless and I was getting nowhere. I decided to take down the sails to spare them, and me, from the swell induced thwacking, and hit the sack. I gulped down as much water as my belly could comfortably handle. I'd learned that a full bladder made the best alarm. If the pressure didn't wake me a wet bunk would. I made sure the mast head light was on and the horizon clear, and dove into my bunk. I awoke at regular intervals to check our status and to pee.

All was well until I heard a loud banging against the hull. Banging on the hull is never a good noise. I flew into the cockpit and found a small, unlit local fishing boat hitting Hanuman's stern. I soon ascertained that they had some sort of line stuck on Hanuman's rudder. I initially assumed that it was their anchor line that I had drifted onto. I knew it was way too deep for anchoring but as we got free of each other, and the problem had passed, I didn't dwell on it further.

There was a flutter of wind and, seeing Orion directly overhead, I knew the sun wasn't far from the horizon. I decided I'd call it a night's sleep, unfurl the jib, and be on my way. For a time, I was. Then I felt Hanuman slow and I saw what looked like the Milky Way light up in the water all around me. Though extremely disconcerting, it was utterly beautiful. As we slowed to a stop, the Milky Way took on a more recognizable form; a fishing net. The movement of the net had set off the dense phosphorescence in the water, outlining the shape of a net that extended as far as I could see in either direction. For a second I thought I might slide over it, but it firmly imbedded itself in the small gap between the keel and the rudder. The same unfortunate gap that had ensnared what had actually been an extremity of the net, in the incident with the fishing boat moments before. I was caught. I didn't like it.

Fortunately the fishermen were half mile off and didn't seem to notice my predicament. I didn't want to look like even more a jackass that I already must have. I furled the jib in an effort to avoid making matters worse.

I contemplated my options for a moment, wishing the net would just go away, but concluded there was no avoiding the mask and snorkel. I wasn't crazy about the idea of jumping into the water in the black of night in the middle of the ocean with all of those hungry sharks who were undoubtedly attracted to all of the struggling fish (and boat) in the net.

I jumped into what seemed like a swarm of fireflies. The phosphorescence was so dense that it cast enough light to allow me an adequate appraisal of the situation. In addition to being jammed in the keel/rudder gap, the net was grabbing onto the propeller. Fortunately, after several soundings, I managed to fee Hanuman, doing my best not to damage the net or become entangled in it myself. Back on board I unfurled the jib and sailed at a 90 degree angle to the net, hoping it was set in a straight line.

I dropped anchor in front of Flores Island the following day. Before I even got a chance to put the sail covers on, ten locals paddled over from their fishing boats and jumped onboard. I figured perhaps that was customary. Fortunately I'd picked up a few phrases in Indonesian and was able to offer them some coffee, actually grown on Flores Island, which they happily accepted. I used one packet, which I think was supposed to brew a pot, per cup. I was still getting the hang of the instant coffee thing. Given the number of people on board, I was only able fill the cups half full with my one pot of hot water. I added some chunks of my molasses cakes to complete the syrupy concoction, and passed it out. *"Terimakasi."* They thanked me and sipped away. Luckily they were the sort of hard living people who could appreciate a thick cup of coffee and drank all but the half inch of sludge on the bottom.

Most took off before long, but one guy with a guitar, and his son, hung out for awhile. We chilled, played music, and drank sludge. They asked me if I was going to see Kilamotu. I hadn't heard of it, but apparently it was the main attraction on the island. I decided to go on my 29th birthday.

It was refreshing and invigorating to be away from the ocean and in the moist tropical jungle. Kilamotu is a National Park with a volcano, which I climbed, surrounded by three lakes of dramatically different colors. According to lore, one's sole goes to a different lake depending on their age when they die, or something like that. I looked down on the lakes from the volcano's rim and tried to decide where I'd want my sole.

I appropriated a bus for the ride home. It happened to be full, but I was allowed to ride on the roof. As it turned out the roof was actually full as well, so two other guys and I clung to a grate on the back of the bus. It was the best 'seat' in the house. I had a huge grin plastered on my face as we snaked through the jungle, ducking for the low branches and bracing for the big turns. Everyone that we drove by was smiling and waving at the white guy hanging off the back of the bus. It was a perfect birthday.

After I'd had my fill of Flores, I sailed on to Rinja/Nusa Kode, which quickly turned into my favorite anchorage. There was no village and no other boats. I had the whole place to myself.

The island of Nusa Kode fills a horseshoe shaped gap in Rinja Island. A well protected 'U' shaped inlet is created between the two islands. I had intended on only staying one night, but the place had an energy that captivated me and I stayed for three. Despite being considerably drier than Flores, the area teemed with life. Deer, monkeys, and Komodo Dragons meandered along the same beach. The reef exploded with life. It was the best snorkeling I'd experienced.

Eventually I pulled myself away from Nusa Kode. It had been a long time since I'd seen any consistent winds, and the passage to Bali was no different.

I hadn't listened to the short wave radio in Nusa Kode, but resumed my evening ritual on the passage. It didn't take me long to figure out that a nightclub in Bali had recently been bombed. The news was a few days old so it took me awhile to piece together the details. It reminded me of when I'd learned of the September 11 bombings just over a year prior. Only these, despite being in a county that wasn't my own, seemed a lot closer to home. Being only 200 miles from the bombings, and who I was, I had a much easier time envisioning myself in a nightclub in Bali than I did in the World Trade Towers. Apparently the assailants drove a van containing K-4 plastic explosives into the nightclub killing between 100 and 200 people and injuring 100 more.

As I sat trying to fathom such an act I noted the large gap that existed between all the Indonesians I'd met and the ones who'd driven into the nightclub in a van filled with explosives. What happened to tolerance? "Perhaps they didn't feel they were getting their share of tolerance," I considered.

There was practically no wind when I heard the news on the radio. I was having trouble just keeping the bow pointed in the right direction. The waning sun left an apocalyptic glow on the soupy horizon. I suddenly felt very vulnerable as I sat bobbing in the dead calm of the windless sea; like Samson without his hair. I was reminded that I hadn't had much wind in the last 1300 miles and that the prospect of wind for the next 2000 seemed pretty grim. I saw before me 5000 windless miles of terrorism before I would arrive in the Mediterranean. I took down the small tattered American flag that hung limp from the backstay, thinking it prudent to disassociate from the western world, and had an intense desire to be in the Med.

It occurred to me that my mom might be getting a little concerned about…well, about a number of things. I was sure she'd heard about the Bali bombing. And, since I'd e-mailed her from Kupang telling her that I probably wouldn't be able to contact her until I arrived in Bali, I considered that she might have thought I was in the night club during the bombings and was dead. Moms have no trouble jumping to such a conclusion. Especially a conclusion that wasn't totally outlandish. Even if I hadn't been killed in Bali, she'd naturally be concerned that I was traveling around in a place where they drive vans filled with high tech explosives into nightclubs on a Saturday night. The fact that my next destination was Malaysia, one of Bush's "axis of evil," probably didn't help. My mom latter admitted that she'd called the Coast Guard after hearing about the bombing, perhaps with the hope that they would go find me and bring me home.

I'd been considering shaving my beard with the hope of greater facial ventilation, having less food on my face (and hence more in my mouth, my mustache had become a major obstacle to food entry), and increasing my odds with the pretty girls in Bali. I'd even purchased some razors while on Flores. After hearing the news about Bali, it occurred to me that in certain circles it might be beneficial to look like a terrorist. "Note to self, 'buy Koran, memorize a few key phrases, possibly in Arabic, and be able to recite when necessary.'" Furthermore it seemed that there was a good chance that there wouldn't be a single cute female tourist who'd stuck around after the bombings.

The odds of picking up crew in Bali, as I'd hoped, also seemed to have been suddenly reduced. In fact, all crew possibilities seemed pretty grim. Brandoni had mentioned meeting me in Kupang. Kupang had, of course, come and gone with no sign of him. During my last working stink in the States I'd met up with Lee, who said he was going to meet up with me in Singapore. That had been after a couple of beers however, and I hadn't heard a word from him since, so I'd pretty much counted him out for Singapore. My English buddy Steve, who I'd met back in the Pacific the season before, was selling timeshares in Phuket, Thailand. Phuket was on the way, so his geography gave him the best potential. He'd had time to get settled however, and had a job, a Thai girlfriend, and a moped, so despite having expressed some interest, I was giving him low odds.

I was glad I wasn't counting on anyone. I no longer needed crew and I was happy about it. I decided that it had been a good thing that Joe left in Australia. If he was leaving, as he'd originally planned, in Bali, I'd have been a nervous at the prospect of having to find crew there. Though content and confident in my singularity, I still wasn't too excited at the thought of sailing up the Red Sea, a notoriously treacherous patch of ocean, alone.

Bali

While laying in my bunk at anchor in Bali, and having the strangest thoughts, it occurred to me that the malaria medication I'd started taking before making landfall in Indonesia might be having a significant effect on my brain chemistry. My normal thought patterns seemed altered. Even my connection with my body seemed off. I noticed I was doing things I would never normally have done. I found the anchor chain not properly secured. I'd apparently not finished the process after dropping it. I would forget I had rice cooking and wonder what 'that smell' was. Most annoying of all; I found myself stubbing the same big toe repeatedly.

Starring down at my thrice opened scab, I wondered if the universe was trying to deliver me some sort of message. I'd begun taking to such esoteric thoughts in my solitude, but the fact that I was contemplating the universe sending me a message through a stubbed toe, bothered me a little.

As I was falling asleep one night, straddling the fine line between consciousness and unconsciousness I realized I couldn't remember where I was. Waking up and not knowing where you are is common enough, but this experience was totally different. Not only could I not remember where I was, I also couldn't really remember anything about myself. The state persisted for longer than I'd ever recalled such a state persisting. I didn't try and resist the condition; I didn't try and find myself. I couldn't grasp specifics, but I had an over-all feeling that all was well around me. During the preceding months, the motion of the boat, and the sounds from above, told me how to react and connected me to the world, but in my quiet state of stillness, my mind and body felt free from the obligation of life. Feeling the soft, yet firm support of the bunk below me, I yielded, allowing myself to be enveloped and given over to an overwhelming experience of empti-ness. My mind tried to explore the state more deeply, think-ing it might have found some new place, unburdened by the realm of repetitive thought, but in doing so felt the cool ebb of memory pour over it. I was reawakened and the state was lost.

As interesting as the mental state was, I decided it might not be ideal for crossing oceans. I concluded that I should cut back on the dosage of the malaria medication.

Years before, while in Uganda, I'd met a peace corp. guy who, along with his cohorts, had been on the same malaria medication for prolonged periods of time. He had numerous stories about people going a little, or a lot, crazy on the medi-cation. I was also taking it when I met him, and thought they must just have been a little mentally weak. Given my condi-tion in Bali, I decided that there really is no beating chemistry. That, or I too, was a little mentally weak, or both. He said he'd cut down his dosage from one pill every week, to one every ten days. I decided to follow suit.

I didn't spend too much time exploring Bali. I just didn't feel like it. There was a nice little yacht club that served most of my needs: food and beer. I spent a good deal of time sit-ting at the bar, just staring out at the water. "You look like you've been out awhile…you got that thousand yard stare," I heard coming from across the bar. The voice swirled around in my head for awhile before hitting the part of my brain that was capable of responding. I came back into the present. "A little while… I guess," I responded, but wasn't able to muster much more than a perfunctory conversation before my gaze was sucked back to the horizon.

My attention was eventually harnessed by a couple of young American girls that appeared in the yacht club one evening. After a period of observation, I was able to surmise that they were doing some sort of internet outreach thing to various schools back in the States. They'd just pulled into the small yacht club marina on a tubby looking sailboat which seemed to have a crew that consisted of three girls and two guys. The crew seemed surprisingly young to have been given such responsibility. I ventured a guess that the whole crew, save one guy, was younger than I.

As I sat at the bar, observing them across the room, I found myself completely enthralled. I had a strange set of conflicting emotions. They appeared so foreign, yet so familiar. They were completely American. Their hair was combed and tidy. The guys were freshly shaved. Their clothes were neat and clean. I could smell them from across the room.

They had a laptop and a few books on the table in front of them. Ashley, one of the girls, was holding up a map and pointing out a few points of interest with the blue glow of the laptop monitor illuminating her face. The image burned into my brain. I could picture it as a poster on the wall of an American classroom, with the words, "Explore your World, log on to www.whatever.com," written across its bottom.

I'd been at sea, or on land among the locals, for long enough to be mesmerized by these fresh faces. Even in the couple of days I'd been in Bali, I was surrounded by a colorful swarthy looking crowd who tended to engage in a lot of cocaine, tattoos, and prostitutes.

Entranced by these young, unsullied faces, I had the desire to just consume them. Part of me also longed to be one of them, making some well informed comment on a point of local interest. Seeing heads nod with understanding and agreement; the blue glow on my face. Beyond that I wanted to fuck one, if not all, of the females; to work their bodies into a sweaty lather and wring out their juices.

I spent no small amount of time studying the women. No nuance was left unanalyzed. Two of them I found particularly attractive. The first was Erin: long blond hair, medium height, nicely tanned skin, prominent, yet non obtrusive, nose, well proportioned facial features, nice B-cup tits, ass that looked a bit soft from too much boat time. Those were of course just some of the basic physical features all of which could ultimately repel or attract my wolfish thirst depending on how they were used. Or rather, how I ultimately perceived them.

She walked with a posture forward gait. Shoulders a little hunched, like she was walking up hill; seemingly very focused on getting where she was going. I figured it was that drive that gotten her where she was. She seemed to walk around with blinders. I wondered if she missed a lot along the way.

I noticed a small tattoo on her foot, nothing that too grandiose. It could be easily covered. I recognized it as Marquesan, freshly done. It looked like the symbol for whale, representing long distance travel, among other things. Did she want to submerse herself in the journey or just have something to take home? Or was she honoring tradition?

Ashley was slightly taller than Erin, with thin, dark, short, wavy hair, medium fair skin, minor freckling on the face and arms, a fairly intense gaze, and blue/green eyes. She was often bra-less, letting her smallish tits splay slightly to the sides. Her movements were much different from Erin's. She was a much more relaxed walker. Her posture was good. She didn't seem so fully committed to the illusion that walking was actually going to take her anywhere. She smoked cigarettes. Observing that act of self deprecation, I decided that she also like bad boys. She considered herself an intellectual bohemian.

The more I watched her, the more I detected an arrogance in her movements, mostly concealed by her ready smile. She probably didn't have to study all that hard to get good grades in school. She belittled others who had to. I decided her parents were wealthy. Erin's parents may also have been wealthy, but still connected more with the working class. I began to feel like Hannibal Lector.

After spending so much time meditating on the girls, I decided it was time to approach their table and actually speak with them. Some of the crew had scattered by that point so it was just Erin, Ashley, and one of the guys, Josh.

We went through the basics to get ourselves acquainted. The vibe was good. Erin, who I hadn't found as attractive prior to the introductions, became more so as the conversation progressed. Oddly, her grandfather had a boat named Hanuman. I learned that she was the captain. I have a weak spot for capable women. Wendy got me by just starting her outboard.

I walked away from the conversation not knowing which one I was more attracted to. I grinned at the serendipity of my predicament. I had the feeling that my odds were better with Ashley. She seemed like she might be more inclined toward whimsical actions. I also sensed that Josh and Erin might be an item.

They would be sailing the same general route as I all the way up to the Mediterranean. I left the conversation with the hope of running into them frequently; curious to see how things might unfold. I decided I must remember not to get myself into any situations I could conceivably regret. I had

had all too much experience with how such things could go. A couple of beers and she's quite her job and is sailing with me and I'm left with that, "what did I just do feeling?" "Note to self, 'learn from past mistakes.'"

South China Sea

Eventually I decided that, although never having really experienced Bali, I was done with it. Ultimately, I was just filling an internal quota for cold beers and meals I didn't have to cook myself. I elected to try and make the 1000 mile passage up to Batam, an island just across from Singapore, in one go. In my head I made the mistake of dividing the 1000 miles in to ten, 100 mile segments that I'd be able to knock out in ten days.

I headed north, staying close to Bali's east coast to avoid the strong current running between Bali and Lombok. Just off the northeast tip of Bali, I estimated there to be over a 100 trimaran fishing boats sailing home after a day of fishing. They all had different colored sails and I felt like I was watching the spinnaker leg of a sailing regatta. "Hmm, perhaps there was more to Bali than the Yacht Club," I mused, but quickly tempered it with a shrug and an, "ehh…."

There were a lot of boats in the Java Sea. I'd venture to say a shit ton. At night I was surrounded by their lights. I was constantly on edge and sleep was fleeting. In addition to all of the local fishing boats puttering around, there were huge steel cargo ships silently prowling through the darkness. Sloppy welds and peeling paint, I imagined them driven by Satan; one red and one green eye piercing the darkness. Trident in one hand, helm in the other, he stood waiting to crush any seaman careless enough to let down his guard.

As the sun set, and darkness fell on my fifth night out, I found myself in the usual predicament of wanting to sleep, but not being able to because I was surrounded by boats. I counted ten little boat lights bobbing up and down around me. To the lights, was added an intensity of phosphorescence I'd never experienced. The bow wave stirred up so much phosphorescence that the jib was illuminated a haunty, glowing green. Every little cresting wave around me was capped like a Christmas tree with a starry light. It became difficult to differentiate between the glowing ocean and the lights of the surrounding boats. I felt like Hans Solo flying the Millennium Falcon through an asteroid field, surrounded by Imperial forces and bounty hunters. Only with no giant worm to take refuge in. To top it all off, there was a raging lightning storm on the distant horizon. I felt like playing some Pink Floyd and charging admission. Unfortunately, the dolphins in those parts are notoriously thrifty.

The Java Sea had a different feel than the other oceans I'd been in; more sinister. Mid day, about half way between Bali and Borneo, I noticed three boats moving around in close proximity to one another. With so many boats in the area, I didn't think much of it. I saw a couple of wooden planks float by and was happy not to have hit them. I continued to observe the three boats. Anything not sun or sea was a pleasant distraction. Two of the boats moved away from the third. I was happy to see them moving in the opposite direction as me. You can never really be sure of a person's intention at sea. The third boat lay not far off my course and I continued to get closer to it. I noticed it didn't seem to be floating quite right. Upon closer inspection, I observed it to be half underwater.

It seemed to be slowly sinking into the sea. I occurred to me that there could be someone on board. I was about 50 yards away and could have seen anyone on deck, but for some reason I had the image of some guy lying in the hold with a knife in his gut. I supposed the boat could have been sinking of its own accord, and the other two boats where there to rescue the people on board, but it seemed odd that the other two boats had taken off right when I arrived, and in the exact opposite direction; a direction that led away from the closest land. In addition, the boat was only half under water when I got close to it, and I'd been watching it for quite some time, so it clearly wasn't sinking all that quickly. One would think that a, not all too rich Indonesian fisherman, would be doing his best to save his fishing boat. If the boat was beyond saving, I'd think he'd be trying to salvage as much as he could off of it.

As I watched the boat fill and become one with the water I felt like I was watching someone die. It was an eerie feeling and I wished for more wind to carry me away.

Eventually the sinking boat faded from view without my ever knowing the fate of its crew. I suspected it was neither the first nor the last shady dealing that took place in the Java Sea. In all likelihood it would remain a secret of the wind.

One night, as I lay in the cockpit, where I slept almost all the time (with one eye open), a loud voice erupted from the VHF radio. "Death to all fuckin' Americans!" The VHF radio had a maximum range of about 30 miles, and the clarity of the voice told me it was well within that range. I was never too relaxed in the Java Sea.

The further north I traveled, the less consistent the wind became. As I rounded the southwest corner of Borneo into the South China Sea I finally caught up with the thunderstorms that had been entertaining me on the horizon for the previous week.

I was excited by the first thunderstorm I encountered. I raced along in the correct direction, which had become less of a given, under reefed sails, howling like a wolf and dancing in the cockpit, as I listened to Macey Gray on the walkman. By nightfall the storm had abated and I was left with a pleasant seven knot wind pushing me towards my destination.

Those conditions didn't last long however. The next day was windless and I was lucky to be able to keep the boat pointed in the right direction. The day faded into a pleasant enough night but before long turned distinctly foul. Enormous thunderheads appeared out of nowhere and over the course of a few minutes my pleasant night dissolved into strong winds and rain of biblical proportions.

I put a quick reef in the main but the torrential rains filled the loose pocket of sail at its foot with so much water that it tore its luff seam, commencing the long slow death of the main, which would come to require constant patching. It was raining so hard that the water level around Hanuman seemed to be rising. I took a brief look down below to confirm that we weren't sinking.

Visibility was seriously degraded. I could barely see 25 yards. Having seen four or five other boats nearby before the storm, I became concerned about their location. That fear was confirmed when I saw one of them burst out of the rain 30 yards from me. Apparently, I'd cut in front of him. By the time I saw him he was passing astern and there was really nothing more to do than say, "That was close," and keep on trucking.

For the next two weeks I experienced many such storms. The wind they brought was always out of the northwest, the exact direction I needed to go. Tacking and reefing seemed to be constant activities. My hands throbbed from pulling on the wet lines. I found myself putting the sheets, the lines used to control the sails, on the winch much sooner than usual, choosing mechanics over muscles.

Prior to the South China Sea I'd never let a squall alter my course. I considered it weakness or laziness. After a week of getting pelted by rain and seeing lightning strike close enough to smell, I would occasionally disregard my destination, and simply sail the course I thought would keep me the driest.

When there wasn't a squall, there was practically no wind at all. Possibly, I'd get a light breeze coming from, once again, the northwest. I set a new daily low mileage record of nine.

After the first week of such conditions my mind sort of shut down. I lost myself in whatever I was reading and sailed on mental autopilot. The South China Sea took its toll on me psychologically. A toll I did not easily recover from.

Everyone I talked to had motored through the majority of that stretch of ocean. I was initially proud that I'd sailed the whole way without using the motor, but it came at a price. A price I wouldn't willingly pay again. Part of the price was that I didn't really care that I'd sailed the whole way. I felt apathetic. I didn't know if I was stronger or weaker for the effort.

Batam

I eventually tacked my way out of the South China Sea and into the Singapore Strait. I reached Batam after 24 days at sea; a significant 14 days over my original optimistic estimate. I'd planned on heading to an anchorage, but decided to spring for a marina. The thought of not having to deal with anchoring and the dinghy was too thrilling of a prospect to pass up. I called the marina on the VHF, found out it was only nine bucks a day, and decided it was in the budget. It was the first time I'd spent a night in a marina since leaving California, aside from the one free night in New Caledonia.

As luck would have it Makulu, the boat containing Ashley and Erin, who I described so intimately previously, was entering the marina at the exact same time I was. Joy of joys! I felt the gods had seen fit to reward me for my tribulations at sea.

I spent a week at the Nongsa Point Marina livin' it up. They had a pool, restaurant, bar, and even a little upstairs air conditioned library/reading room type place.

As a guest of the marina I was allowed to sign for everything. I hadn't had much experience signing for things and found myself thoroughly taken with it. I felt like James Bond...

"Beer… cold, not warm." Without Money Penny to keep me in check I spent more money than intended but had no regrets.

During my week of lounging I spent a considerable amount of time with the Makulu crew. It turned out that my original estimation of Ashley and Erin was way off. Hannibal Lector I was not.

Ashley, age 28, was quite a hard worker, an overachiever even. As I mentioned, the Makulu crew was doing some sort of educational outreach. Consequently they were always working on a paper, article, report, or some such thing. Ashley was the sort that couldn't relax knowing that she had something to do. In fact, I imagined it a rare time when she was able to relax at all, perhaps never. She smoked, drank diet coke compulsively, and I intuited that she'd voted for George W. I was opposed to all of those things, yet I found myself smitten by her. She had an intensity I found pleasantly amusing. The way she moved her diet coke soaked lips when she talked was also endearing but I couldn't help but wonder if I would've been as attracted to her in different circumstances; if I hadn't spent so much time toiling by myself at sea or if there had been some other women around.

Despite not having really gotten past each other's basic personal statistics, I sensed she lacked that combination of youthful exuberance and inner calm that I needed to be deeply attracted to someone. Regardless of feeling that I could never have a truly rewarding relationship with her, I found the way she moved her lips to be enough to warrant my continued interest. Besides, I couldn't resist.

Regarding Erin, I was at least right about her relationship with Josh. Aside from that, I was just as off in my original estimate of her as I'd been with Ashley. Given her relationship with Josh, I put her off of my libido radar.

I spent much of the week at Nongsa Point clinging to the Makulu crew in an effort to regain the mental equilibrium I'd lost during my months alone. I actually started to feel some-what lecherous. They always had something to do, and I was just sort of hanging around. I found all of their running around very amusing. "We're going to wash a baby elephant," they exclaimed with glee. "They can't wash themselves," I thought as I let out a little grin that almost transformed into a chuckle.

While sitting alone with Ashley in the air conditioned reading room one lazy afternoon she informed me that their crew had talked and was considering lending me a crew member so that we could convoy to Thailand. I'd been plan-ning on anchoring every night to sleep as I hugged the coast of Malaysia heading up the Strait of Malacca. I was actually excited at the prospect of getting a full night's rest every night.

The Strait of Malacca has a long history of piracy. Makulu's logic was that if they lent me crew I wouldn't have to stop and sleep (one can't safely sail and sleep in the confined area of the Strait) and we would be able to sail straight through the more dangerous areas together, hoping for safety in numbers.

The way things unfolded, I didn't really end up responding to the proposal. Aside from being a little hungry for company, I wasn't sure if I was ready to have one of them in my space. I was also concerned that they might not find the living condi-tions aboard Hanuman up to the standards with which they'd become accustomed. While a considerably better sailing ves-sel, Hanuman lacked many of the creature comforts and the all around 'niceness' of Makulu.

The idea of convoying also sounded a bit restrictive. I didn't really want to alter my pace or itinerary to match Makulu's. They had a significantly different agenda than I. They were all about seeing this and seeing that, while I was content see whatever passed before my eyes.

One generally couldn't expect too much wind in the Strait of Malacca and trying to daysail all the way up the coast in the extremely light conditions could take forever so motoring was to be expected. I knew Makulu would be putting the throttle down and motoring through as quickly as possible. I didn't want to push Big Red any harder than necessary, and I felt that I probably wouldn't be voted in as Admiral of our fleet, hence not entirely in control of the pace.

Paramount to the whole notion of crew lending was the question of who I'd be getting. I did my best to question Ashley on the matter without it seeming as though I was really interested. "Of course it wouldn't be Erin or Josh since they're the captain and the first mate," she responded. Josh had actually captained the boat for a stretch in the Pacific, so I doubted that one couldn't handle the boat without the other. "Not to mention they're bumpin' uglies," I thought. "Of course," I replied. "So it would probably be you or Jess (the other girl onboard), since John is the camera man," I ventured. "It would probably be Jess or John, since they haven't been getting along too well," she retorted. That wasn't exactly the scenario I had in mind and the whole topic just kind of died there. "Pretty windy out there." "Yup."

While I ended up leaving Nongsa Point without anyone from Makulu, I didn't leave totally crewless.

Somewhere around the middle of the Pacific I developed a bug 'problem.' At least the Australian quarantine officer thought it was a problem. I had to fumigate the boat before I was granted entry. I didn't personally see it as problem until the bugs started making off with a significant portion of my food.

The fumigation, I decided, had only managed to kill the sick and the weak, leaving a stronger, fiercer breed which began to flourish in the South China Sea. The predominant variety was what I called, 'Speedy Gonzalesus (Spedius Gonzali).' They were in the roach family, but significantly leaner and faster than the average household variety.

Bugs of the flying variety also started to proliferate in the South China Sea. Normally any flying type bugs didn't last long in the open ocean, so their presents made me suspicious of their origin. I imagined a seething infestation of maggots in the bilge. After some digging around, my nose led me to a plastic bag full of what had previously been carrots in the back of one of the cupboards. It had commenced rotting in tropical fashion. I gagged as I dumped it overboard. I wanted to inspect it closely for life forms but I didn't have the stomach for it. The flies disappeared shortly thereafter.

The roaches weren't so easy to get rid of. They'd infiltrated every nook and cranny of the boat; they were fully entrenched. At night, when I turned on the light in the galley, the counter came alive with the herd. I initially called it a swarm, but they progressed to a size and level of organization where the term no longer seemed appropriate. After a while, the larger, cockier ones no longer scurried off when I turned on the light. They just ambled off to the nearest crevice. I even caught one trying to stare me down. It seemed as though I had to fight for my food. I would cut up an onion, leave it on the cutting board, turn off the light to save power as I went back to the cockpit while the burner heated up, and when I returned to put the onion in the hot oil, it was covered with roaches. When I turned the light back on most would take off, but the bolder ones, who were trying to gobble down whole pieces of onion, got added to the hot oil. "Protein!" It wouldn't have surprised me to see them making off with a whole plate of food; like ants in a cartoon.

I didn't take such abuse without a fight. When I turned on the light at night I reached first for the cutting board and brought it down wrecking ball style on the flat surfaces, leaving many pan caked corpses in my wake. After that, I finished off any stragglers with both fists, 'whack-a-mole' style. I started out leaving the carcasses where they lay, as a warning to the others, but found that the roaches were just as happy to dine on their dead as they were to dine on any of my cuisine. After that I left the corpses laying there out of pure laziness.

I confirmed the rumor that they could still produce off-spring even after they were dead. After smashing what looked like a pregnant female I put her in a cup and watched as her abdomen erupted with little eggs that, over the course of a couple of days, turned into little roaches. Further studies reveled that if I smashed them really thoroughly, the eggs would be smashed and killed as well.

The fumigation in Australia clearly hadn't worked and I'd just read *Silent Spring* by Rachel Carson, who wrote about the side effects of pesticides, so I decided to look for a new approach. In addition, the 'bug bombs' were somewhat expensive. Despite a warning that I might ultimately end up with an elephant problem, I decided that biological control was the way to go. All I had to do was figure out who eats bugs. I arrived upon geckos.

I pontificated on my biological control idea with Ashley and John over dinner. As I articulated my plan I directed their attention to the numerous geckos ornamenting the walls and ceiling of the restaurant. "See, all I need is one of those guys and all of my problems will be solved." Skeptical but interested, they took a moment to observe the various geckos moving about the wall.

Our eyes were drawn to a specific pair as they performed a violent mating ritual. The male, presumably, mounted the female, again presumably, and started biting her neck and head. There was more biting, and some convulsing, when the geckos parted with the ceiling and went crashing to the floor not far from our table. I decided that such an opportunity might not again present itself, so I seized the moment, got up from the table, and pounced on the geckos. I'd like to say that I nabbed them on the first try, but that wasn't the case. I didn't want to crush them so I pawed at them gingerly, and with a little hesitancy about making any more of a scene in the restaurant than I already was. I eventually managed to capture one, though in the confusion of the scuffle I wasn't sure whether it was the male or female. Thus I shanghaied myself a crew member, Kama Sutra.

The Malay Peninsula

With my new crew and a couple of sacks of fresh produce, I left my utopic existence at the Nongsa Point Marina and headed across the Singapore Strait. The Singapore Strait made the Torres Strait look like an old country road. 50 huge ships, cruising along at 20 plus knots, on fixed courses, were in view at any given time. I was accompanied by decent wind and, for the first part the crossing, a favorable current, but I was anxious to get through to more hospitable waters by night-fall so I sailed with the motor running for maximum mileage. We moved along at the thrilling speed of nine knots. A great improvement over the two knots I'd been averaging for the previous several months.

With the changing of the tide and the waning of the wind our break neck pace came to an end, but "no matter," I thought, "Big Red in still chugging along." No sooner had I finished the thought than the chugging turned to sputter-ing followed by, "clunk, clunk, wheeeeez," and a heavy silence replaced the comforting rumble of the engine.

The grave quiet had an ominous effect. I paused for a moment to take it in and formulate a plan. 30 seconds of thinking can often replace ten minutes of running around banging elbows, not accomplishing anything. I figured I probably had an air leak in the fuel system. Determining the location of the leak was the real challenge. I decided where I thought the leak was most likely to be and used a jerry can of diesel and some spare tubing, and just bypass the whole area. Between frequent dashes into the cockpit to make sure there weren't any steel beasties bearing down on me, I fashioned the jury rig. After about 45 minutes of knuckle skinning and profuse sweating I had things in place and was relieved when she fired back up. Big Red managed to get me to my first anchorage, but the relaxation I'd been feeling was replaced with a subtle, gnawing tension deep in my gut.

With the boat at anchor, I inspected the fuel system more closely for leaks. I decided I probably hadn't seated the primary fuel filter properly after I'd changed it at Nongsa Point. I speculated that a little gap had allowed a trickle of air into the system. I reseated it, got rid of the jerry can rig, bled the system, and called it 'perfect.' Recalling my experience with such situations in the past however, and despite the fact that the engine seemed 'fixed,' I felt the need to admit it may in fact not be. The air could have been coming into the system from any number of areas. The filter was just my best guess and the easiest to remedy.

I continued up the Malaysian coast, mostly motoring by day, due to an extreme lack of wind, and anchoring by night. It turned out I hadn't fixed the engine problem, but the air leak was slow enough so that I only had to stop and bleed the system once or twice a day. It was annoying knowing that the engine could give out at any time.

After a couple of weeks of that routine I arrived in Port Dickerson Marina, where I anchored in the small bay outside the marina. I was pleased to find Makulu in the marina. I also happened to arrive the day before Thanksgiving and tacked myself onto an invitation by 'Heart Song,' another American boat, that had been extended to Makulu. I found myself dining in style on an air conditioned yacht. Fortunately I'd met the 'Heart Song' couple in Nongsa Point and they seemed happy to have me.

Ashley had stopped by another boat on her way to Heart Song, where she managed to get a little tipsy, which turned into drunk after few glasses of wine with dinner. I found this exceedingly amusing. She eventually had to leave prematurely.

I normally have the tendency to overdo it on both alcohol and food in such situations, but after sailing alone for so long my body was always a little more 'on alert' and I had less of a tendency to get carried away by my gluttonous side. Even when physically off the boat a part of my mind was always on it, noticing if the wind picked up or shifted direction; remembering how securely the anchor seemed set and the proximity of any potential hazards.

The company was extremely cordial and slightly formal. We all made some sort of congenial excuse for Ashley's behavior; the sort of behavior that was tame when compared with the antics that had taken place on Hanuman in previous times. Normally in such situations I would've been waiting for her to pass out so that I could chief her, but I followed the tone set by my hosts; when in Rome.... "It was probably the air conditioning," I commented with a straight face. "It can dry out your lungs, preventing proper air exchange, depriving the brain of oxygen. Seen it once, seen it a million times."

I wasn't long in Port Dickerson. Makulu and I took off at the same time, and were planning on heading to the same anchorage that night. We had some decent wind and I actually turned the engine off for a stint, a nice change. The pleasant breeze turned squally, drenching us with rain. Makulu reported seeing a waterspout.

After the squall passed Makulu called me on the radio and said they'd decided to skip the anchorage and carry on. I was a little disappointed, but not surprised, and stuck to my planned anchorage.

I continued to make my way north, sailing/motoring by day, and anchoring by night. It wasn't an especially stimulating segment, but it was novel to sleep through the night.

Late one afternoon, a couple weeks north of Port Dickerson, I saw a sailboat on the horizon behind me; Makulu. This was a pleasant diversion from my head space and made me much more excited for the anchorage ahead; which they were also headed to.

After a night and day together at a beautiful anchorage we both made the short sail north to the island of Langkawi. As luck would have it a new marina had just opened and was giving away a free week's stay, a T-shirt, and beer.

The second night we were there, Ashley, John, and I shared a taxi with a few other 'yachties' to the other side of the island for a night of drinking. We found a couple of bars on the beach which had a lot of island type bar games to keep us amused.

As the evening progressed and the warm glow of alcohol over took us, Ashley and I gravitated toward each other in a fashion common to such situations. Gazes were held a split second longer than was polite. Limbs that strayed into contact were not pulled back, but left to linger. Before long we were arm in arm. It felt good. I'd been isolated from physical and emotional contact for so long that I fully enjoyed every nuance.

We eventually made our way down the beach from the bar and, before long, were rolling around in the sand. We proceeding to kiss, caress, and grope. She was a biter and devoted substantial energy to gnawing on my lower lip. It was a bit painful, but I was down. I'd recently been reading the Kama Sutra and realized that biting might play a larger role in the 'love making' process than I previously calculated. I wondered how trim she kept her fingernails, thinking I could be in for even more pain.

We alternated between kissing and talking, giving the experience an added intimacy.

While I was enjoying the biting, I thought I would try and tease a gentle kiss out of her but she didn't seem to have it in her. I satisfied myself with the biting. The biting seemed to complement her somewhat neurotic behavior.

In one of her biting frenzies she managed to sink her teeth into the beach and we both ended up with a mouthful of sand. Ultimately our make out session ended in spitting.

After getting most of the sand out of our mouths we made our way back to the bar where John had passed out with instructions to wake him when we were ready to go. We spat some more and got a taxi back to the marina.

The following day, Ashley, John and I rented mopeds and toured the island. I discovered that I'd given Ashley a hickey; probably in an attempt to hide from her teeth. John arrived on scene with a big grin on his face and was quick to comment on it.

The day was full of mirth and we had a great time. I can't help but laugh at myself when I'm on a moped. Ashley and I had a few moments alone together and I thought about recommencing our physical relationship but I wasn't getting a strong enough vibe. I considered the possibility that she wasn't all that into me and I'd just been the nearest one around when her buzz tickled her horny bone. The idea didn't devastate me but I was hoping for a bit more fun before we parted ways.

Makulu left the next day. I stayed, feeling I had to get the most out of my free weeks stay. Before leaving however, I was approached by Ashley with a big smile. She said they'd only be sailing around to the other side of the island, and that we should meet up at the bar we'd been to two days prior.

I taxied over with a few other young sailors who'd been racing on some super fancy racing boat. As the evening progressed, I noticed that Ashley seemed to be spending more and more time with one of the guys from the race boat she'd just met. I didn't think too much of it, assuming her not to be the type to go after some other guy with my hickey still fresh on her neck. It seemed a little too trailer trashy for a yachtie. I figured wrong, confirming my suspicion that a narrow margin exists between a trailer and a yacht.

Eventually Ashley and the pretty boy boat bitch disappeared. I didn't see them leave together, and, at first, just figured they happen to both be emptying their bladders. Time passed however, and I got a bad feeling in the pit of my stomach. I couldn't take the waiting and had to leave the bar. I really wanted to rise above my feelings of rejection and leave without wallowing in self-pity, but I just stood outside the bar, dazed with disbelief. In my weakness I just roamed around the place, hoping what I knew to be true, to be proven false.

As I stood on the side of the road, trying to force myself to start down it, Ashley emerged from a dark area across the street, a few twigs poking out of her thin hair. "You headed out?" she asked, in a recently sobered, pseudo-nonchalant voice that thinly veiled her guilty conscience. "Something like that," I replied weakly, still unable to actually start leaving. As Ashley and I bathed in an awkward silence, the tired looking pretty boy emerged for the same dark corner Ashley had. He made some comment about the ferocity of the blood-sucking mosquitoes, unwittingly drawing what I viewed as an ironic parallel to my situation, and ambled back into the bar. At least the mosquitoes had mercifully left me to my own devices. Feeling I'd been granted resolution, I started down the road.

Langkawi is a fairly large island. Walking across it in the middle of night is no small feat. I had a lot of time to think. Fortunately I've always found walking a good stimulant for thinking.

While I'd been quite fond of Ashley, I knew that I could never tolerate her diet coke drinking, cigarette smoking, type-A personality in any sort of a long term arrangement. "In reality," I thought, "things couldn't have worked out better." What easier of a way could there have been to avoid commitment.

Thailand

Once my free week expired I shoved off from Langkawi, bound for Thailand. I stopped at two uninhabited islands and stayed a full day at the second. I spent the morning playing Robinson Crusoe, but fell into a deep boredom in the afternoon, feeling disenchanted with the island life and hanging out by myself on a deserted island with little to do.

The following day I sailed to Ko Phi Phi, an island not far from Phuket. Its steep cliffs and lush vegetation where striking, but I'd brought my apathy over from the last island and was considering not going to land at all until a couple of local boats with young topless tourists motored by. I was instantly jerked out of my funk.

I cracked a hot duty free beer from Malaysia and began unpacking Sputnik. A few minutes later I looked up while pumping the dinghy and saw a ferry boat entering the bay. The rails were lined with beautiful women waving at me enthusiastically. I started pumping double time and sweating like a hog. I dug through the medicine cabinet in the head and found an ancient stick of Old Spice deodorant. It had dried up considerably since I'd used it last and when I removed its cap the deodorant sprung from applicator onto the floor. I fished the shrunken waxy oval cake from behind the toilet, plucked off a couple of pubic hairs that were clinging to it, and rubbed it around in my armpits. "Perfect!" I downed the rest of my beer, chucked Sputnik in the water, and strapped P.O.S. (Piece of Shit, the outboard) onto the transom.

The outboard had been on a gradual decline since I'd purchased it used in California two years prior. When Joe and I got it out in Australia, after it had been sitting unused for six months, we found it inoperable. I spent hours trying to get it working; using cursing as my primary tool.

I had it in the cockpit and was taking apart the carburetor, when a small piece fell out of it and quickly rolled into the cockpit drain, never to be seen again. I shrugged my shoulders, "oh well, maybe it wasn't all that important." I eventually got it to start, but it would only run for a few seconds before cutting out. Joe and I mostly conceded to paddling to and from Hanuman but we eventually developed a theory that the piece that had fallen into the cockpit drain was responsible for fuel flow regulation. Painstakingly, we honed a system where by one could regulate the fuel flow into the carburetor using the fuel shut off valve. Open for "one Sputnik, two Sputnik, three Sputnik." Close for "one Sputnik, two Sputnik,… seven Sputnik." "Repeat." The system mostly worked, but by no means guaranteed success. It was especially touchy at night. I theorized that there was an electrical problem that was exacerbated by the moist night air. The theory was strengthened by the fact that I would occasionally receive a sever shock. It also leaked fuel, which combined with the potential electrical problem, made me wonder if POS might at some point explode. I didn't dwell on the thought however.

A mere ten pulls on the cord and POS sputtered to life. I had a hefty callous on each hand from spending so much time pulling on the cord. To top off POS's POSness, Brandoni had lost the gas cap back in the Pacific. I'd replaced it with a wooden plug.

The one nice thing about the whole setup was that it was light. Pulling it up the beach on Ko Phi Phi was no problem. I also didn't worry too much about it being stolen. I did, however, frequently arrive at the dinghy to find people had used it as a trash receptacle.

Ko Phi Phi was touristy. Fortunately, touristy was exactly what I was in the mood for. I was tired of deserted anchorages and uninhabited islands. Ko Phi Phi was perfect. It's a small island with no cars or roads, only footpaths. I'd had many great experiences with all of the locals I'd met in Indonesia and Malaysia, but was ready to hang out with some backpacker type tourists. Ko Phi Phi had no shortage. After months of relative solitude, my life suddenly took a 180 degree turn and I was basking in the glow of hot women and cold beer.

I walked around, scoping out the place. It was still fairly early in the day and the nightlife hadn't gotten going so I pulled into a small restaurant and had a beer and a pizza; heaven. After my pizza I walked around some more and then decided to just pick a place, make camp, and see what unfolded before me. There was really no one in the bar I chose, but the Scandinavian waitresses where attractive, though not exceedingly friendly. They'd clearly become calloused by the overt advances of oversexed European backpackers.

Eventually the place started to fill up; lots of Swedes. It turned out that I was in a Swedish/Scandinavian bar. Everyone in the place was speaking Swedish. It was odd as hell. I would never have guessed when I woke up that morning that I'd be at a Swedish bar in the middle of Thailand. It seemed weird for a bunch of Swedish kids to come all the way down from Sweden only to hang out in a bar with a bunch of other Swedish kids, but I loved it.

I befriended a Swedish guy and we decided to see if we could wrangle up a couple of girls. I was in the process of pointing out a couple of potentials to him when he grabbed my shoulder and whirled me around. "No, no, I've already got a couple over here." He led me back to a table with four stools and two Swedish chicks, one of which looked like she must have been a model. I'd picked a good wingman. After some conversation, I was on the dance floor with the modelesque one, Sofia. Dancing got closer and slower and eventually led to the infamously classy act of making out on the dance floor. The veil of anonymity was as intoxicating as the alcohol and I was living in a consequence free society. So was she, it appeared.

After the Swedish bar, named 'Carlito's' for some reason, closed we made our way to another bar kissing and groping along the way. On a whim, I asked her if she wanted to go back to the boat. Despite things having gone so well between us thus far, I didn't really expect her to say yes, but to my delight she did.

We launched Sputnik under a perfectly starry sky. POS was like a misbehaved pet waiting to make me look like an ass in front of someone. After a good 50 pulls I handed Sofia a paddle, the straighter one. Fortunately the idea of paddling amused her, and we were off. The passage took awhile, models and paddling..., but it was a pleasant night and I was in no hurry.

Back on Hanuman I quickly ducked down below and turned on the light to give the roaches a chance to scatter. Fortunately there weren't many. Past their bedtime I supposed.

I dragged some ragged bedding material onto the fore-deck and was relieved when Sofia commented on how romantic it was. Months of solitary contemplation and scrutinizing introspection dissolved into simple desires of the flesh as we watched the stars fade into the dawn.

I'd been excited to get to Phuket and meet up with my English buddy Steve but I decided to linger on Ko Phi Phi for another day soaking up Sophia's company.

I eventually pulled myself away and sailed over to the island of Phuket. Steve introduced me to a whole other side of life. Simply put, Thailand is like no other place.

After a week of debauchery in Phuket, Steve and I decided to sail back to Ko Phi Phi for New Years Eve. I really hadn't gotten enough of the place. We determined that we ought to have costumes for the event. After a couple of warm beers and some head scratching we arrived upon Togas with tinfoil head ornaments, the old standby.

We started out tame, having a couple of quite drinks, looking a little overdressed to be sitting so casually in a half empty bar. Five different people asked to have their pictures taken with us. As things began to heat up we made our way to the Reggae Bar, where they had nightly Thai kick boxing fights. I thought it a questionable call to have a bunch of drunk people getting all riled up watching a live fight, but who was I to cast judgment.

We progressed from beer to Thai whiskey and Red Bull. Thailand is the birthplace of Red Bull and it is said to be doubly potent there. We drank them by the bucket full, literally. They actually pour the concoction into a small bucket, jam in a fist full of straws, and hand it to you.

The actual stroke of mid night came and went without much notice. Things just steamed forward, or at least Steve and I did.

The dance floor didn't seem like enough to vent our energy so we made our way into the Thai boxing ring and started wrestling. Others saw the appeal and before long it was a free for all. Our Togas and head dresses took a beating. Things wound down after Steve sprained his shoulder.

The night becomes hazy at that point. I woke up the next morning on the beach with an intense thirst and a dull hangover thankfully muted by the fact that I was still drunk. Fortunately I still had of few bucks in my pocket and got myself a milk-type drink, very soothing to the stomach and head, that Steve had introduced me to.

The night came back to me as I sucked down the sweet beverage. I remembered meeting a girl named Nicole, who I'd invited to sail with me, and decided to see if I could find her place and have her fill in the gaps in my memory.

I arrived at Nicole's hovel at the way too early hour of eight am. She was surprised to see me, but interested. We went for a short hike. I was pleased to find myself not interested in her sexually. I was much more interested in finding crew than a girlfriend. I renewed my invitation to sail and to my surprise she said she was interested and keen to think about it.

I spent the next hour wondering around looking for Steve. We'd gotten separated as we tended to almost every night we went out. I couldn't find him and went back to the boat for a nap. He eventually was dropped off on Hanuman by a local boat. He'd woken up on a couch in the lobby of one of the nicer hotels. The staff had covered him with a blanket and let him sleep. Thai people can be very accommodating.

Nicole turned up at the boat shortly after and Steve reintroduced himself to her, having no recollection of meeting her the night before. She looked over the boat, flipped through the pile of pictures I'd accumulated, and decided she was in.

The next time I saw her she said she was with some friends who were also interested; an American girl, a Dutch girl, a French girl and an Aussie guy who was hooking up with the French girl. That would definitely be exceeding comfortable capacity on Hanuman, but I was willing to squeeze all of the girls in.

Ultimately all of the girls backed out except Nicole. Chris, the Aussie, stayed on as well and I had myself a crew.

Many of the details of the time I spent in Thailand were lost in an intoxicated, glutinous haze, and probably incommunicable. Thailand is matchless. Boundaries are blurred, laws are negotiable, and everything is for sale. The Thai people display a unique blend of beauty and kindness, with a dose of corruption and harshness, creating an enchanting land of both strangely lovely and strangely revolting possibilities.

In the peculiar may-lay of shadow and light, the three of us did manage to haul Hanuman out of the water and paint the bottom before leaving. The time gave us a good chance to get acquainted with each other and the boat, before heading out into the Indian Ocean.

Chris decided that we all needed new nicknames and christened himself: 'Dr. Cock.' He considered himself quite the ladies man and I got the feeling that he may have been calling himself, at least in his head, 'Dr. Cock,' for quite some time. Somehow I got assigned 'Captain Fellatio' and Nicole was stuck with 'Admiral Anus,' as a tribute to her irritable bowel syndrome.

Indian Ocean I

Apart from the brief passage from Ko Phi Phi to Ko Phuket, Dr. Cock and Admiral Anus had never sailed. For the first three days Nicole was a slave to sea sickness. She occupied the mid-ship berth (the cripple den), which was the most spacious and comfortable at anchor, but lacked the security of the of the two aft quarter births at sea.

We started off with trailing winds in a rolly sea. We ran under the jib alone, which didn't offer much stability. Consequently Hanuman rolled through a substantial arc from side to side.

On the first night out as I sat on watch, quietly contented with the new phase of my journey, a pained voice yelled up from below. "How the hell do I stay in the bed?" Nicole's voice was filled with tortured frustration. She'd been thrown out of her bunk and was lying on the floor. I could make out a pair of eyes in the shadows looking up at me from a tangle of bedding. I offered her my bunk but she thought it a little too cave-esk for her liking. "Make like starfish," I suggested. A grumbling let me know she wasn't satisfied with my response. "Do you want me to empty your puke bucket?" I offered.

"I don't care," she replied meekly, in a voice heavy with resignation. "Glad I'm not her," I thought, taking another swig beer.

Two days out, she started asking questions about the Nicobar Islands spread out across the skyline to the north. "So… the only way to and from those islands is by boat?" she queried. "No, there's surely there's an airstrip," I hastily retorted. As I did so rust flew, as the gears in my head broke free, analyzing the nature of her question. I feared that she might demand an emergency stop, and quickly regrouped, "but it's probably just a small private airstrip…and you need special visas even to stop there… and I heard about some civil unrest in the capitol… potential coup d'état unfolding… an all around bad place to be currently." I shrugged, shook my head gravely from side to side, and gave her a look hoping to convey my powerlessness in the situation. "Oh," she replied, as her glimmer of hope crumbled. She pulled her puke bucket closer, as a frightened child might a favorite stuffed animal.

On the third day Nicole was a new woman. She emerged from her bunk with a new glow on her face, though still claimed she'd be parting ways with the boat as soon as we got to Sri Lanka.

Days passed and Nicole became more and more comfortable. Our point of sail changed, making Hanuman more stable. We saw dolphins streaking through the phosphorescence, sipped wine at sunset, and caught two huge fish. "Maybe I'll go onto Egypt," Nicole blurted out on the eight day.

Chris loved it from day one and was fully committed to sailing all the way to the Mediterranean.

Sri Lanka

After nine grand days of sailing, we arrived in Galle, Sri Lanka. We'd made good time. For the previous four months I'd been dreaming about the consistent monsoonal winds and it had been a delight to experience them. My daily mileage average jumped from 40 to 115.

As regulation dictated, we anchored in the outer harbor and radioed the navy, requesting entrance. We'd been informed that the inspection officers liked to confiscate various items they found, like cigarettes and booze. We'd hidden our four bottles of Thai whiskey, not wanting them to turn into two or three. Chris was a smoker, but he'd left Thailand with only one pack, forcing himself to quit when he it was gone. Consequently, we didn't have any cigs to confiscate. We didn't really have anything in surplus to quell officialdom's confiscatory desires, save one item; toothpaste.

We'd done a big shop up at a warehouse type place in Thailand and had ended up with an eight pack of toothpaste. We decided to leave boxes of toothpaste around the boat, hoping to assuage the inspectors.

Before long a boat came out and a couple of officers boarded Hanuman. "Any cigarettes?" "No." "Alcohol?" "No." I eyed one of the toothpaste boxes sitting by the sink and gave my left eyebrow a conspiratory lift. Apparently they weren't interested in dental hygiene. They had a quick look around, didn't see anything that interested them, and the inspection was over. We were granted entry into the inner harbor.

Sri Lanka had been plagued with an on-again off-again civil war for the past 19 years between the Tamil people of the north, who were originally brought over by the Portuguese (who, among others, occupied Sri Lanka for a time) from India, as laborers in the tea plantations, and the Senegalese people who were the 'original' inhabitants. The Tamils wanted independence. The Senegalese didn't want them to have it. People don't freely give up what they feel they deserve. Empathy always seems in short supply. Hatred and vengeance are easily triggered.

At the time of our arrival there was a cease fire and the new Senegalese leadership seemed promising. The country was far from at peace however, and every night they strung a net across the entrance to the inner harbor and dropped depth charges in the outer harbor to discourage any Tamil Tiger frogmen from swimming into the inner harbor with explosives.

With Hanuman secured to the wharf, we decided to undertake an inland exploration. Our first foray into the interior was by rail. The train filled quickly. I occupied a standing spot by the door. As the train swelled with passengers, I found myself slowly getting pushed out the door until I was just kind-of hanging onto the side of the train. I loved the lack of safety standards, and what my spot may have lacked in safety, it made up for in ventilation and views. The only drawback was that I frequently got whacked by passing vegetation.

After a few days of training and bussing around, we found ourselves at the base of Adam's Peak, 'The Holiest Mountain in Sri Lanka.' We'd also picked up a couple of English travelers who decided it was much easier to come along with us than to figure what to do for themselves. They more than earned their keep by entertaining us.

At the top of Adam's Peak is believed to be the foot print of Adam (as in Adam and Eve,) Mohammad, Buddha, Shiva or Mickey Mouse; depending on your faith. I was pulling for Mickey.

A well placed pub prevented us from actually starting the ascent until just before sunset.

Adam's Peak had inspired many other pilgrims who'd also shown up for the journey; people of all ages and segments of Sri Lankan society, many of whom were shoeless. We had no idea it was such a popular undertaking. The first mile of the journey snaked through wall to wall shacks that had been erected to sell the would-be pilgrims the necessary accoutrements for the climb. Sandals, shoes, water, food, offerings to your God of choice, and all sorts of commemorative knick-knacks were available.

The idea behind such a late start was to see the sunrise from the top. Rather than waking up at two in the morning to start the hike, I decided we should bring our sleeping bags and sleep at the top, positioning ourselves so that watching the sunrise was a simple matter of opening our eyes. It also saved us a night of paying for accommodations.

After considerable toiling, the five of us arrived on the summit in varying degrees of condition. It was a steep climb. Chris, the last Boy Scout, insisted on being prepared for every eventuality, bringing his full backpack along with his belly pack. I was more of the 'fast and light' school of thought, and just brought my sleeping bag and a bottle of arrack; the local spirit (for medicinal purposes only of course). I enjoyed the hike. Chris enjoyed the toil.

At the summit, even in the middle of the night, there was a constant procession of people going past the footprint. It was covered by plexi-glass and surrounded by a steel fence. I didn't get a chance to really study it, but I thought it had a mousish look to it.

The summit wasn't what I'd envisioned. Everything was a little on the ghetto side; lots of crumbling cement. The power lines that lit up the foot print, and various other areas, definitely weren't a tribute to the skyline.

We found an unoccupied (we weren't the only ones with the sleep on top idea) area, that didn't smell too much like urine, on some stairs to lay our sleeping bags. The stairs were only about three quarters of a foot wide, making sleeping a bit of a balancing act, but I managed to get a few winks before sunrise.

After the sunrise we decided to descend the longer, less travel path down the other side of the mountain. It seemed like a good idea at the time.

About half way down, Nicole, Damien (the English guy), and I decided to stop and roll a joint. The English chick and Chris continued on, thinking that if they stopped for too long they might not get going again.

While Nicole rolled the joint I decided to bash through the foliage and find myself a nice place to take a crap. Bad move. I came out relieved but with something moist feeling clinging to my eyelid. I attempted to brush it away but it didn't move. I suddenly got the idea that it might be a leech. I made a couple of frantic attempt to remove it but had no success.

"Damien, is there a leech in my eye?" My spastic rubbing motions had somehow moved the wet thing from my eyelid onto my eyeball. He looked at me with a seriousness that told me that in fact I did have a leech in my eye. I made a few panicked attempts to pinch it off of my eyeball but only managed to tear out a handful eyelashes. Damien then went in with his own filthy digits but succeeded only in further bludgeoning my eye.

We took a step back. "What do we have?" Damien asked. Nicole gestured to bottle of warm Sprite we'd just purchased at the last rest stop. "I guess we could try pouring Sprite on it," Damien offered. There was a moment of silence as we pondered the idea, before a round of "no that's just stupid" closed the subject.

Meanwhile the leech was still in my eye, presumably sucking my eyeball blood. We took another moment to reevaluate. "I'll go for help," Damien blurted, reaching for his backpack. "Get back here you pussy. Go for help?…phuff," I rebuffed. Damien just wanted to flee the scene.

In the interim, Nicole had magically produced a pair of tweezers she probably usually used as a roach clip.

The tiny leech was none too easy to grab. It had suckers on both ends of its worm like body and was capable of 'walking' around on my eye.

Nicole refused to get near my eye with the tweezers. She actually only had one working eye herself, due to a birth defect, and her depth perception was lacking. It was up to Damien, whose previous solution had been to run away.

I braced my head against rock so I couldn't squirm, Nicole held back my eyelid, and Damien went in with the tweezers.

Needless to say it wasn't the best view I'd ever had. Despite having the leech on my pupil, yes it had walked onto my pupil, I could still see quite clearly out of the eye. I could actually see the leech wriggling around in the foreground and Damien, with a gob of sweat giggling from his nose and a violently shaking hand grasping a pair of tweezers, in the back ground. "Feel free to brace that hand on my face," I suggested.

While Damien was prepping himself, a couple of Sri Lankans walked by. They didn't speak English but the situation spoke for itself. They peered into my eye. We pleaded for advice, hoping this sort of thing happened all the time. They nodded their heads with a gesture that seemed to say, "Yeah, you're screwed," and walked on.

We went back to work. Damien said the leech was swelling, presumably with my blood, and thought it might be easier to grab. "Great."

After about 20 minutes of grabbing, poking and prodding, Damien managed to tweeze the little bastard out. "I got it," he howled. It was naturally a joyous moment. "How does my eye look?" They both peered in. "It's a bit …bloody." "A bit?" I queried. "Well actually about three quarters of the 'white' part is blood red. "Hmmm."

My eye felt raw but my vision was only slightly blurred and …hell, I no longer had a leech in my eye, so I thought life was pretty good. "Let's smoke that joint!"

The hike ended, we spent a few days with extremely sore legs, and I got a lot of redundant questions. "What happened to your eye?" "Nothing… why?"

We eventually made our way back to the boat. My eye healed and I returned to 'normal.' Although I did wake up one night in an especially dark hotel room thinking I was blind. "Nicole, Chris," I blurted out in the darkness, "Can you see anything? I think I'm blind!" It occurred to me as I spoke that I probably wouldn't be blind in both eyes, but the die was cast and I'd provided Nicole and Chris with lasting amusement. "Mike, are you blind?" they would bellow after a few beers.

Nicole decided she would continue on to Egypt and shaved her head for the occasion. Chris shaved his head as well. I hadn't cut my hair in over a year and had a respectable beard going so we made quite a trio.

Sri Lanka to the Maldives

The ocean felt welcoming after three weeks on land. The breeze drifted through my hair and emptied my thoughts as Sri Lanka sunk below the horizon. Bob Dillon's, 'Blowin' in the Wind,' wafted out from the cockpit speakers. My mind followed the music, the sound of the sea against the hull, and the gentle rustling of the sails. Hanuman cut an easy path at a good pace in mellow seas. She was happy to be back at sea as well.

We were all feeling the effects of our ceaseless activity. Our last couple of nights we'd discovered a beach bar/restaurant with a rope swing tied to a palm tree that hung out over the ocean. The palm was tall and the rope was long, allowing for a satisfyingly extended swing out over the water; at which point you could jump in or swing back to land, hovering just above a breaking wave. After a joint or two the experience became surreal.

The restaurant served good food, large cold beers, and upon request, joints. We partook in all they offered and made our way to the rope swing. I was obsessed with the swing. As a result, my hands became so blistered that I could barely pull a line. Being the captain, and having a certain amount of stubbornness, I insisted on doing so despite the intense and embarrassing pain. I ruptured most my blisters on the first day. After 'showing that I could do it,' I spent the rest of the day watching the slow stream of puss ooze out of the furuncles and accumulate between my finders where it turned into a sticky paste.

We were all in recovery mode. Just about every day full of physical activity had been topped off with a night of excess. Nicole sat in the cockpit with an angry scowl on her face and looked like she was about to barf. After a couple of days in the sun, her freshly shorn head had taken more rays than it could handle. Her head had erupted in blisters that burst, dried up, and began to resemble a moonscape. Chris and I gave her no end of grief for her condition. We'd peer down at her head and make faces like we were about to hurl. She didn't find our antics nearly as amusing as we did. She started wearing a bandana. "I liked you better when you thought you were blind," she stated aggressively.

Chris began to take personal offense to the presence of the roaches and armed himself with a can of what he called, "fuck off." The Aussies have an adorable way of describing things in their simplest and most direct terms. Another amusing trait is that they add a 'y' to at least one noun per sentence, giving a humorous touch of adolescence to every statement. "Mate, hand us me sunnies (sun glasses) and a beer out-a-the esky (cooler)."

Watching him through the companionway from the cockpit, he looked like a boxer; jabbing with the bug spray and retreating. He held a shirt over his mouth for protection. I was a little concerned that he was spraying the 'fuck off' on our food, but he was a man on a mission and I left him to it.

It was a hopeless struggle however. We couldn't hope to defeat the roaches, only to reduce their numbers. We really needed a comprehensive battle plan. We needed Norman Schwarzkopf. In truth, we were living on their boat. They had the numbers, the organization, and the will.

The Maldives

The passage to the Maldives was quick and painless and we arrived feeling well cleansed of our Sri Lankan excesses. We avoided the capitol of Mali, and its hefty check in fee, only stopping at Ulegama, one of the islands in the north.

Ulegama had only one simple Muslin village. Outsiders weren't allowed to stay overnight on the island. The village consisted of a handful of houses organized around a couple of sand streets. Exploring the area took only a portion of a day. We used most of our time to make repairs on Hanuman that had been neglected in Sri Lanka. Chris fabricated a rather elaborate awning to replace the disintegrating bed sheet that had been in use since Mexico.

We snorkeled by day, though found the reef to be more dead than alive and played Jenga and drank Thai whiskey by night. I thought it absurd when Nicole bought 'Jenga' in Thailand. The idea of trying to balance a bunch of wooden blocks on a rolling boat seemed preposterous. However, the anchorage was fairly well protected and the occasional roller just added an extra element to the game. It wasn't wise to linger on your turn. The sea could lose the game for you before you even got a chance to touch the tower.

Eventually we felt we'd experienced all that we were going to in the Maldives and raised anchor, bound for Yemen.

Passage to Yemen

The passage from the Maldives to Yemen was about 2,200 nautical miles, a significant chunk of ocean. Back at sea, my head felt clear and my belly light. We spent our first day out bobbing around, wondering when the Monsoonal winds would fill back in. "Do you think we'll still be able to see it [Ulegama] in the morning," Nicole pondered. "It looks like it's actually getting closer," she continued. "It does kind of look that way," I admitted, looking up at the wind indicator, before returning my eyes to my book with an ambivalent grunt. Fortunately we weren't able to see Ulegama the next day. A solid breeze filled in during the night and carried us along at a steady pace for the next couple of weeks.

It was great to have crew again, but as is so often the case, to gain something new I had to give something up. The challenges I faced with Chris and Nicole on board were completely altered. Sailing the boat no longer presented much of a challenge. With favorable winds and two crew members I crawled into my bunk after a night watch knowing I'd get four hours to myself with only the occasional interruptions for sail adjustments.

The greatest challenge that I faced was Nicole's personality. I often felt as though she wore a negative filter between herself and the world. It was like she was waiting to interrupt every action or statement with a negative rebuff. Chris or I would make some casual statement, with no negative connotation, and she'd suddenly get all bent out of shape, offended, and often lash out with some scathing remark. Her reasoning could be so illogical. I was usually able to just let it go, but on one occasion I lashed out.

I'd never yelled or even raised my voice at anyone on the boat before, but Nicole struck a nerve. "Shut the fuck up!" I heard coming out of my mouth. I wasn't even aware of its coming. It simply demanded release. It was triggered by something completely trivial. We were placing bets on when we would arrive in Yemen and she couldn't accept the simple rule that whoever guessed closest to the arrival date won. "Well… that's not fair. My day is in between your days so I have less…" Nicole attempted to say before I lashed out at her.

Nicole challenged my being in ways I wasn't always prepared to deal with. As a result I found interacting with her to be strenuous and I frequently did my best to avoid it.

I knew she hadn't grown up with the most love a child had ever received and I guessed that she'd probably built up defensive barriers to protect herself. I surmised that her defensiveness closed part of her mind. She often seemed so wrapped up in herself that she missed the basic things that were going on around her.

She also had a strong need to prove herself. A quality I'd begun to take note of in people in general. I assumed it must have arisen from some sort of insecurity. I certainly never felt that anyone on board had anything to prove to me.

Physically leaving Sri Lanka was an organizationally complicated process. We had out two anchors, one line to a mooring buoy, one line of a floating excuse for a dock, and two lines running to a large cement jetty. We were in a tight little horseshoe shaped area, and surrounded by other boats. The situation required some coordinated movement to make sure we escaped without damaging Hanuman or any of the adjacent boats.

I'd originally assigned Chris the task of using Sputnik to collect all of the lines at the correct time, but Nicole interceded. "Can't I do that, I never get to do anything." I initially responded, "Yeah, sure, go for it," but as she was climbing down into the dinghy I changed my mind. Nicole was inept at paddling the dinghy solo, and to have her retrieve the lines would've been a liability to Hanuman. I called her back and reassigned the task to Chris, who'd quickly gotten comfortable with paddling (which wasn't as straight forward as one might think; you could easily just spin around in circles), and could quickly untie knots and handle lines. With a side wind blowing Hanuman into the boat next to her, things had to be done as quickly and efficiently as possible. It wasn't a good time for learning.

Departing went well. We were able to get under way without incident and I congratulated everyone on a job well done. I always strove to hand out compliments in such situations. Entering or leaving an unfamiliar harbor in a big heavy boat, with no brakes, can often be tricky. I never took success for granted.

"I didn't get to do anything!" Nicole ejaculated in an angry tone. I did my best to control my tone and volume, but didn't throw any punches with the content. "I won't increase the risk to Hanuman or our journey simply to make you feel good. There is a time to learn skills and a time use them. You haven't learned them and that wasn't the time to fumble around. As I said from the beginning, you can learn as much or as little as you want and make the journey into whatever you desire but I won't perpetuate any illusions when it comes to the security of the boat."

I felt bad for her, but also felt that my decision had been the right one. Why wouldn't I choose the best person for the job? It wasn't some sort of children's sporting event, where 'everyone gets to play.' And she had done something. She'd pulled all of the lines on deck as Chris fed them to her. It simply wasn't the job she wanted. One must master the simple tasks before one gets assigned more complex ones. It's always worked that way at sea. Nicole had had ample time to learn if she'd really wanted to.

She tended to get frustrated whenever she was trying to learn something. It was like she was just waiting for things not to work out so that her anger could lash out. She would end up battling herself instead of a knot. The fact that she was constantly stoned probably didn't help matters. She'd been a chronic stoner for the last six years. I felt she just needed to watch what was going on around her and be a little more patient with herself.

Despite feeling that Nicole's negative defense systems closed her mind and prevented her from learning as much as she could (and from just being happier), I still admired her for trying and for committing to the experience, and enjoyed her company the majority the time. She had a warm, compassionate side and an unassuming demeanor that all of the people we met along the way found easy to engage.

After a week and a half of sailing, the wind increased and changed direction, compelling us to beat forcefully into it. The main started opening along one of its seams. We took it down and Chris and I swap shifts sewing for a couple of hour before we could raise it again.

I came up for my watch the next morning to find that the Aries rudder had snapped off and was dragging behind the boat on its safety leash. "The steering seems a little off," Nicole commented. I wasn't too impressed that she hadn't noticed something so major. I imagined waking up with water flooding into my bunk and Nicole saying, "The boat seems a little wetter."

I had spare parts for the Aries and could have fixed it, but to do so underway, I decided, wouldn't be worth it. Nicole held my ankles while I dangled off the back of the boat to rescue the Aries rudder.

The Aries had been steering almost the entire time since leaving Thailand. Chris and Nicole had never really hand-steered. I'd done my share and wasn't at all excited about the prospect. It's easy to get spoiled. While hand steering isn't 'all that bad' it can get tedious when you have to do it eight hours a day. It's also requires time that can't be spent reading or spacing out.

I did my best to bill it as a good learning experience. "You can't fully appreciate sailing until you spend some quality time behind the wheel." We still had a good five or six hundred miles to go, so there would be ample steering time for all.

The following day a huge wave ripped the bow light off. "Oh well, we have other lights. Some of which still work," I commented, mostly to myself.

With Nicole's birthday rapidly approaching the weather began to be of concern. We feared the rough conditions would interfere with the grand feast we had planned. Fortunately the weather eased just in time and we were able to celebrate in style.

Chris decided he would learn, with stunning success, how to bake a cake. He managed to produce a double-decker chocolate cake with chocolate frosting. It probably could have been a triple-decker if he hadn't consumed so much batter in the process.

I baked four pizzas, with dough made from scratch, and busted out a few beers and a bottle of Sri Lankan arrack.

During the night the wind dropped to nothing, which was good for Chris and me, since we passed out during our shifts. We probably both did a few circles in the night before our heads jerked to attention and we realized that we were pointed towards the Maldives.

Entering the Gulf of Aden changed our outlook on life. The Monsoonal winds that had carried us along so consistently, deserted us. Compounding the bothersome lack of movement was the Gulf's notoriety for piracy. It was impossible to fully ignore the feeling of being a wounded gazelle on the savannah.

Many of the sailors that we'd met were going through in convoys, hoping for safety in numbers. Some even came up with code names for communicating on the two-way radio. I was never sure what the point of that was; as if a pirate would know one boat name from the other. I could just hear the pirates, "Oh, don't bother with 'Coco Puff,' I'm sure they don't have anything worth stealing."

I decided we'd go it alone. I didn't see how we could stay with another sailboat for 2,200 miles, and I felt 'safety in numbers' might be just an illusion.

The calm that began on the night of Nicole's birthday persisted into the next day. My policy of not using the motor unless necessary was well known to Chris and Nicole, but I could see Nicole's desire for it in her eyes. The wind came and went and we continued to sail on whatever little breeze we received.

The calms unraveled Nicole like a ball of yarn. The days following her birthday continued to be light and our daily mileage dropped dramatically. She started freaking out. The, "I just want to be there," feeling overwhelmed her. She spent a substantial amount of time in the head (bathroom) with the door closed. It was the only private area on the boat and I guess she wanted to be alone. I didn't know what she was doing in there and was afraid to ask. She was also having trouble with insomnia and the idea of being attacked by pirates. To top it off she was on the rag.

I didn't know what to say to her except, "we'll get there eventually," which only seemed to irritate her more. "I don't control the weather," I insisted. She wasn't convinced, and telegraphed a sneer indicating that she felt I'd created the situation. "The wind doesn't usually drop off completely for more than three days in my experience… five days at the most. No time at all, geologically speaking," I stated with assurance. Chris chimed in with: "Bob's your uncle," a common Aussie euphemism he'd adapted to fit our 'bobbing' situation. "Bob's my uncle," parroted Nicole, in placid resignation.

"Wham, wham, wham." Three knocks on the cockpit above head brought me out of my dream world and into reality. Three knocks was the signal for 'on deck immediately,' though I couldn't recall anyone ever actually using it.

I was on deck in one swift motion, honed by repetition. It was bright as hell, and an elongated moment passed before I could see anything, but the intense rays, muted only subtly by Arabian dust, did little to veil the obvious tension partnered with the triple knock.

Chris was at the helm. There was just enough wind to keep Hanuman pointed in the right direction. The seas were calm. "Small motorboat coming right for us… rapidly," Chris said, as he pointed at an outboard powered skiff planing towards us about a mile off. I quickly fired up Big Red, to give us the ability to maneuver, handed Chris his 'beatin' stick,' and grabbed my own.

The beatin' sticks weren't necessarily the most obvious choice for a weapon. We had a machete but it was so dull and rusty that I figured the best it could do was give the pirates tetanus. An undesirable condition to be sure, but not an immediate solution to our problems. The Hawaiian sling, with its three pronged spear tip, seemed like a reasonable choice but I feared that in a close quarters combat situation it might not be too effective. There was also the possibility

241

that any weapon I started out with could end up in the hands of the pirates and I wasn't too excited about getting speared or machettied. Hence the beatin' sticks. Chris took down the sunshade to increase visibility, and swing radius.

Nicole was alert by now and looking up through the companionway, waiting for encouraging words. "Man the two-way radio and to be prepared to send out a mayday," I ordered. We decided she should stay below to conceal the fact that we had a female, albeit an ill tempered one with an oozing, puss covered, shaved head, onboard.

The boat continued its rapid approach. We could make out two people onboard. The boat speedily closed to within feet of us and then cut the engine and dropped out of a plane only barely before hitting us. Their wake bitch slapped Hanuman's quarter, sending a minor shock wave through the boat.

The two youngish black guys occupying the 16 foot long open boat with a 70 horse power outboard came right next to us. I was forced to turn Hanuman a few degrees to avoid being hit. The guy in the front of the boat was standing up. He was lean, with bulbous knotty muscles and prominent cheekbones, and wore a stoic expression. The salt on his dark black skin gave him a grayish hue. The other guy, sitting in the stern with one hand on the outboard tiller, was stringier, with an annoying, somewhat deranged grin plastered on his face; like he was up to no good and knew it, but couldn't hide that he was enjoying it. Like a Labrador licking a child's ice cream cone.

They both eyed us heavily before speaking. Chris had set his beatin' stick on the cabin top within reach and taken up residence amid ship doing his best to look large and imposing.

I waved and offered a hello. We really had no idea what their intentions were. Chris played the tough guy and didn't say anything. "Hello…water?" they responded. They asked for water but their eyes darted around in the dark manner of those who were interested in something far more coveted than water.

We'd heard about this trick. According to lore, in such situation the approaching vessel would ask for something and as soon as you turned your back, they would jump onboard and start tearing stuff off your boat.

"We don't have any extra water," I said. "Food?" I again replied in the negative. "We are fisherman…water?…food?" I shook my head, noting unnervingly that they didn't have a single item of fishing gear on their boat. All they had were a bunch of rocks. I speculated on what the rocks were for. Optimistically, I estimated that they could be used as fishing weights. Pessimistically, I observed that they appeared an ideal size to be used as hand thrown projectiles; putting them in the weapon category. They did seem to be scattered fairly evenly around the boat, which I took as a good sign. I reckoned that if they were going to throw them, they would've each had a pile next to them. "Then again, planing across the gulf surely would've scattered any piles," I thought.

They continued to ask for food, while doing circles around us in their boat. They repeatedly forced me to alter course to avoid hitting them. Eventually they stopped asking for things and just circled like sharks.

As this was going on we noticed a group of three or four similar boats about a mile off. They were stopped and appeared to be huddling. Just as we though our fate was about to get worse we heard the buzzing of a plane over head and saw a large, four propped, military plane coming towards us. It approached and began to circle. The guy driving the boat pointed up at the plane and then to us with a questioning tone. Despite having no idea where the plane had come from, Chris and I both nodded in affirmation that they were here for us. Seconds later the two-way radio came to life, "small sailing vessel this is coalition warplane so and so." We made contact and they asked us if we were having any problem. I replied, "not at the moment, but we aren't sure of the intentions of the boat circling us."

The boat zoomed over to the group that was conferring a mile off. The coalition warplane continued to circle and eventually the group of boats motored back to the north where they'd come from and the plane left as well. We called it 'crisis averted' but kept the beatin' sticks in the cockpit permanently.

Thankfully the wind picked up not long after our encounter and we happily put some distance behind us.

The following day we were able to pick up a spotty plea for help on the two-way radio from a cargo ship who was attempting to outrun some pirates. The reception wasn't that clear, so it was hard to make out what was happening, but it seemed that the ship had been boarded and shots fired. We never learned their fate. The fact that we could hear it on the radio meant that they were probably less than thirty miles off, a fact that I neglected to share with Nicole.

We later learned that a few yachties had been robbed. We got firsthand accounts of a how a very entrepreneurial boat, illegally transporting Somalians to Yemen, had stopped along the way to do some pirating. Bambola, a boat we would later meet in the Red Sea, was boarded my men with AK-47's who jabbed their guns into the stomach of Michael, the captain, and demanded money. They made off with 600 bucks and an expensive SSB radio, but not before parting the rigging of Olf's (Olf was a German single hander sailing in convoy with Bambola) boat, as they fired their riffles into the sky.

The wind was sufficient to keep us moving at a tolerable rate and, a few days after our encounter, we were attached to a couple of rusty old mooring balls in front of Aden, Yemen.

It was April of 2003 and America had invaded Iraq. Mostly, people didn't care where we were from or what we were up to, but we did have a couple of people curse at us from a distance, "all fuckin' Americans go home."

A local guy, who had latched onto us as our guide, told us to tell people that we were French; apparently they were the only white people who were popular in the region. We were anchored in the same bay the USS Cole had been when it was blown up a couple of years prior. "What? We don't even speak French," I contested. "Nobody else does either," he countered. We shrugged, *"Viva la France."* On the flip side, most Yemenis had the wisdom to separate a people from their leader and treated us very well, regardless of where they thought we were from.

Aden marked the halfway point, longitudinally, of my circumnavigation. But having the Red Sea looming before us made it seem like a poor time to celebrate; that, and we were out of alcohol.

The Red Sea

The Red Sea is only 1100 nautical miles from top to bottom, but is well known for serving up plenty of punishment. Typically the southern half sees southerly winds and the northern half, northerlies. We left Aden with the hope of favorable conditions for at least the first portion of the transit.

On our second day out we sailed through the narrow southern opening, *Bad al Mandeb* (Strait of Tears), into the Red Sea. I found myself extremely glad that we weren't going the other way. I read ten knots on the GPS speedometer as we surfed down a wave's face in 25 knots of wind. "At this rate we'll be in the Med in a week," I stated with a dubious grin. Chris and Nicole were sea wise by this point however, and barely grinned at my feigned optimism.

The winds mellowed over the next few days and their southerly direction became less consistent. I'd hoped for more easy miles before we had to start working for them.

Conveniently, the east coast of Sudan and Egypt are flush with protected anchorages. Small pockets within the reef, called *marsas*, with their narrow entrances, provide great protection from heavy seas. The narrow channels into the *marsas* can be difficult to navigate, necessitating an entrance planned around good visibility, when the sun's angle doesn't create too much glare. Eyeballing a route is the only reliable means of navigating through the maze of reefs. Occasionally, local fisherman had pushed small sticks into the reef around critical areas, as channel markers, but they couldn't be counted upon.

Marsa Ibrabam, in southern Sudan, was our first anchorage in the Red Sea. The anchor chain jammed, offering an inauspicious welcome to Sudan, as Chris was trying to deploy it. But we sorted it out and got ourselves secured without ramming into the reef.

Camels on shore lifted their heads to check us out briefly, before returning to their grazing. A dry, scrubby expanse extended behind them. It was exciting to be in such an exotic locale, but a feeling of disenchantment had enveloped me and I was having trouble enjoying the new environment.

I felt both the weight of the miles behind me and the miles before me. I was also a little sick of my crew. We'd spent a lot of time together in close quarters. Nicole's presence alone was occasionally enough to annoy me. She could be so difficult to interact with. I sometimes found it painful just to talk to her, like banging my head against a wall. The noise she made when she chewed seemed to drive me crazy. She was on the rag again and the pad she wore made a diaper-like sound when she walked that seemed to echo around in the tranquility of the anchorage. She stepped over me as I lay in the cockpit and my skin crawled as I imagined something dropping down on me. Ironically, when I was stepping over her, after pissing off the rail, and apparently not shaking sufficiently, I actually shed a few urine droplets. "I think I just got peed on," she deadpanned in a rare moment of stoicism. "Ops, my bad," I replied, trying unsuccessfully not to give in to Chris' bubbling laughter.

Chris could annoy me on a different level. He was one of those guys who really liked to be right. If he was right, everyone was going to know about it. If he was wrong, he would go into absolute silent mode until the situation had passed and he had another opportunity to be right again. I felt like half the time he was just waiting around for me to make some sort of mistake so he could snicker and tell me how he would have done it.

Ultimately I felt Chris and Nicole were both great people, and when they were at their best, I loved to be around them. But the absurd amount of time we spent together, the constant subtle stress of being in an ocean where we could be attacked by pirates, the palpable hostility of a region about to erupt into war, and the concern of somehow getting stranded in the middle of nowhere, coupled with a lingering fatigue brought on by my increased vigilance made necessary by the narrowness of the new ocean, left me shorter of compassion and hotter of temper. Chris and Nicole of course felt this also and so occasionally we all pretty much hated each other, and possibly even ourselves.

We spent just a night in Marsa Ibraham. The water wasn't particularly clear, and getting out the dinghy and going to land didn't seem worth the effort, so we pulled anchor and took off the next morning.

The wind was light and we alternated between sailing and motoring, in order to make our next anchorage by nightfall. The southerly winds, which had been so accommodating in days prior, had deserted us. The *marsas* were spaced close enough along the southern portion of the Sudanese coast so that we were able to sail by day and anchor at night.

As we motored into our second *marsa,* through a more complicated channel than the first, Big Red gave the chortle that I'd become all too familiar with, and promptly died. The reef was only a boat length away. Chris dropped the anchor on the double, with a short scope. I'd gotten in the habit of leaving the main up when I was motoring into an anchorage,

249

just in case the engine conked out. We let it flog in the light breeze as I invoked some 18th century medicine, giving Big Red a quick bleeding. Fortunately she fired back up and we pulled the anchor off the reef and made our way into the *marsa*. Before we reached my target anchor dropping area, she started sputtering again and wheezed to a halt. We managed to coast in and dropped the hook.

I spent the following day puzzling over the engine. After going over all of the fuel lines, and not being able to conceive of a location that air could be entering, I removed the lift pump and poked and prodded it, thinking that the problem might lie in its inner workings. I hoped to find some obvious problem, like a fingernail blocking a valve. Not being familiar with how it was supposed to look, and not finding a fingernail, I just hoped that I'd inadvertently fixed it. After getting things back together I fired the engine back up. She ran as normal and I just hoped for the best.

The engine problem added to the overall uneasy feeling. In addition to needing it for the passage north, the transit of the Suez Canal loomed ahead. Passing through the canal requires two days and 120 miles of motoring. One has to obtain a transit captain and maintain a certain pace. Breakdowns in the canal become a very expensive affair.

With the engine 'fixed,' Chris and I swam to land to explore the sand and scrub. We found a yellow camel's scull slowly turning to dust in a dried salt pond and pried a couple of large, phallic looking teeth out of its jaw for souvenirs. Chris wasn't sure how, but he was confident his tooth would get him laid. He didn't express the sentiment, but I could see it in his devilish grin as he inspected the five inch tooth cradled reverently in his palm.

The following day we headed out in the company of two other boats. While not many sailboats transit the Red Sea in a given season, they all follow pretty much the same path.

We tended to see the same boats on a fairly regular basis and camaraderie not common in other oceans was formed.

The wind was out of the north but from a decent angle so we were able to sail towards our destination without excessive tacking. We kept the motor running however, to try and gauge its level of 'fixedness.' It ran for four hours before I shut it down and called it "perfect."

We continued our northward journey, sailing by day and anchoring by night. If we came across a pleasant anchorage with good snorkeling and spear fishing, we'd stay an extra day and enjoy it. Sometimes we felt the need to make some miles so we'd only stop for the night and be on our way in the morning.

We eventually reached Suakin, Sudan, a port of entry, requiring us to go through the whole checking in riggamarole.

We radioed Port Control as we approached and received instructions in rapid broken English. I had no idea what the guy was saying. I glanced at Chris and Nicole, hoping that perhaps they'd caught more than I. They returned my questioning glance with shrugs. I asked the Port Control guy to repeat himself several times and could tell he was getting frustrated. I sensed he was gesticulating wildly with his hand as he tried to explain what he wanted me to do. In addition to being unclear, he seemed to change his mind in mid stream. The situation may have been exacerbated by a large cruise ship, which seemed quite out of place in a town that consisted entirely of shacks and tents, that was closing in on us from behind. I suspected he just wanted us to go away so he wouldn't have to bother with us.

After some more shoulder shrugging, and driving around in circles, a tug boat came up next to us in order to drop a doctor off to verify that we weren't carrying the plague or anything. The tug driver kept motioning us to stop as if all I had to do was step on the breaks. If I put Big Red in reverse

I knew the bow would yaw to the right and I didn't want the tug, lined with car tire fenders, to rub against Hanuman's supple fiberglass. Also, if we stopped moving we wouldn't have any maneuverability and we'd be at the mercy of the tug driver who, given the dents the side of his steel boat, seemed comfortable bumping into things. I actually wanted to come up next to his boat and hoped he'd stop. Consequently, we ended up circling each other like animals about to strike. We never reached an agreement on the matter. I continued to idol forward and he continued to alternately gun his engine in reverse and forward, sending turbulent white water into Hanuman's propeller. "It's okay if the doctor falls in the water, just don't let that piece of shit hit Hanuman," I informed Chris and Nicole, who were at the rail ready to fend off.

Both on and off transfers went smooth enough. The doctor asked us a few questions, "anyone peeing blood?" and was off.

I only had large scale charts of the region. The whole Suakin area could have fit on the head of thumbtack so I didn't really know where to anchor. I pointed in a vague direction and asked the doctor if he knew where the anchorage was. "Yeah, yeah," he replied, without actually looking where I was pointing.

I had another look at the charts, hoping it would reveal more than it did the first time I'd eyed it, but the chart was a copy of a copy of a chart and the whole area just showed up as a dark smear.

We proceeded further down the channel, hoping that things would become obvious. We eventually came to a 'T'. Neither way looked more appealing than the other. Water depth remained good. I shrugged and decided to go right. Just as I was doing so, some kids on the beach started waving their arms frantically and pointing to the left. "Left it is," I said, shrugging my shoulders once again, and threw the wheel over to port. After coming around the bend, we found our-selves in our own little private bay and dropped anchor in the 30 feet of extremely tranquil murky water.

Anchored in Suakin, Sudan

The peninsula that separated our bay from where we could have ended up was covered with the half eroded rubble of 1300 year old buildings, complete with camels grazing the shoreline; a nostalgic contrast to the shackish looking build-ings that lined the mainland. I wondered what had become of the previous culture. Although not so much that I actually bothered to find out.

An agent was required to check in with officialdom. We hired the only one. Sudan was one of the most expensive countries I'd checked into. I'd long since discovered that there was never any relationship between a country's GDP and their check-in fees. Fortunately, Nicole, Chris, and I split it three ways, so it was a fairly manageable 30 bucks each.

After checking in, we took the beach and made our way to a small restaurant to sample the local cuisine. The ratio to flies to humans in the little dirt floored shack was about a thousand to one, but it was clearly a place that the locals ate. Not that any non-sailor tourists seemed likely to be coming through Suakin. Despite the flies the food was delicious and we waddled back the boat with full bellies.

After digesting my first Sudanese meal I made a couple of strong cups of coffee, looking for a caffeine buzz to give my mental state a little shaking up. The altered state brought me out of the funk I'd been experiencing and I started to feel much better about the trip and life in general.

As I lay on deck, under the African stars, I had a chance to reevaluate my prospective. Chris and Nicole had their only personal dramas going on, just as we all do. I decided my mistake was making their dramas my own. In addition to causing myself aggravation I was probably compounding theirs.

Despite a few short lived minor revelations, when the caffeine wore off, I felt, on the whole, a general sense of apathy toward life. Few things seemed that exciting or that devastating. Neither the present nor the future seemed to hold any interest. I felt as if I could almost fade out of life all together. The feeling was a little unnerving but I found that there was something about being satisfied with any given outcome in life that I found liberating. I was free from desire, and hence, disappointment.

But when one feeling ebbed, another would flood, and I was overcome with the vague notion that I should be cultivating a greater depth of appreciation for all the unique and beautiful moments that surrounded me. I wanted to see the magic in the mundane. I wanted to feel it when the cool morning breeze tickled my shirtless shoulders. I wanted to hear it when that same breeze rippled the placid *marsa* as the sun dipped down behind the Sudanese mountains. I wanted to taste and smell it in my first and last sip of Ceylon tea.

I wanted to see it when I looked at Nicole and Chris. I wanted to see it in my own reflection.

Philosophizing and actual living often seem to resist amalgamation. Having an idea about something, and incorporating it into one's life, are totally separate things. On the boat we found ourselves so constantly engaged with each other and the journey that taking a step back didn't always happen; perhaps for fear of falling off the boat. Getting myself to a point where all of my thoughts and actions originated from a place of clarity, compassion, and understanding, unclouded by my mental baggage, was rare and fleeting, but felt good, though foreign. When I was able to manifest that state a certain part of my brain wanted to rebel against it, preferring its old comforts. Comforts that weighed down my heart, furrowed my brow, and left me feeling hateful and weak, but that nourished my feeling of self importance.

After doing some inland exploring by bus and getting supplies from an open market where one of the vendors showed us a picture of Osama Bin Laden while giving us a thumbs up, smiling, and nodding his head up and down, we pulled anchor and continued north. We anchored behind the protection of an offshore atoll for a couple of days of good snorkeling before leaving with the hope of sailing for a few nights nonstop and making some miles.

The second day out however, the wind started to howl and, after an uncomfortable and slightly scary night, we headed to a nearby anchorage. Nicole was elated that I was flexible about stopping earlier than originally planned. She seemed to have gotten the idea that I'd sail into a storm until it tore the skin off my knuckles. I wasn't sure how she'd formed the idea, but I was happy to demonstrate that I didn't go to sea just for the pain of it.

We started down the long channel of Khor Shinah, wondering where exactly we were going to anchor, when we came around a bluff and saw more boats at anchor than I'd seen since Thailand. "We'll anchor there, I guess." I wasn't impervious to my 'magnetic anchor' theory.

Nicole was happy to be with so many other boats. Chris and I were comfortable with extended silences but Nicole was a social person who didn't revel in the quiet as we did.

We were pinned down for several days waiting for the wind to die. We made the best of it, having an elaborate, by sailor standards, dinner one night with Ewan and Lisa who we'd met previously on their boat Pollux. Olf, the gay German single hander who Nicole was in love with, and Alex, the straight German crewing on the pirated boat, Bambola, who Nicole had a crush on, were also in attendance.

For the occasion I baked some herb bread which had become 'my thing' and Chris made a cake. After his success with Nicole's birthday cake, Chris had gone hog wild with the cake making. He baked one about every other day. When on land, getting Chris' cake baking supplies was a major priority. Fortunately, life at sea had made Chris adaptable, so he could make do with whatever was available. We all loved Chris' cakes and were starting to develop the physique to attest to it. Nicole had what she referred to as a 'gunt,' a condition in which the gut and the cunt meld into one. Chris and I decided that we had 'gicks.' It didn't matter; we were way more in love with the cakes than our bodies.

Nicole made her 'cheesy pasta;' a delightful combination of processed Kraft cheese, canned tuna, flour, and pasta. It was one of our favorite meals.

Ewan and Lisa still had some booze left over from Thailand. Nicole, Chris and I had been dry for way too long so we relished every sip of the straight whiskey.

THE RED SEA

The following morning the wind had died and there was dew on the deck (which Ewan said was supposed to indicate wind coming from the south), so we headed out in the company of four other boats, including Olf's, Pollux, and Bambola.

We snaked our way through the channel back to sea, where we found a gentle breeze filling in from the northwest. We raised the main but kept the motor going. Before long the wind veered and started coming out of the NNE and we tacked, let the jib out, and cut the engine.

Over the next half hour the wind piped up to 20 knots. As we reefed we noticed, one by one, all of the other boat tacking into a nearby anchorage. The next anchorage was only ten miles away and I decided that we'd keep on going as long we could; hoping to at least make it there.

Nicole had just prepared a meal that we were in the midst of shoveling down. It took only five minutes for the waves to catch up to the wind. A wave hit the starboard bow and sprayed my food, convincing me that perhaps anchoring wasn't such a bad idea. I was anxious to get away from the convoy we'd somehow become a part of but decided it wasn't worth four or five hours of pounding into a head wind just to make ten miles. And ultimately there wasn't a rush. The sooner I got to the Med., the sooner I'd start blowing through what money I had left.

Marsa Wasi

Marsa Wasi was a minor scene. Boats were crisscrossing all over the place, some dropping anchor, some pulling anchor because they weren't pleased with their first set. Olf was buzzing around the whole *marsa* looking for shallows. Having neither windlass nor crew to help him pull his anchor he always found the shallowest place he could.

Eventually everyone settled in and I got out my mask and snorkel, ostensibly to check the anchor. Saying I was getting in to check the anchor unburdened me from company when I went snorkeling afterwards. Nicole hadn't actually been in the water for quite awhile. She was worried about an infection on her foot. And it wasn't that I didn't enjoy snorkeling with Chris, I just wanted to indulge in the complete freedom that the water can provide; without the restriction of having a companion. Plus I cherished what sparse alone time I could create.

I found the snorkeling to be some of the best I had experienced; spectacular colors, a good variety of soft corals and sponges, and a healthy density of fish. On the down side there were a shit ton of jellyfish. But after a few bounced off my face, I realized that they didn't have much of a sting and I began to enjoy swimming though them. It was easy to zone out in a school of jellyfish, forgetting where and who I was; becoming one of them.

Back on Hanuman an afternoon fatigue had set in. Chris' limp feet hung out of his bunk. Nicole had dragged my blanket onto the foredeck, where she lay curled in a ball; the wind ruffling the blanket's edges as she slept. A pleasant serenity had swept over the boat. I sat in the cockpit and soaked it in. A dry, yet surprisingly cool wind was blowing off the Arabian Desert and across the Red Sea, sending ripples into our *marsa*. The wind anesthetized my mind, taking any cares across the water and off into the Sudanese mountains where they dissolved into the desert.

My perception of the calm serenity, where all things seemed to be vibrating in harmonic synchronicity with the wind, yet not really moving at all, was broken as a dinghy entered my field of view. Four people headed towards Ewan and Lisa's boat, Pollux.

The sight seemed so at odds with all I was experiencing that I felt something was wrong. I'd previously turned off the VHF radio, because static was filling Hanuman with an annoying buzz, but decided to turn it back on just in case something was wrong.

"May-day, may-day, may-day, this is sailing vessel Pollux. We have a person who has stopped breathing." The calm voice then gave the coordinates which I instinctively started to write down before realizing that the odds of there being a Pollux other than the one in the *marsa* with us, broadcasting a 'may-day' within radio range, were astronomical. I looked out the companionway at Pollux 300 yards away.

Chris jumped out of his bunk asking if I'd gotten those coordinates. "It's Pollux... they're right there," I replied, still unable to believe that there could be something wrong on Pollux.

Chris was a very 'take charge' sort of guy and wanted to get on the VHF right away. I suggested we wait to see if a doctor or someone with any actual medical knowledge responded to the 'may-day'. "This is what I've been trained for mate," he announced. I'd been under the impression that he was a surveyor.

We waited for a brief moment and then Chris got on the radio and made contact. "We could use any help we could get," pleaded the guy on the other end of the radio. The gravity of the situation stank in for me at that moment. I'd initially pictured a hoard of people jammed in Pollux' small saloon pulling out their hair, yelling a bunch of different things to do. I thought we might just make things worse, but after hearing the guy on the radio I knew we had to get over there as quickly as possible.

Chris had been living for this moment. He started taking charge of the scene on the radio before we even got there. "Get me over there," Chris demanded, as though expecting me to conjure up a helicopter.

Unfortunately Sputnik was stowed and deflated so there was no way to 'get us over there' very quickly. The fastest way, I decided, was probably to swim. "Get me over there," Chris yelled again, but to no one in particular. He sounded like some crack specialist being sent in to defuse a high tech bomb that only he could handle. We managed to flag down Ben, a kid from the boat 'Why Knot,' to give us a ride. Nicole decided to stay behind. "Nicole, if you're not confident with CPR, it's better not to come," Chris stated with authority. I saw it as another one of his 'I'm the man' sort of comments, but I was happy for her not to come, as it fell in line with my 'too many people can be more of a hindrance than a help' theory.

Ben dropped us off on Pollux and into a whole different world. Climbing off the dinghy, I could see through the companionway and caught glimpses of a prostrate Ewan underneath various others performing CPR. Lisa was in a state of controlled hysterics, moving furniture around to make more room. "Calm down and have a seat," Chris commanded Lisa. I waited for him to slap her and possibly give her a good shaking. She actually wasn't all that frantic and the table did need moving.

Descending into the main saloon, we got a full view and the situation. Ewan was lying on his back, limp. Olf, it turned out, was a nurse and was giving chest compressions while Alex and Kelso (from 'Why Knot') were alternating breathing into Ewan's mouth.

Ewan's neck and upper chest were blue. His face was yellowish and his eyes open. Things did not look good.

Chris started switching off with Olf and I got in rotation with Alex and Kelso. I came in after a short stint by Kelso. It was a 'full on' experience. Ewan's face was speckled with mucus, saliva, and some red chunks, which I figured to be either coagulated blood or the beets he had been eating prior to his collapse.

I pinched his nose, tilted his head back, lifted his chin, covered his open mouth with mine, and blew. His blue chest heaved, animated, life-like. I brought my mouth away from his and air bellowed out with a shocking flapping noise; like someone snoring violently. The smell was pungent and heavy, and stuck in my mind long after the image of Ewan's face faded. It reminded me of a digested version of a bean sprout salad we'd eaten the night before. Though was more likely a combination of the beets, which were a matter of concern to Lisa, who conjectured may have caused an allergic reaction, and whatever chemicals his body was producing, or had produced, in the heat of the cardiac failure. In addition to the smell, the intensity of being so close to his empty, open, cold blue eyes was saturating. After several breaths I rotated off, more out of a desire for a break from the powerful intimacy of the situation than from any real sense of fatigue.

We'd gone through three or four breathing rotations when, on Alex's shift, blood started coming out of Ewan's mouth when he exhaled. I wiped the blood from Ewan's face between Alex's breaths. Alex's cheeks and chin were splattered with blood. We all began to silently acknowledge the futility of the situation. "No one has to continue if they don't want to, given the blood," Chris informed us. I don't think anyone was too concerned with infection, but we were all thinking that this might be 'it,' and our CPR began to tail off. We made cautious eye contact with one another during exaggerated pauses between breath and compression. "Olf?" beckoned Lisa, who was in the cockpit being comforted by a female friend from another boat. She lunged towards the companionway unable to grasp why we were stopping and was gently pulled back by her friend. "Olf?" she repeated. We all saw the fear in her deep set eyes and wordlessly resumed CPR. The charade continued only briefly however. Kelso, who was the most senior member of our team, patted Alex and Olf on the shoulder, "Guys…guys, I'm stopping it." We all looked up in a daze. "He hasn't had a pulse since we began," Kelso continued, shaking his head gravely. We all nodded. It was over.

We lifted him onto the settee, put a sheet over his body to the neck, and supported his head with a pillow. I believe we were all wondering if we should cover his face or not. It was the sort of situation we'd only read about, or seen in the movies. Kelso eventually put a small towel over his face.

Lisa looked down, saw what had happened, and let out a bone curdling screech. She came down, took the towel off his face and cried in disbelief. She moved away for a moment and I thought she said to cover his face, so I did. In reality she'd said, "Don't cover his face." I apologized for the misunderstanding. I certainly didn't want to add aggravation to her agony.

I felt that perhaps I should be crying like some of the others but I just felt dry and empty. I was in a daze, still in disbelief. Ewan was only 31 years old. He'd just invited Nicole, Chris and I over for dinner the previous night, and shared the last of his whiskey with us.

We had no idea why he died. Lisa said they'd just eaten a can of beats, laid down to take a nap, and a short while after, he sat up and called to Lisa. Moments later he had a seizure and collapsed. Lisa screamed over to Olf, who was anchored nearby, and he swam over and started CPR while Lisa called for help on the VHF.

When Ewan and Lisa were visiting Asmara, Eritrea, Ewan had gotten sick on two occasions. He had to be taken to the hospital and given fluids but the doctors didn't seem to be able to find anything wrong with him. The day prior to his death he said he was feeling all right and had done a long hike and gone snorkeling.

When the may-day was broadcasted, some Sudanese authorities and a US warship were contacted on a SSB radio. I didn't learn the contents of the conversations but neither party seemed to be of any help. Prior to Ewan's death, I had the poorly thought out impression that when someone was dying everyone around would drop what they were doing, put expense aside, and in the case of the US warship, send a helicopter with a medical team to the scene to help. Realizing there were probably plenty of Sudanese dying with little help from anyone, and a war being waged in Iraq with countless people dying and suffering, I slowly accepted that in the grand scheme of things one sailor's problem was not the world's problem, or even concern. It wasn't a particularly comforting realization.

After Ewan, who'd suddenly gone from being an individual to a body, was made to look comfortable on the settee most of us filed into the cockpit. Lisa talked to him down below about the times they'd had and the times they should have had. Various people went down to comfort her and returned to the cockpit in tears.

Only the night before, Lisa and Ewan had announced that Lisa was pregnant. They had conceived the child consciously three months prior in Nua Relia, Sri Lanka, in a cozy inn next to a tea plantation.

Eventually Ben gave me a ride back to Hanuman. Lisa was taken to one of the other boats, and Chris and Olf stayed behind on Pollux because Lisa didn't want Ewan to be alone. Nicole and I made dinner for the four of us and brought it over to Pollux. Even in the heavy shadow of death Nicole and I still managed to get into a fight over the ingredients of the meal. Despite my moments of realization about how I should interact, my rapport with Nicole had only become more strained.

Once on Pollux we decided to eat on Olf's boat. Pollux cockpit was rather small and cramped for the four of us and the idea of eating down below with Ewan wasn't too appealing. We did roll him over however, to get at his last bottle of Bundaberg rum. We figured he'd want us to have it. We had a small wake with the last of Ewan's rum, told Ewan stories, talked about death, the afterlife (or lack thereof) and laughed.

On the following day the grieving ended for all but Lisa, and logistics had to be addressed. We couldn't just shove Ewan into the sea with the last stitch threw his nose as they'd done in the old days. Beyond that, Lisa was in no condition to take off solo in Pollux.

Eventually (getting the doctor to the remote townless and roadless area where we were anchored took a couple of days) a doctor, required by the Sudanese officials we contacted on the SSB radio, came to collect Ewan and take him to a hospital where an autopsy could be performed before sending his body back to New Zealand for burial. Lisa would fly back with him.

There was still the huge matter of how to get Pollux to a reasonable locale. We couldn't, in good conscience, just leave her anchored in Marsa Wasi. Chris volunteered to help bring Pollux north to a marina in Hurgada, Egypt. In fact he even volunteered to do it by himself.

Chris had learned much during our journey from Thailand, and we all admired his bravery and desire to be of help, but sending him out alone on a boat he was unfamiliar with into the Red Sea was more than we all though prudent. We'd planned to stay in convoy as a group, in order to be of assistance to whoever was on Pollux, but we also realized that when you're at sea and you get in the shit, you're there by yourself. The marina was still 400 miles to the north; not a trivial distance, especially in the Red Sea.

After several days on the SSB (short for Single Side Band, a two way radio with much greater range than a VHF) we made contact with a boat south of us who had an extra crew member willing to join Chris. The only problem was that they were well south of us, so we'd have to wait several days for them to catch up.

Sue, Lisa's friend who'd accompanied her to the airport, returned. Apparently the autopsy on Ewan was inconclusive. The doctor said he died because his heart stopped; which is of course, simply the definition of death. She returned with a few bags of fresh produce to split among the boats that'd been waiting. It had been over a month since any of had access to fresh vegetables. Hanuman was down to a couple of potatoes and a few onions. On top of that, our canned goods supply had dwindled to a few cans of mint flavored peas and syrupy lynches. We'd also run out of sugar, meaning an end to Chris' cake making spree. We went through cake withdraw afterwards, but decided it was for the best.

Tension slowly crept into our group as a prime weather window came and went without us. 'Why Knot' departed, since there was really nothing more they could do, and because they had people waiting for them further north. They contributed 80 liters of diesel towards Pollux' journey. Pollux had a good little engine that could really push her along. The plan was to rely mostly on the motor, which many boats had been doing for quite some time anyhow. 'Why Knot' was wished well and sent on their way but there was a sense that several other boats wished to accompany them. They stayed out of an obligation they may have been beginning to question.

The subtle tension that blanketed Marsa Wasi surfaced when the food that Sue had brought was distributed. The details elude my recollection. Perhaps the vegetables didn't divide nicely into the five piles representing the five boats that'd stayed behind. There was yelling. It started to resemble an episode of Survivor. I'm sure many could have listed several people they'd have been happy to vote off. I usually tried to stay as quiet as possible at our regular group meetings to avoid any soap-operaish interactions. Chris usually vocalized his thoughts actively at the meetings. I both admired him and found many of his ideas rather juvenile.

I developed a pleasant routine of spear fishing (which had become necessary to turn plain rice into a decent meal), reading, and lounging around. Boats came and left 'our bay,' as we'd deemed it, while we waited. Seeing a new boat come into the bay was always an exciting event; certainly one worth setting my book down for. Chris, Nicole, Olf, Alex, and I became a tight sub group of the original Marsa Wasi crowd. We were all on the younger side and shared ambivalence towards leaving right away. We also had a lack of alcohol in common. Every new boat entering the *marsa* was potential prey. As a boat tacked and made way for our bay I'd stick my nose in the air, "sniff, sniff, whad-a-ya' think they got?" "Maybe rum…I think they have rum," Olf stated optimistically. "I like rum," I replied approvingly, as I nodded my head. "Girls, I smell girls," Chris added.

Girls never arrived. They rarely do in the middle of the desert. Arrack, a cousin of rum, did show up. Dave, a young American guy, was sailing with his aunt and uncle and had been dying for someone to drink the Arrack he'd been carting along since Sri Lanka with. We were happy to help and added Dave and his Arrack to our nightly card playing and roach killing ritual on Hanuman.

Eventually Mustang Sally, with Pollux' other crew member, Giovanni, arrived. Naturally we had to wait several more days for a weather window before we could head north, giving Chris just enough time to discover that he couldn't stand Giovanni. It had been decided that Giovanni would be captain, having more experience, which didn't make matters any more pleasant for Chris.

Never the less, Chris packed up all his shit and moved into his new home the night before we were to leave. I wondered if he would be returning. In addition to being unhappy about losing a friend, I also had some selfish misgiving about seeing him go. Nicole had decided she was leaving, "for sure this time," when we got to Safaga, Egypt, which would leave me crewless. In addition to not wanting to sail alone from there to the Suez Canal, I'd also been hoping to preserve some of my long since depleted funds by splitting the cost of the transit with Chris.

Fortunately Nicole and I had been getting along a little better. We had a lengthy talk one evening, which seemed to help. Also her crush on Olf, despite the fact that he was gay, seemed to make her more pleasant to be around.

We woke up to a light but steady breeze out of the north, which usually predicted even stronger winds out of the north as the day progressed. But after three weeks at anchor, we decided we were ready to head out and put Marsa Wasi behind us.

Northern Red Sea

Less than two hours out of Marsa Wasi the wind started howlin' out of the north and we all dove into Marsa Gwiliab for shelter. We'd only covered eight mile but were relieved to be in a new spot. It wasn't much, but it felt like progress, and separated us from the tragedy of Marsa Wasi.

We were pinned down for another three days in Marsa Gwiliab. I rarely left the boat. I spent most of my time reading, shifted my position occasionally to increase my comfort level, and dozed off between chapters.

Nicole swam over to the other boats, chit-chatted, and returned to Hanuman at the end of the day to fill me in on all of the gossip.

The final destination for Pollux was supposed to be Cyprus, where it was hoped that Lisa would be able to sell the boat and make a decent profit. Stewart, from Essence, had volunteered to take the boat from Egypt, where Chris was headed, and deliver it through the canal to Cyprus. Giovanni had volunteered to go with him but, after a few days on Pollux, decided he had some pressing issues back in Italy and couldn't do it. Chris had volunteered to go all the way to Cyprus on

Pollux if Nicole was willing to stay onboard Hanuman. He even said he'd still be willing to pay half of Hanuman's transit fees. Given Chris' generosity I felt a little guilty for my selfish concerns regarding paying the transit fee all by myself.

After three days, where we frequently experienced 35 knot gusts, we had a weather window and headed north. We made it about 12 miles before we were blown into Marsa Umbilia. On the way in Big Red went through its all too familiar death rattle and shut down. Fortunately Marsa Umbilia had a much wider opening than most of the *marsas* we'd been to so we were able to sail in and anchor without Big Red.

I spent the rest of the day 'fixing' the engine. For lack of being able to find any other problem I decided that my secondary fuel filter was clogged. "My diesel could be dirty," I figured, "clogging the filter prematurely." I replaced the filter and she fired up nicely. I ran her for half an hour and called it good.

The following day, with the motor 'fixed,' we head back out to sea. There was potential for one more anchorage before crossing foul bay, where no anchorages existed, but conditions were favorable so the whole group, anxious to get as far north as possible, continued on.

By mid day the wind still hadn't come up and we motored along under bare poles. I couldn't relax with the motor running. My ear was trained on every rise and fall of the pistons. And then I heard it, that first little sputtering that diagnosed death. I mourned briefly as Big Red took her last breath, gasped, and wheezed to a halt.

I took my usual moment of evaluation and decided on a course of action. I went through the usual bleeding process but no air bubbles were produced. Fuel wasn't getting to the engine. I decided there was either a clog or a problem with the lift pump.

I was a bit relieved, now that the engine had actually broken down. It seemed a respite from just waiting for it to fail. When it was running, all it could do was break down. Once it was broken, things couldn't get any worse (regarding the engine), only improve.

I'd dropped off the convoy and they called me on the radio to see what was going on. "Just a little engine problem… should be able to fix it… go on without us." Nicole wasn't too excited about the "go on without us," but the fleet didn't need any more encouragement and continued on.

Since I'd just changed the filter, thinking I had a clogging issue, I decided to proceed forward with the thought that it was the lift pump. I went back to the old faithful jerry can method, bypassing the main fuel tanks, with the additional feature of hanging the jerry can above the engine. I started a siphon, so that gravity could do the lift pump's job.

Back in Australia, after Peter Perfect had saved my ass helping me fix the engine, he mentioned, out of the blue, that one could bypass the lift pump by using a jerry can to gravity feed the engine fuel. For some reason his off handed statement had stuck in my head, and as I tied the jerry can into place I imagined him winking at me; like old St. Nick in *T'was the Night Before Christmas*. As Peter floated around in my head I imagined him as an over grown cherub sent to help me on my way.

As I madly wrenched away, covering myself in diesel, a powerful noise that sounded like thunder underwater gave me a jolt. I ran up on deck and was relieved to see we weren't on a reef. "What was that," Nicole asked. "I have no idea but I don't like it." It was a deep cracking that sounded like depth charges going off nearby; or at least what I imagined depth charges sounding like. There were no ships with in sight. I shrugged and went back to work on the engine, enveloped by an eerie feeling that made me want to get Big Red going, as much to cover up the strange noise, as to get us moving.

In my agitated state I almost slipped and fell on the diesel I'd spilt as I maneuvered around the engine. After a few more minutes of knuckle skinning and tying things in place, we managed to get Big Red fired up and we were on our way.

Problem solved? Who knew, but we were moving and no longer able to hear the strange noise so all seemed well enough.

A few hours later the wind built from a favorable direction and we shut down the engine. It was nice to turn it off, rather than to have it simply die. It gave me the comforting illusion of control.

The rest of the fleet continued to motor sail and slowly pulled further from sight. Nicole sighed longing as Olf's boat slid below the horizon. It was refreshing to be on our own, at least from my perspective. Most of the group was trying to make it to Sharm Luli before sunset the next day, when our weather window was supposed to slam shut.

Ras Banas

Nicole and I arrived at Ras Banas, Egypt the following day. Despite favorable winds, we decided to anchor based on the weather forecast. I was tempted to continue on, since conditions were perfect, but knowing the kind of ass wupin' the Red Sea could generate, I decided to play It safe. I questioned my decision as the sun set and a gentle wind blew from the south. But in the middle of the night a nasty northerly filled in, breaking the anchor snubber, and I knew we'd chosen wisely.

The wind blew tirelessly for days. I was mildly anxious to get to a place where I could e-mail and let people know I was alright and still going to make it to the Med., but other than that I was perfectly content to be right where I was. My occasionally intense desire to get to the Med. had vanished. I was still excited for it but I felt I could see clearly how it would play out. I deemed the Red Sea more exotic and less predictable. It was the hunt. The Med. would be the feast. And as much as I loved feasting, I was blissfully submersed in the hunt. My mind was clear and ready to take on any challenges placed before it. I felt a strong inner energy even though I'd done very little in the way of exercise and probably wasn't in that great of shape. I believed that I was right where I should be and that there was truly nowhere to go. The wind howled but I felt safe and cozy in the little haven that Hanuman created for us to read and play Scrabble.

It would also have been a great environment for eating if we'd had any decent food left. We were down to rice, pasta, flour, and bunch of little packets of curry paste. On the upside I'd quickly lost the 'gick' I'd acquired during the era of cake. I actually reveled in being low in food; relishing every little luxury we were able to create.

In addition to being extremely low on food we were down to our last little bottle of kerosene to run the stove. To make matters worse Nicole spilled enough kerosene to cook for days while she was filling the stove's reservoir. I observed the debacle wordlessly, knowing anything I might say would only aggravate the situation.

We were also dangerously low on water. Fortunately some friends, Joanna and Dell on Limbo, with a water maker had pulled in the same day we did and offered to make us water. Jo seemed a little starved for feminine company and invited us over for dinner. It started off with a glass of white wine; chilled white wine no less. I could've been satisfied with just the white wine but it was followed by pasta with meat sauce. Meat sauce! I hadn't had any non-fish meat in months. I swooned as its fatty juices coated my mouth. The pasta was accompanied by fresh baked bread, covered in some delicious seeds, and a salad. A salad! Ahh… the wonders of refrigeration.

During our meal time conversations I'd been trying to down play the low level of our provisions, due to some sense of pride, but Nicole seemed eager to let them know where we stood. I forgave her since it lead to Jo and Dell donating three angry looking potatoes, two cans of tuna in oil, a small browning cabbage, and a rusting can of water chestnuts. These items might seem like a rather modest offering while one is gazing into the cluttered depths of their refrigerator, wondering what will satisfy that post dinner craving, but in the middle of the Red Sea they changed eating from a chore to a delight. We'd come to believe that after a good 20 or 30 shakes, Italian seasoning transformed from a spice to a vegetable.

We busted into the tuna first. Normally I'd drain the oil overboard, but in our calorie starved state, only pooh was getting dumped overboard. We couldn't just shovel the tuna down without cutting it with something for more bulk, so I made up some crepish type things out of flour, water, and baking soda, which we decided resembled a tortilla. We added the tuna, along with some shaved cabbage and spices, and called it a fish taco. "Ohh, captain, you've really outdone yourself this time," Nicole moaned with delight. Standards were low.

I spent an afternoon staring at the can of water chestnut until it finally hit me. I dove into the spice cabinet and started digging around. The spice cabinet was still quite formidable, so it took some digging, but eventually I found the half used packet of tempura powder that I was looking for. Fortunately we still had vegetable oil, so tempura battered water chestnuts were on. The stove produced a nice hot flame capable to heating the oil up to a good temperature; never a guarantee. Often times all it could muster was a sputtering smoky flame which left the cabin top black with soot and the pasta hard. The stove could require a scientific exactness, combined with a Zen-like focus, to get it going well, or sometimes, going at all.

We pulled the golden nuggets of deep fried goodness out of the oil and dipped them in a sauce I'd whipped up from a random assortment of spices. We decided that as long as the oil was hot we should add fries to the mix. We cut up one of our angry potatoes and chucked it in. "Fuckin' delicious

Fellasio!" "Yeah, nothing like a bit of grease to lift ones spirits." "I won't even mention how great this would be with some katsup," Nicole couldn't help but add. By 'some' Nicole meant like half a bottle. "If you didn't consider it a food group we might still have some left," I added. "I do love my catsup," Nicole followed with a grin.

The group of boats that we'd been traveling with was anchored about 50 miles to the north and getting pretty antsy to move on. They were beyond the range of our VHF but Joanne and Dell had been in communication with them on their SSB radio.

The weather report for May 30th, 2003 called for calming winds. The 'poke my head out of the companionway' report on the 30th said it was still windy as hell. We learned later that day that the northern group had decided to take off anyhow but was regretting it as they pounded through wind and wave. I experienced a brief moment of being left behind before remembering that I was right where I was supposed to be. I could see the wistful look on Nicole's face as she thought about Olf, her gay love interest, sailing further from her.

We anticipated leaving the following morning, hoping that the weather window had just been a little delayed. I checked the engine fluid levels to make sure everything was kosher. I wasn't in the habit of checking the coolant level. It had never needed topping up. Nicole looked over my shoulder as I went through my routine. "Aren't you going to check the coolant?" "Nah, the coolant's never given me any problems," I responded casually. Checking the coolant didn't require more than twisting the cap off and looking in the reservoir so, in favor of prudence, I decided to check it. Bone dry, not a trace of coolant. "Fuck… that's not ideal."

In a heady moment of contemplation I'd decided terms like 'good' and 'bad' were too subjective to be of value so I chose 'ideal.' In truth, I was thinking, "that fucking sucks, definitely not good at all."

Optimistically, I filled up the reservoir with some premixed coolant and water that I had lying around and hoped everything would 'be just fine.' I started the engine, vented the system, and shut it down. The reservoir was still full, which seemed like a good sign. Which is to say: 'it seemed ideal for the functioning of the engine.'

We awoke to a dewy dawn. The deck was muddy from all of the desert dust that had accumulated during our windy week at anchor. I had to dive into the cool water to untangle the anchor chain that had wrapped around numerous coral heads. Nicole muscled up the slack.

One of the most unanticipated aspects of the Red Sea was the temperature. I'd expected it to be sweltering. I imagined my bunk being a merciless sweatbox. I'd visited Eritrea in the summer a few years prior, via land, and the air temperature had been barely tolerable. The water offered little relief. We arrived in March and it was downright chilly. The water, while not 'cold' by most standards, hovered around 73 degrees. Add 20 knots of wind and snorkeling excursions became brief.

After an hour of untangling I was back on board, a bit bloodied, but free of entanglements. We motored out from behind the protective point and back into the open ocean. A few camels looked up briefly before returning to their chewing. We felt invigorated to be moving again after a week of vegetating. The idea of heading to Safaga, an actual town where we could fulfill our capitalistic imperative to buy things, like food and beer, was exhilarating.

A breeze came up just as we cleared the headland and I shut down the engine. I was relieved to find the coolant reservoir full. For the remainder of the day we tacked north in a steady breeze but as the sun set it was reduced to a whisper. We sailed until we could no longer keep Hanuman pointed in a consistent direction and, after confirming all the fluid levels, decide to fire up Big Red. "Click… click, click, click." It had been ages since Big Red had refused to turn over at all. Nicole contained the sense of dread she surely felt.

It was a different sort of clicking than I'd experienced in New Caledonia after getting stuck on the reef but I thought it couldn't hurt to try the old screw driver on the starter trick. It only resulted in more of the same clicking. Nicole looked on with hopeful dismay. She was ready to be in Safaga where she planned on ending her journey. If she could have gotten out and pushed she would have done so.

I had the feeling, which was unfortunately the basis for most of my engine work, that the engine, for some reason, wasn't getting enough juice. The clicks sounded weak; like the engine was getting enough power to click, but enough not to actually turn over. I traced the path of the starting wires giving them a little tug and shake where I deemed appropriate. Eventually I got to the main negative battery breaker. I'd been suspicious of its condition for some time. I gave it a good couple of back and forths, went back to the ignition button, pressed it, and was relieved when I heard the roar of the engine. I gave Nicole one of my 'see, no problem' smiles, coupled with a little 'everything seems to be just fine' shoulder shrug, and we were off. "I couldn't do it like you do," Nicole proclaimed with weary relief.

We motored through the night, pumping diesel out of the main tank, with a small, frustrating hand pump, into a jerry can, which we then poured mostly into the jerry can hanging from the ceiling. We repeated the procedure every hour or so.

Big Red still lacked gauges so we wouldn't have any warning if it lost coolant and overheated. I instructed Nicole to smell for any change in engine temperature. "Smell?" she snorted. "Yeah, smell. Everything smells different as it heats up. Take yourself for instance." I imagine Nicole took my

OK…

instructions as, "hang out in the cockpit and fantasize about life on land."

We shut the engine down every four hours to check the coolant level, feeling that by the time it started to smell different, it could be too late. The first shut down went fine but the second revealed an empty reservoir. "That sucks," I offered in a slightly defeated tone. Nicole surveyed the situation silently with a look of disapproval. I decided to be cautious and avoid using the engine. "I guess we just have to sail from here and hope for the best." I filled the coolant reservoir just so it would be ready. But when I checked it later that day it was empty, despite the fact that the engine hadn't been run.

The second night out brought us within striking range of Safaga and when the darkness faded on the following morning a few sun bleached buildings were visible in the distance. Unfortunately the wind was light and our progress slow. Safaga was an Egyptian port of entry and we wanted to be able to clear costumes quickly and have Hanuman in a secure anchorage so that sunset would find us with beers in our hands.

We slowly inched our way into the heart of the deep bay that boarded the commercial port and customs. Entry regulations required us to tie up to the main pier for the checking in process. Our plan was for Nicole to fill the coolant reservoir with water (we were out of coolant at this point) just before I started the engine. We'd then motor up to the pier and get Hanuman tied up quickly before all of the coolant drained out. Nicole would also stand by down below to do a refill if she saw vast amounts of water coming out of the water pump, which we'd determined was the leaking point.

"How things lookin' down there?" I asked after starting the engine. "Fine…I guess." "Everything smell all right?" I ventured. "The engine smells fine, I reek." We eased our way up to the pier, managed to tie up to a dock designed for 100 foot steel boats, and promptly shut down the engine which, interestingly enough, hadn't lost any water.

After marching around in the dust for a couple hours clearing customs, we sailed through a tight shallow channel to the anchorage area and anchored rather sloppily under sail; not my proudest moment. I wanted the anchor to be well set so I dropped it while we still had some momentum in order to use our speed to dig it in. Having more speed than prudence dictated, I ended up dragging the anchor along the bottom until it grabbed a rock and jerked the chain violently, almost talking off a finger.

"Perfect! Let's go get some fuckin' beers." It had been a long day and we were relieved to be done with officialdom and have the boat anchored; to 'be there.' Thankfully POS fired up after only a dozen or so pulls and we made our way to shore. We didn't have to walk more than 50 yards before we found a bar attached to a dive shop.

I'd only managed to get in a couple of deep, can denting draws on my beer before a portly looking Egyptian named Abrahim sidled up to our table and started talking at us. His porn star mustache saddled his chubby smile as he gave us the once over. I hadn't slept much the night before and just stared straight ahead, feeling the acquiescent resignation of a saddle sore pony at a fair about to be taken for a ride. I had no interest in taking to him. I answered his questions as briefly as I considered polite. He went through the list of all the things he could get us if we needed them. I did need many things, but at that moment, none as much as dry land from which to contemplate the horizon and a cold beer. I also had a certain affinity for wandering around a dusty unfamiliar town tracking down the little items I needed for the boat. Short of that I preferred asking taxi drivers where to find things. I was always skeptical of people who approached me offering help. It may sound cynical but nine times out of ten they were looking for something from me rather than for me.

Nicole, a natural talker, prattled on with Abrahim. I was content with the arrangement. It initially allowed me to just sit, stare, drink, and listen. Annoyingly, my apathetic voyeurism ended with Abrahim's question/statement. "You hungry? I take you guys to my cousin's restaurant in town. Great food... not expensive." By the look of us, he probably felt it wise to tack on the 'not expensive.' "No, we'll just get something around here," I said, using a full sentence for the first time. I had no desire to get wrapped up in his world. "No, nothing good to eat around here, all very expensive," he retorted shaking his head as though the idea were ludicrous. "We'll just eat back at the boat," I countered. "What kind of food does your cousin have?" Nicole asked as she considered our options on the boat. That was it, we'd shown interest, his teeth were set.

I shot-gunned the back seat so I that didn't have to talk. The car ride was enjoyable. I was amused to move through space so effortlessly. Dinner was fine. Abrahim ended up eating most of the food that we ordered. It wasn't all that cheap however, and I got a rather confused look from the owner of the restaurant when I referred to him as Abrahim's cousin. "Not actual cousin...like cousin," Abrahim responded to my quizzical expression. We were eventually deposited back on the beach with a grin and a lighter wallet. "I will see you tomorrow," Abrahim said, waving goodbye. I was sure he would. He had his teeth in. The scuba bar was closed. We sputtered back to Hanuman, appallingly sober, in the half deflated dinghy.

We spent the next couple of days eating at the nearby restaurants which served inexpensive pizza (pizza!) and wine and getting things for the boat. Abraham did prove useful in finding a place to get replacement seals for Big Red's water pump. He also got a few other things for us, all of which, of course, came with an undisclosed commission. I had nothing against paying for a service but detested the feeling that I was grabbing my ankles as I was doing so.

Feeling good about fixing the engine, or at least its most broken part, I decided to chance leaving Hanuman unattended for an overnighter to Luxor to check out some Egyptian stuff. Nicole had made arrangements to fly out of Luxor so we took a bus together and parted ways on arrival.

Later that day, as I walked lazily along the Nile, I saw Nicole jump from the back of a horse drawn carriage, run to the edge of the sidewalk above the Nile, take a quick picture, and start running back to the carriage. "Hey, Nicole." She threw me a panicked, confused glance. "Fellasio!" she screamed giving me a bear hug. It felt like we'd been separated for longer than three hours. I joined her on the carriage. "I've got to get to the travel agency. I missed the first flight and I've got to get on the next one to meet up with my ticket back to Canada." She got a ticket but ended up having several hours to kill. We chartered a *felucca* and sailed up the Nile while we were served tea. I got to steer.

Sailing up the Nile in a felucca

To the Suez

After getting Pollux to Hurgada and a trip to the Pyramids in Giza, Chris, thankfully, made his way back to Hanuman. "How were the pyramids?" "Kick ass mate." "Cairo?" "Real shit-hole aye." "Any chicks? "Met this one Canadian bird, made out a bit, but that was all. Had a husband or something." "Ready to hit the Med?" "Hell yeah mate."

After provisioning, and another 'fuck-off' assault on the roaches, we pulled anchor feeling eager for the Med. It wasn't quite ready for us however.

The first day out was agreeable and we tacked back and forth across the narrowing Red Sea in a pleasant breeze, contemplating the fruits of the Mediterranean. Night fell as we approached the narrow northern segment of the Red Sea. We kept a vigilant watch and tacked frequently to avoid small islands and reefs. The wind increased throughout the night and we battled our way northward under heavily reefed sails, taking a beating as we did so. The beating was familiar but not welcome and we traded watches exchanging only grunts and pertinent information. "Ship at ten o'clock, moving north." "How long has it been this fuckin' windy?" "Half hour." "Hmh."

During the predawn dog watch, a seam in the upper main parted from leech to luff, leaving a gaping hole in the main. It was way too rough and we were way too exhausted to contemplate fixing it on the go. Flying just the staysail and a small portion of the jib, our speed fluctuated between negative one and one mile an hour. It was time to put Big Red's new water pump seals to the test. She fired up nicely, always a good sign, and I throttled her up until I saw an average of 3.5 knots on the GPS. I didn't want to push her too hard and blow out the new handmade seals on the water pump. The guy who made the seals said to come back if they didn't work so I didn't have full faith in them. And 3.5 knots would be enough to get us to the next anchorage before sunset.

It was as a long slow slog but we found ourselves anchored on the west coast of Saudi Arabia by late afternoon. We were exhausted but wanted to be off at first light so we got to work sewing up the main. I started the process but passed out mid stitch so Chris finished it off, doing most of the work; it was a long seam. I woke up just after sunset, still sitting upright in the settee.

We weighed anchor at sunrise and were rewarded with a delightful day of sailing in moderated wind and mellow seas. We were still beating to windward, and having to tack back and forth, but the effect was more relaxing than tiring. As night fell and the wind lightened we found ourselves close to the Egyptian coast, trying to get the most out of the tack we were on. I went below to plot our position. "Looks like we've drifted into region marked, 'unexploded mines, keep clear,'" I commented. Chris peered down at me to see if I was joking. "Well, I reckon we ought to tack, aye," Chris replied, nonchalantly. "Yeah, I guess, but we're only on the edge of the mine area and we're doing so well on this tack," I added. "Yeah, but then it only takes one mine, aye mate." "True."

TO THE SUEZ

We didn't make many miles over the course of the night, but enough wind remained to keep us moving in the right direction and, after our experience two nights prior, we were happy to just enjoy the tranquility and gaze up at the stars.

The Suez

After another day of pleasant sailing and oil platform dodging we found ourselves entering Port Suez. There the tranquility of the day ended. I radioed the port authorities and the headache of the canal transit began. The guy at the other end of the radio informed me that I needed to select a canal transit agent before I even entered the port. I didn't think that was true but felt wasn't in a place to argue. As 'luck' would have it the, presumably bribed, radio operator happened to have an agent standing by and within minutes he was being dropped off, while underway, on Hanuman by a pilot boat. Chris and I managed to get tied up to a couple of moorings while our agent prattled on about all that he could do for us while failing to help us get moored up in the slightest. Once we got ourselves secured we found that our agent had morphed into four agents, now perched like pigeons on the edge of our boat. "Where did all these people come from?" I asked Chris as I returned to the cockpit after securing the bow line. "They paddled over on that sawed in half barrel." We eventually managed to shew off our agents, but only after they got us to agree to allow them to represent us.

We spent a few days getting Hanuman ready for the transit and waiting for our agents to get our affairs in order. Canal Authorities came out to the boat and measured Hanuman to assess displacement. The whole process seemed ridiculously overly complicated. It appeared they were using the exact same forms and procedures for sailboats as did for freighters. One of the forms asked us for the dimensions of our cargo hold. The two guys spent about an hour and a half measuring everything they could. Chris and I stood by rolling our eyes. "Why on earth would they need to measure the sink?" Chris queried. "I think they're measuring the engine compartment (which was right under the sink) but I have no idea why." Eventually they finished up and left without asking for any baksheesh. Despite what we considered and absurd charade, they actually came across as very professional.

We were expecting a visit from our agent the following day with the results of our measuring, used to calculate our transit fee, but he never came. Our transit date had been set by the Canal Authority for the following day and we had the distinct notion that our agent might be waiting until the last moment before giving us our bill so that we would have no choice but to comply. We spent the day trying to track him down but had no luck. We did run into one of the other agents who tried to get us to ditch our agent and use him. "You see, where is your agent now?" he goaded. We were pretty annoyed with our agent but something about the new guy's white suite and gold rimmed teeth and matching sunglasses didn't scream, "Trust me." He looked more like a drug lord from Miami Vice as he climbed into his Mercedes Benz, also gold rimmed, than someone I wanted to trust with my money.

Just as we expected, some guy from the agency we'd hired, someone who we'd never seen before (they always seemed to send out a guy we hadn't met so that the he could plead ignorance to the promises of the previous guy), showed up and gave us our bill. After talking to other sailors we had a pretty good idea of what we should be paying. The number he gave us was twice our estimate.

Chris went off on him; standing up and winding back his head before ejecting, "bull shit," like a sneeze. "Where did you come up with these numbers," I added. "Not my numbers, they just give them to me," he replied. "Who just give them to you," I demanded. "The Canal Authority." "What paperwork do you have from them?" He was only holding a copy of my ships documentation. "Look here," he said pointing to the largest number on the page, which had apparently just been doubled and multiplied by 100. "That's absurd, the Canal Authority is supposed to determine a number based on the measurements they took." The agent, or the agent's cousin, or whoever we were talking to, had started off very calm and composed but Chris and I assaulted him with our good cop bad cop routine. Chris dropped 'F-bombs' while I calmly pointed out the absurdity of his conclusions until he got flustered and started stuttering. "B-b-but you just, just have to pay. You are leaving today. The pilot is c-c-coming." I could see that he was getting nervous about having to go back to his higher ups without the cash. Chris and I went silent and just stared at him. "You, you have to pay he pleaded." "No!" Chris and I stated flatly in unison. "Then you can't leave today," he replied grasping at the final straw he hoped would break us. "Then we won't go today," I stated, looking not just at him but through him. By this time, the canal pilots where being dropped off on the various boats that were starting the transit that day. We sent our pilot away and the lackey agent left as well, glancing back at us with a hang dog expression on his face hoping that we might call him back with a change of heart.

Later that day one of the higher up agents came by and we had it out all over again. He was more authoritative than the last guy, one gold tooth severing as an insignia of rank. Chris played the 'bad cop' again, standing toe to toe with our agent, exchanging saliva heatedly. Chris hurled one insult after another at him. The agent feigned offended, countering Chris' accusations by simply saying the opposite as him. "You're a fucking liar!" Chris stated with finality, pumping out his chest. The agent looked to me for relief and I decided to jump in before Chris started in on his mother. "Okay, okay. The numbers you gave us clearly didn't come from the Canal Authority. We just need to get these numbers adjusted," I stated as calmly as I could, hoping he would see my soothing command as salvation from Chris' onslaught. "Well, you can get remeasured if you want but…." "Fine," I said cheerily.

The Canal Authority returned the following day and we asked them about the numbers our agent had given us as they began the remeasuring process. We found there to be no correlation between the numbers our agent had given us and those determined by the authority. We didn't have any real doubt that we'd been lied to by our agent but it was nice to have the Canal Authority confirm it. "What do you think about this?" I asked the Authorities. "You have to talk to your agent," they replied, looking rather uncomfortable with the subject.

Our agent returned later that day with a big smile, acting as though nothing had happened. Our new numbers were half what they had been. I looked at him questioningly, wondering how he could be behaving in such a nonchalant manner given it was now plain as day that he'd been lying to us about the old numbers. We'd gotten what we wanted so I decided avoid a fight and not press him on the subject. "So we'll be leaving tomorrow?" I asked. "Yes." We paid him, got a receipt, and he left.

He returned later that night as we were reclining with some friends in the cockpit drinking wine. It was dark, I was relaxed, and certainly in no mood to deal with him. "You need to pay a little bit more." "What?" Chris screamed from the other side of the cockpit. The agent stayed low in his boat trying to shield himself from the sight of Chris. "Yes, the Canal Authority said they made a little mistake and you have to pay more." "No," I replied wearily. He waited for a second to see if something would follow my 'no'. I waited for the same reason but the 'no' seemed to sum up everything I felt so I left it at that. "Yes," he said, "you can come down to the Canal Authority and they will tell you." I hesitated, wondering if he was bluffing. "Come, come, I will show you." He sounded a little too excited about taking me to the authority to be bluffing but I decided I should see it through. He was actually only asking for about ten bucks but I wanted to confirm that he wasn't just fucking with me. We went to shore, got in his car, and drove down to the Canal Authority building. He tried to make some small talk, asking why we couldn't all just get along and be nice to one another. "We could get along if you hadn't lied to me repeatedly and tried to steal my money," I stated without emotion, putting a damper on the small talk.

We arrived at the building and walked up to the office. I was a little concerned that there might be some thugs waiting around the corner. It was dark and it seemed like an odd time for any government employees to be hanging around the office. Fortunately, none materialized and we made our way up a couple flights of stairs and found the guys who'd measured Hanuman sitting at their desks, clearly only pretending to work. "Fine, so they're in on this one too," I thought. I let them explain why I owed more. I didn't really pay attention. They could say whatever they wanted. I paid the agent and went back to the boat.

Kindly I'd been saved a half glass of wine. "How'd it go captain?" Chris said as he wrung the last of the wine into my coffee mug. "Did you have to grab your ankles?" "Yup,"

I replied, after mopping up the wine that was dribbling down my chin. "I figured as much. At least we'll be gettin' out of this shit hole tomorrow, aye." "Aye."

Fortunately we were spared any further visits from our agent. A canal pilot was dropped off the next day and we motored into the Canal. Our pilot turned out to be a congenial fellow. We'd heard and read numerous stories about the pilots being assholes; constantly asking for more money and generally being overbearing. He said he usually worked in one of the control towers. Perhaps that contributed to his lack of bad manners and general decency. He even let us put up the main a time or two for more speed, but never complained about the speed we motored. We'd been told that some pilots tried to push the boat as hard as possible so that they could get home earlier.

At 10 pm, after 60 miles of motoring, we arrived in the Port of Isabella, finishing the first half of our transit. We dropped our agent off on the dock with an envelope full money, as was customary, and a pack of cigarettes. We'd read it was best to put the money in an envelope and hand it over only when the pilot was leaving so that he didn't have time to debate the sum. Our pilot just thanked us with a gentle smile, not even looking in the envelope. Chris and I made our way to the anchorage relieved to have made it through the first half of the Suez unscathed.

Some boats chose to have a layover in Isabella, in order to see the pyramids, but Chris had already been there and I was ready for the Med so we just stayed the night. A new pilot was dropped off the following morning. He hopped on Hanuman without introduction, or an explanation for being an hour late, and started shouting out orders. "Go there…no there…here, I drive." I hesitantly relinquished the wheel. The previous pilot hadn't insisted on driving at all. He immediately jerked the throttle lever all the way up. Big Red let out an angry roar and a cloud of white smoke. After swerving away from the reef he throttled back down and threw it in reverse. "Whoa, whoa, whoa…how's about I drive and you just tell me where to go," I said firmly, nudging him out of the way. I took over and we eased back into the Canal, hugging the left bank in order to give the enormous ships plenty of room.

Five minutes into the Canal our pilot got a call on the VHF. After some rapid fire Arabic, he said we had to go back because there was a large convoy of American war ships transiting and no other boats were allowed to go through next to them. "How long," I asked. "One hour, maybe." I couldn't help but wonder if we'd be in this predicament had he not been an hour late.

We anchored up just outside of the main channel and waited. It was hot, we were anxious to get going. Our pilot was extremely disappointed that we didn't have a refrigerator with cold cokes. He asked for something to eat. We offered to make him some rice but he scoffed at the idea. He seemed to have the idea that he was on a cruise and that Chris and I were there to serve him.

After two hours of hanging around, we got back under way. We motored through monotonously long and straight sections of canal. I set the electronic auto-pilot to get a break from steering but the pilot started pressing the correction buttons incorrectly, almost sending us into the bank, so I disengaged it and resumed hand steering. The pilot constantly asked us to increase our speed and we continued to refuse. When I went down below to check on the engine he tried to get Chris to increase our speed, as if he and Chris were on a team conspiring against me. He would even try and just reach over and raise the throttle. A stern glance sent his hand retreating and brought a sleazy, 'oh you got me,' smile to his face that spread his smarmy mustache past the width of his rat like narrow set eyes.

Darkness set in and we motored on. Around mid night we arrived in Port Said. As we entered the harbor area the pilot got on the VHF and started chatting away in Arabic. "There is police coming to check your papers," he reported. "Oh no you don't. You just called one of your mates to come get more baksheesh," Chris shouted down to him. He shook his head furiously, "No, no baksheesh, is the police maybe trouble if you don't have papers." But he couldn't keep that shit eating grin, which told us he was full of it, off his face. "We're not giving any fucking money to any of your mates," Chris repeated. The pilot got back on the VHF and shouted out a few lines, but as he was doing so a police boat, complete with sirens and lights, came blasting out of the darkness. Chris and I looked at each other and shook our heads. "I hope they've got fuckin' fenders," I mumbled. The police boat did a couple of fast laps around us before coming up along our starboard side. "Bullshit," Chris grumbled through clenched teeth.

A chubby policeman in a shabby uniform, with buttons taxed by his heaving belly, clomped on board with a grin that fell somewhere between that of a child on Christmas morning and dope fiend about to get a fix. I handed him some random boat papers. I didn't think it important that they weren't the papers he asked for. I chose the ones that I had the most spare copies of. He glanced at them briefly and laboriously climbed down below. He moved slowly, careful not to overlook anything that he might want. I think the disappointed looking pilot conveyed to him that we weren't the most willing of targets. I gave him a pack of cigarettes and he left looking unsatisfied, sloppily shoving the papers I'd given him into his back pocket.

Happy to be rid of the police, we continued further into the Port Said area, wondering when we would be rid of our pilot. Eventually a small boat came up next to us to pick him up. We handed him his envelope of money and a pack of cigarettes as the small boat motored next to us. "Lots of money?… hundreds?" he asked, his rat faced grin expanding beneath his beady eyes. "Hundreds?" I shouted. "Time to go," Chris stated, chuckling his bag into the boat next to us. "Lots of money?" he repeated over his shoulder, as Chris started helping/pushing him onto the small boat. "Get out of here," Chris demanded, prying the pilot's fingers from the rail. "More money?" he chirped one last time through his fiendish smile.

Chris and I breathed a sigh of relief as the last of the 'hand in your pocket' mongers left our lives. As much as we knew 'that's just how it is in Egypt' we were thoroughly relieved to be done with it. "To the Med!" I bellowed, as we pumped the air with our pelvises. "Damn glad to be done with that bull shit mate." "Fuck yeah!"

There were numerous channels out of the Port Said area but with a bit navigating we managed to find our way into the open ocean (the Med!) and get the bow pointed towards Cyprus.

The Med

Prior to entering the Mediterranean I received many e-mails from friends interested in the sailing its fabled waters. I decided to send out a group response, giving people some idea what to expect should they sign on.

Dear friends,

As Hanuman approaches the Med, it seems that many of you are interested in exploring its enchanted waters. I thought it wise to give you the low down on life aboard and what to expect.

Living 'Accommodations:'

There's one door. It leads to the head (bathroom). Any notion of personal space or privacy should be abandoned at the dock. There are a few places to sleep, the exact number of which depends on ones love of sweating. My bunk, which I am constantly renaming, receives very little ventilation. I christened it the 'Sweat Pit' while crossing the equator for the first time. If it was hot on deck it was a sauna in the bunk.

Extended 'Sweat Pit' conditions transformed it into the 'Salt Marsh;' constantly damp to wet, with layers of salty, oily sweat. During one of the roach uprisings, I coined it the 'Roach Motel.' Unlike the roach motel on TV however, the roaches checked into and out of my hotel as freely as they please.

In an effort to remedy the moisture situation I recently pulled the mattress up on deck in hopes of airing it out. The mattress is of dubious quality however, and when I returned it to 'The Cave,' another name I have for the bunk, a mountain range had sprung up longitudinally down the middle of the mattress. The range eventually became known as 'Roach Ridge.' I now have the option of sleeping on the 'North' or 'South Bank' (Hanuman is usually sailing west.)

The airing out seemed to have no negative effect on the roaches. In fact their numbers seemed to actually increase. I hypothesized that it may have been getting a little dank in there even for them. They writhe all over my body at night. The motion of 'grab, squish and chuck' has become automatic. I fear they may worship me as some sort of deity. I brought a bag of cloves and some cinnamon sticks into the Motel, hoping to freshen things up. I fear they may have just used it as nesting material.

Incidentally, Nicole and I recently read a book about a guy in a Bangkok prison who had a roach crawl into his ear and lay eggs. The eggs hatched in to larvae, grew (presumably feeding on his innards), and his neck ballooned out, with what looked like a baseball, under his skin. Eventually a fellow inmate lanced his neck and the larvae came pouring out. Nicole and Chris now sleep with earplugs.

In rough conditions, with the sun well hidden behind a ceiling of gray, I referred to it as 'The Womb.' While peeling off weather soaked clothes and crawling into it, there is no other place in the world I'd rather be. In such conditions falling asleep seems to take about two seconds.

In addition to my bunk there is a matching one, minus Roach Ridge, on the starboard side, known as the 'Piss Bunk' for reasons I won't go into but I'm sure one can imagine. These bunks are big enough for one person who likes to sweat or a couple (married of course, no sinners allowed on Hanuman) who love to sweat.

The two aforementioned bunks are in the aft section of the boat. As we move forward past the navigation area and the galley we arrive in the communal area/cripple den. This area consists of two settees (couches) with a table in between them that can be lowered to create a largish sleeping area on the port side. The table actually hasn't been in the up position since Mexico. With the table down, a somewhat well ventilated area, padded with many molding pillows and blankets, can accommodate two people relatively comfortably or possible even a ménage a trios (provided, once again, that they're all married.)

The starboard settee is only about five feet long, thus works well for one hobbit.

Forward of the common area is the head and the fore peak (aka: the garage) which is mainly used for storage. To my knowledge no one has attempted to sleep in either of these places. The floor can accommodate about three.

While at anchor sleeping on deck is the norm. Some have slept on deck while underway but they must remember that they are in a 'working' area of the boat and are subject to being pummeled by waves, stepped on, kicked, and hit by lines. No apologies will be made. On rare occasions they have been pissed on and consequently pissed off. What's that rule about peeing into the wind? There are no real rules on Hanuman, more just guidelines.

At anchor I prefer to sleep on the side deck, which affords me the luxury of simply rolling over to pee without having to stand up. It's the little things.

I haven't placed any upper limits on crew numbers. I've sailed with as many as seven, which could definitely be described as crowded, but there was still a little room on the floor. One also has to remember that, while underway, at least one person is always on watch, creating more room down below.

Lifestyle/Living Conditions:
Those of you who've received my past e-mails and didn't, or have yet to, hit 'block sender,' will recall that I signed on, or better stated, 'shanghaied,' Kama Sutra the gecko to manage the roach population. Unfortunately it turned out that Kama Sutra was more interested in free love and was ill prepared for an adversary of the magnitude of the roaches. When I ceased to hear his pleasant little chirping, I suspected that a couple of suicide roach fundamentalist took him out. One must remember that these roaches have survived numerous aerial (aerosol) bombing sorties and countless hand to hand (or hand to claw) skirmishes and are a rugged breed who've been separated from their terrestrial brethren for generations. In their isolation these nautical roaches (speedius gonzali), having been denied access to the education and culture of their more privileged cousins, have resorted to fundamentalism; forcing us to launch operation: 'Total Roach Annihilation.' We are hoping to obtain some WMDs and we'll wait for no resolution before attempting genocide.

Of course one has to consider the consequences of one's actions. As it stands, the roaches are a large part of our daily lives and, in addition to our bowel movements, discussion of them constitutes the majority of our conversations. Without the roaches we might not have anything to talk about. Or perhaps conversations regarding flatulence and bowel movements would simply take over.

Personal Hygiene:

This pretty much begins and ends with the toothbrush. Apathy sets in for everyone at some point. The sooner you succumb to it the easier life becomes. There actually is a shower on board but it hasn't been used since San Francisco. Few crew members have even been aware of its existence. Water is limited and so is the power required to pump it. Any surplus water is mixed with sugar, yeast, and rotting fruit and made into grog. Any surplus power goes into the ten-disc changer. Hanumanians much prefer to be dirty, drunken rockers than clean, sober dullards.

Ultimately, the ocean is the perfect bathtub and washing machine and you can be as clean as you want, though I personally have been wearing the same shirt since Australia. Those who don't know me by name most certainly refer to me as the guy in the red Hawaiian shirt. I figure at some point it reached a filth equilibrium and now as much foulness comes off of it as is collects on it. It really isn't that dirty however, at least from my perspective, I believe there to be something magical about rayon.

I also have fairly unscrupulous habits regarding cleanliness in general. On more than one occasion I have had food torn from my hand and thrown overboard. "You're not eating that." "Mutiny!" "Mongrel!…you just picked it off the floor and it's got mold on it." "The floor is no dirtier than anywhere else and I wasn't going to eat the moldy part." "Sure you weren't."

In Australia, Joe and I coined the term 'ground food,' and it continues to constitute a significant portion of my diet. I consider it necessary for a healthy immune system. Babies stick everything in their mouth for a reason. Who's to say the fountain of youth isn't gutter water?

What was the point of this e-mail? Ah yes…crew. Anyone still interested?

Despite, or perhaps because of, the e-mail I still had a few people who decided they were in. "Should I bring some bug killer?" was the only response of concern that I received.

The Med decided to reward us for our Red Sea struggles and we coasted into Cyprus under a starry sky after only a few quick, yet comfortable, days of sailing.

Cyprus

Chris and I had a few days to unwind before the new crew arrived. We celebrated Chris' birthday over the course of a few days; going out on the town, drinking gratuitously, and getting to know Cyprus. We learned that Cypriot men are very protective of Cypriot women, whether they know them personally or not.

Drinking my tenth or twelve beer, I lounged in a white plastic chair, enjoying the mild Mediterranean air in a pleasant our door bar, with two cigarettes hanging out of my mouth while chatting up a healthy looking olive skinned Cypriot girl. Chris and I, along with a couple from another boat we'd met in the Red Sea, were soaking in the night, reveling in the refreshing European atmosphere, when a group of Cypriot guys stormed over to us and began yelling aggressively in our direction, though mainly me, in heavily accented English. I stood up, assuming there had simply been some sort of misunderstanding, and waved my hands in front of me in the universal, 'I don't want any problems,' fashion. "No, no, no," I repeated simply. They weren't quelled by what I thought was a very calm and reassuring gesture and I was given a solid shove backward. With my chair right behind me, I topple backwards over it and became somewhat entangled in it; essentially turtled. Chris stood up in a statue like fashion, "enough," he commanded. Apparently the 'enough' quota hadn't quite been filled in the Cypriot's eyes and one of them threw a fist at Chris which glanced off his cheek. "Is that all you got mate?" Chris inquired, thinking he was in an Arnold Schwarzenegger film. Meanwhile the other guy with us threw a plastic chair at our attackers and picked up another, using it in lion tamer fashion, "back...back, get back," he shouted. Just as I untangled myself from the chair, some bouncer type guys from the bar stepped in, broke things up, and told us we should probably be on our way.

"What happened," I inquired as we limped off. The other guy with us complained of his foot hurting. I thought he was playing it up until we saw him the next day with a cast and crutches. "Oow... that sucks," I commented sheepishly. "I feel kinda' bad about his foot," I said to Chris when we were alone. "Ahh... the wancka' shouldn'ta been throwin' chairs mate," Chris explained consolingly.

New Crew

When Brandoni, Pat, and Carly arrived the real party began. Brandoni had broken it off with Sara, the girlfriend he'd had in the back in the Pacific, and after spending a year in school getting his teaching degree, was ready to do a little womanizing. He made a perfect wingman for Chris, who considered himself a maven when it came to the seduction of the fairer sex.

Pat and I had played water polo on the same team in high school and college, had taken several 'coming of age' trips together in Alaska, and had lived together for three years. If I were into categorizing friends, he would've fallen into the 'best' category. I'd also spent a lot of time with Carly, Pat's wife. Along with my girlfriend at the time, and Pat, I'd traveled with her through Africa by bus. I was the best man in Pat and Carly's wedding.

We were all well acquainted, and were well reacquainted even before the duty free Tangueray was uncapped the night I met them at the airport. Carly was sopping up the unchewed pasta that Pat had barfed down the front of his shirt within 12 hours of arrival, a typical arrangement. "It's fine, just leave it there," Pat pleaded from behind glassy eyes. Carly ignored him, peeling off his shirt and using it to mop up the mixture of marinara, Tangueray, and digestive juices on his face. "Must have been the jet lag," Pat explained the following morning as he hunted for his toothbrush.

Wanting a bit of distance from the boat, we rented a car and toured the island, smoking hash out of an apple as we did so. As we wound our way across the island we found ourselves behind a car occupied by a pair of seemingly attractive girls. They waved at us in their rear view mirror. Brandoni's mind raced with the possibilities.

Before long, we found ourselves amid roadwork and forced to stop behind the girls. Brandoni decided he would jump out of the car and go talk to them; a ballsy maneuver by any standards. The rest of us waited, slightly embarrassed, yet thoroughly intrigued, while Brandoni chatted with the blond on the passenger side. The fact that she hadn't shoed him away immediately seemed a good sign.

From what we could see, things seemed to be going well. Traffic movement began to resume and Brandoni was still plastered to the side of the car. We were on the verge of honking when he came running back with a huge grin on his face and a little slip of paper in his hand. "Well?" we asked in unison. "They're Russian," Brandoni beamed, with the delight of a child who'd just received a Red Rider BB gun on Christmas morning.

He'd gotten their number and we were to meet up with them that night in Ayia Napa, the party hub of Cyprus. We were all exhausted after a couple days of partying, and lingering 'jetlag,' and looking forward to a good night's sleep, but Brandoni's enthusiasm didn't leave any room for negotiation. We slept in the car on the way there.

After finding a cheap room and getting some dinner, Brandoni called the Russian chicks and arranged to meet at the most recognizable landmark, McDonald's.

Pat, after downing a craft of wine, complained of jet lag and passed out early; leaving Chris, Brandoni, Carly, and I to head off in search of the Russian chicks. Chris, Carly (who obviously had no real interest, other than her own amusement, in meeting up with the Russian chicks) and I were a bit tired and felt the energy required to meet new people seemed not worth the effort. Once again we allowed ourselves be carried along by Brandoni's enthusiasm.

"I'm just going to stop in here. You guys go on ahead," Chris said about a block away from McDonald's. "What… what are you talking about? McDonald's is right there. What about the Russian chicks man?" "I'll meet up with you guys later. Go on ahead," Chris replied furtively. We shrugged and continued on.

We did a little 'walk through' to make sure they weren't inside scarfing down chicken nuggets, before sitting down on the stone wall at the base of the golden arches to wait. I suddenly realized why Chris had stayed behind. The awkward feeling that I was back in high school hanging out in front of the 7-eleven, waiting for some girls that might not come, overwhelmed me. "How long are we going to wait here," I queried. "Just a few more minutes," Brandoni replied, clearly unfazed by the situation. The girls had obviously always shown up back when he was in high school. He was probably the guy with the keg and the parents who were out of town. "Okay, we'll give them until 8:30." "Deal."

Before long they did arrive and we exchanged awkward introductions and asked a few strained questions to try and establish some sort of rapport. Of the two, one was distinctly hotter that the other, though they were both attractive. The hot brunette had a glamorous err about her and the confident penetrating gaze of the alpha female. The blond was more school girlish and reserved, though clearly eager to make our acquaintance. The conversation had slowed to smiling and head nodding when Chris arrived on the scene. "Hey… how ya goin'," Chris ejected, in an exaggerated Aussie accent from his huge smiling face, with the air of just happening to run into us. "Jackass," I thought with a grin, amused by his tactics. He'd clearly just been spying on us from across the street (talk about highschoolish) waiting to make his entrance, letting us play the fools as we waited under the jaundice glow of the giant 'M.' It worked however, and with his cool kid clothes and animated head back laughs he wooed the Russians into warm smiles and girly giggles. "How's about we go in git us a few cocktails," lured Chris, but they were already hooked and we were on our way. We headed off towards the bars, Chris leading the way with large arm gestures and more head back, mouth open cackling. Carly and I trailed behind with knowing bemused head shaking.

The night progressed. Brandoni tied one on, and as we walked through a bar looking for a bathroom, he slapped some chic's ass. I apologized profusely, defusing the situation, but I was thinking it was time to get Brandoni back to the room before he could get himself, and me, into any more trouble. Fortunately, however, he managed to get himself under control and continue with the evening.

I watched Chris and Brandoni interact with the Russian chicks, wondering how things would pan out. Chris hung back playing the cool guy waiting for them to come to him. Brandoni was all over one of them one minute and distracted by some other chick who walked by the next.

Eventually Chris and the brunet seemed to pair up as did Brandoni and the blond, if only by default. Despite there being two of us, Carly and I began to feel like a third wheel as Chris and Brandoni worked there various games, so we took off on our own to go have a drink elsewhere.

Carly and I got along well, enjoying our time together. I'd even allowed the Russian chicks to develop the impression that we she and I were a couple. I was a bit leery of the Russians chicks and didn't want to get involved with either of them. Carly and I had been close before she arrived but for some reason we seemed to gain an intimacy that we hadn't previously possessed. We eventually decided that we were done with the down town scene but not quite ready to call it a night. We concluded that we should see if we could find a hot tub to poach in one of the bigger hotels. We never found one, though not for lack of trying, and didn't end up stumbling back to our own hotel until dull gray of the predawn was upon us.

'Three zip," Chris declared the following morning, referring to fact that since he'd gotten on board Hanuman he'd managed to have sex with three chicks while my efforts had been considerably less successful. He was also excited to check Russia off the list of countries yet to be defiled. "How bout you Brandoni?" I asked. "I ended up making out for awhile with some random chick I met on the walk home." "Was she hot?" "I really don't remember. It was dark. I doubt if I could pick her out of a line up, but we'll go ahead and say she was," Brandoni responded, finishing with a grin.

We eventually made our way back to the boat and after a couple more nights of partying, during which four legs frequently writhed in the opening of Chris' bunk and Brandoni and the blonde Russian chick became better acquainted, we set off for the Greek island of Rhodes.

Rhodes

Rhodes was magnificent and we, all being natives of relatively young nations, marveled at the ancient city. But ultimately our lives digressed to more of the same shenanigans that had taken place in Cyprus. Chris and Brandoni tracked down a pack of Finnish chicks and we had a little party back on Hanuman. Chris and Brandoni already had their legs wrapped around two of them when one of their roommates arrived. Henrika, who as it happened was several times more attractive than either Chris' or Brandoni's Finnish chick, just kind of fell into my lap.

"Five one," I announced to Chris the following day. "Actually mate, that's six one," Chris corrected. "What, who was number five?" "That Dutch chick… from the other night." "Oh yeah, that anorexic one." "Nah, she was haut mate."

Despite being distracted for a few nights by the Finish chick, I still felt myself being pulled toward Carly and had even begun to feel what I could only describe as a crush on her. There was of course the obvious fact that she was married to my best friend, so I never had any notions of nurturing the feelings, but I wasn't so strong as to be able to fully let them go either. I told myself that we were friends and that I simply enjoyed hanging out with her. Certainly there was nothing wrong with enjoying hanging out with a friend, I concluded. However, one night when we ended up heading back to the boat alone together, having become separated from Chris and Brandoni (Pat having charged too hard and gone down early, as often happened), we found ourselves lingering on the dock longer than proper decorum dictated. While no lines were crossed, there was a whisper of something beyond friendship that I had to struggle to ignore.

Boarding Hanuman, Carly quickly discovered that Pat had pissed their bed… for the second time so far on the trip. The first time hadn't been as bad. Pat had only wetted the shorts he was wearing and the Therma-Rest he was sleeping on. The second time he'd not only soaked the pants he was wearing, but all of the bedding under him as well. Carly was none too pleased with him and ended up sleeping under a towel in the cockpit.

Santorini

After waiting a couple of days for high winds to abate, we cast off. My mom and her swim team were coming to Greece for a swim meet and the plan was to rendezvous in Santorini. The sail to Rhodes and all of the time living aboard had accustomed the new crew to sea life so the passage was considerably easier on everyone than previous passages and further puking was avoided.

Carly developed a quick grasp of the workings of the boat and impressed me by knowing what lines to pull when. I didn't trust Pat to flush the toilet. He'd never had any natural aptitude for things mechanical, nor any interest in learning. I recalled having to put his bike chain on for him on more than one occasion back in high school. If his bike had a flat tire it was considered broken until he could take it into the shop to have it fixed.

We met up with my mom and the swim team shortly after arriving on Santorini. It was good to see her for the first time in over a year. As usual she gave me some new clothes to replace the rags I'd been wearing. She also brought a new lift pump for Big Red, so the red jerry hanging from the ceiling below decks could be stowed and the constant aroma of diesel eliminated.

We all rented scooters and tore up the island. The pure joy of riding around a hilly Greek island on scooter can't be overstated.

Brandoni had been keeping in touch with his Russian chick via e-mail. "Hey Chris, the Russian chicks said they might want to meet us in Crete (our next destination)," Brandoni offered. "I don't know mate," Chris responded skeptically. Brandoni eventually convinced Chris to agree to the idea, Brandoni could be rather persuasive, and they arranged to meet up with the Russian chicks in Crete.

The day before we were to head south to Crete, Brandoni met a couple of American chicks late that night at a bar and invited them to sail with us. They were a bit hesitant, but Brandoni ensured them that the captain was, typically, more sober than he, and that they would be perfectly safe. They were still reluctant, but Brandoni sped away on his scooter, falling only once, and said he'd come by the next day to get them. Again, Brandoni could be rather persuasive.

The following day Brandoni had forgotten when and where (and quite possible who) exactly he was supposed to meet, but managed to hunt the girls down never the less.

I only learned of Brandoni's invitation on the morning we were to depart and wasn't convinced there would be any American chicks showing up. Pat gave them a 15 percent chance. I gave them 20. Against our odds, Brandoni pulled up in a taxi, a little past departure time, with a couple of American chicks and their back packs in tow.

Mark, aka Raw Dog, who Pat and I had played water polo with back in college, now swimming with the masters, also decided to sign on for the sail down to Crete, where we would be reuniting with the team. I'd been hesitant to have him along, as the boat seemed full enough, but after he declared,

"I fully expect to be awake, puking and suffering the whole trip," I decided he might be alright. He also managed to make it to the boat, a good sign, despite the intentionally vague directions I'd given him. And early, no less. After introductions the eight of us loaded up for the 75 mile overnight sail and pulled out.

Once out of the Santorini wind shadow, an obliging breeze from the northwest accelerated us to a comfortable steady pace. Conditions were idealic. Beers were passed around, and life seemed like it couldn't get much better. Recounting the tribulations of married life and his baby daughter, Raw Dog commented, "You have the best life ever." I considered explaining that it wasn't always like this, but just smiled, thinking he might prefer the illusion. Rather than lament about his missed calling as a sailor, Raw Dog was intent on soaking up a lifetime's worth of experience in the next 70 miles. "Does that fishing pole work," he asked. "It does…," I responded, thinking, "but only if I set my beer down and let the lure out." His enthusiasm was infectious however, and after finding a place to wedge my beer where no one would pick it up and slam it, as was par for the course, I let out the line. Raw Dog had taken over steering duties as well.

Brandoni and Chris were busy jockeying for position with their fresh meat. I was deeply relaxed and well lost on the horizon. Pat and Carly were hanging out on the side deck, taking in the wind. Raw Dog was left the only person interested in being at the wheel. "Let me know if you need a break Raw Dog," I offered, intentionally unconvincingly, hoping he wouldn't take me up on the offer, but not wanting him to feel like a slave to the helm. "Alright," he commented standing behind the wheel, slightly exaggerating the motion of the ocean as he swayed back and forth, head tilted back with an expression of relaxed contentment on his face. "Nother beer Raw Dog?" I asked, reaching for one for myself. "Naw, I'm alright for now thanks."

"Zzzzz," the reel screamed. My head jerked aft. "Fish on! Fish on!" I yelled, a little louder than usual to heighten the drama of the situation. I quickly wedged my beer and untied the rod letting out a few whoops as I did so. The rod got passed around so that those who wanted to could have a chance to fight the fish. Eventually we had ourselves a decent sized Big Eye on our hands.

Raw Dog, despite his nick name, was a relatively mild mannered sort of a character but the writhing fish in the cockpit evoked his inner caveman and before I knew it he was tearing off large chunks of the fish and eating it raw. I considered that even the freshest of fish could still be riddled with parasites but decided it wasn't the time for logic and, at his request, handed him some of the discarded fish skin so that he could bite off the meat still attached to it.

As the sunlight faded we added the Big Eye to the fried rice that we'd made and doled it out in the rag tag assortment of eating vessels I'd accumulated. The beer ran out but we still had plenty of wine and alcohol to consume. Brandoni and Chris where in the midst of classic pre-mating, courting rituals. It was amusing to watch things unfold right before us on the cabin top. Both Chris and Brandoni where more keen on the blond, though I thought the brunette more attractive. Treaties were forged, alliances sealed. Brandoni ended up with the blond and Chris the brunette. I was happy to see Brandoni with the blond as I feared that he might always be left with Chris' discards. Chris wasn't initially into the brunette but she seemed to be responding to his big Aussie laugh so he started in with his standard pre-mating tactics: finger tips 'accidentally' resting on a forearm, soft talking close to the ear; subject matter of little importance, use of the rolling motion of the boat to feign accidental bumping of the torso, see if she pulls back, a little stroking with those fingertips already poised for action, and most importantly, "would

316

you like another drink?" "Yes please," responds the brunette, with coquettish smile. Repeat that sequence of events several more times, lower the sun, and Chris is chalking up number seven, bareback in the piss bunk.

It takes Brandoni an extra day to close the deal, owing to his tendency to drink to the point of losing focus, both literally and figuratively. Five minutes after declaring that he was going to stay up all night, Brandoni was passed out… classic.

I'd seen such scenarios unfold before so I established a watch order early and got some sleep while hitting land wasn't an immediate concern. Sleeping areas were scarce. A two person watch was maintained so more berths were available and so that Brandoni didn't pass out during his watch like he had on the passage to Rhodes where he ended up taking a four hour watch, only 15 minutes of which he could account for. I paired Chris and Brandoni up with their respective mates, figuring the scent of fresh meat would keep them alert. Sleeping spaces were still scarce however and at six foot five, Raw Dog probably didn't catch more than a couple of winks in the hobbit bunk. Fortunately he regarded this as simply an enrichment of the whole experience. I found him brushing his teeth with salt water in the morning. "We can probably spare enough fresh water for tooth brushing." "Ah, that's all right. I know you guys only have so much fresh water." I was on the verge of commenting that we weren't in the middle of the Atlantic, but I respected the consideration, not always a given on Hanuman, and just nodded.

The wind slowly died as the sun came up and before long we found ourselves coasting through a submarine exercise area. I'd seen it on the chart but it didn't say that entry was prohibited. To avoid it completely would have necessitated a longer passage. I figured I could safely shave off its edge.

A military helicopter wasn't a welcome sight. It informed us over the radio that we were in a military testing area. "Oh really?" I asked, playing dumb, and said that we would alter course. Thankfully that was the end of it and we were tied up to the dock in time for lunch.

Crete

The port authorities weren't too happy that we arrived with three people that weren't on our crew list. They seemed especially concerned with the two girls who we thought were 'American chicks' but who actually held Israeli passports. "You can't just take people from Island to Island without consulting the harbor master," I was informed. "But there wasn't a port authority on Santorini," I argued. He seemed concerned that the girls might be terrorists or something and brought them in for questioning. Eventually he eased up and after a day of prohibiting them from leaving the island, ideal for Chris and Brandoni, let us off the hook.

Chris had his own concerns. Having never had sex with an American, he thought he'd just checked one off the list. "She's Israeli," I informed him, "she doesn't count." "Yeah mate, but she's spent her whole life in America." "Maybe, but if she doesn't have the passport she doesn't count," I retorted. "Well what if she had two passports?" "Then you would get credit for two countries," I offered. He couldn't find fault with my theory but wasn't happy about it.

Chris and Brandoni had more pressing issues however. "What are we going to do about those Russian chicks?" Chris asked Brandoni. "Oh shit, I totally forgot about the Russian chicks. I say we just ignore them and hope they don't find us." Chris rolled his eyes but agreed, deciding he was more interested in having sex with his new American/Israeli chick. The new chicks were also considerably more low keyed and down to earth than the Russian chicks. I didn't get the vibe that they wanted anything more than a good time.

They continued to hang around for a week. "I've gotten some angry e-mails from the Russian chicks," Brandoni confided when they weren't around. "Apparently they're here and wondering where we are." "That's not entirely too surprising I suppose," I replied. Brandoni was joyously wrapped up in the present and not giving too much thought to the ramifications of his actions.

I discovered that Chris thought he was living in a consequence free world as well. "You still have those day-after pills lying around you were talking about mate?" Chris inquired, in a tone as close to sheepish as an Aussie can get. "Yeah, you need'm?" I inquired, with a huge grin on my face. "Might be a good idea."

I could vaguely understand Chris not using protection, but I had a hard time imagining the girls not insisting on it. "Brandoni, have you been using protection?" I inquired. "Well... not every time. I used the old coitus interruptus once... but then I jabbed it right back in afterwards." "You guys are nuts," I said shaking my head. But I couldn't help laughing. "Yeah...," Brandoni replied almost wistfully, as if he'd been thinking about bygone days, instead of just the night before.

The Summer Solstice

The Summer Solstice began with an open water swim organized my mom's coach. Pat, Carly, and I had taken it relatively easy the night before so we were able to make it to the beach in the morning. Chris and Brandoni were more committed to their exploits with the American chicks, and passed. I managed to come in fourth overall which I was rather pleased with, given that most of my working out had been in 12 ounce increments. Pat came in shortly after me and puked on the finish line, living up to his recently acquired nick name, 'Sir Puke-a-lot.' "Jet lag," we all agreed.

The open water swim was followed by a swim meet in the Crete club pool. I decided that we needed to put together a Hanuman relay team. The excitement of the events set the tone for the day. Pat, always happy to get started early, was suckin' down beers in the bleachers before we were even up to race and maintained the pace after we finished.

After the meet, the Crete team put together an authentic Greek BBQ with heaps of great food and plenty of ouzo. Our relay team, consisting of Pat, Carly, Brandoni, and I, got together for a team photo. Carly and I were next to each other and as we squeezed in for the picture somehow her hand and wrist got linked around my elbow. After the photo Pat got up and Brandoni slide over but we stayed put, arm in arm. We stayed together for longer than just a moment and even though I felt Pat's eyes on me, and I knew I should pull away, I was slow in doing so, entranced by a feeling that trumped logic. I saw my mom look over at the two of us and wondered what she was thinking. Did she think nothing of it, just a couple of friends arm in arm, or did she pause for a moment and say, "…hmmm?" I was still deluding myself into thinking it was just a friendly physical gesture. And if there was a little more to it than that, well… certainly nothing would come of it.

We were introduced to some traditional Greek dances which were fairly simple but, given our condition, amazingly difficult to master. A few drinks later, much to every ones amusement, Brandoni started in with his break dancing; an inevitable product of music, alcohol, and venue. He started off looking pretty sweet and then… 'WHAM,' he hit the floor at terminal velocity. He repeated the maneuver to the same effect a couple more time before the numbing effect of the ouzo wasn't enough to mask the pain and he limped off the dance floor and fell back into his chair. We began to sense that we might be keeping our hosts up; most of the swimmers had retired long before the break dancing got going, so we decided to take our party elsewhere. Plus, all of the beer was gone.

Gaps in recollection prevent a completely accurate summation of the events that followed but I do recall passing around the few warm beers we had lingering in the backpack and urinating in less than discrete locations. There may have even been some simultaneous walking, peeing, and drinking going on; always a sign that one is on the right track. Somewhere along the way Pat decided to head back to the boat. I didn't know if it was because he'd had a row with Carly or because he'd just hit the wall. "Jetlag," we all intoned as he set off for the boat. The rest of us, Carly, Brandoni, Chris, the two American chicks, and I, were a bit tired after a full day of activity but decided that, it being the summer solstice and all, we should see the evening through.

We decided the most cost efficient course of action was to buy some beers in a shop and drink them in the park. After a few prolonged games of pig, using a crushed beer can and a trash bin, we started walking in no particular direction. Somehow Carly and I found ourselves divided from the group and sitting on a water front bench. I stretched my arm out on the bench behind her and she leaned in. Our conversation started casually; the swim meet, the summer solstice, and the antics of Chris and Brandoni, but took a turn for the more serious when Carly asked, "Mike, what do you think of me?" I wasn't quite sure how to interpret the question. I told her that I thought she was a great person and that over the years of knowing her I felt I'd seen her transform from a fairly self absorbed trivial (I didn't use those exact words) girl into a very impressive women. I explained that it was a change that I'd never expected to see but one that I was impressed by. I said I was stoked to share a future as her and Pat's friend. "I don't think it can work out for Pat and me," she stated flatly. "What?" I was genuinely shocked by her statement. She said she'd seen the end of their relationship coming for awhile and that she didn't think things could be salvaged. I hugged her in the manner of consoling a grieving friend and kissed her on the cheek. And then our lips met, and an era ended.

We pulled back, shocked at our behavior, in a 'what did we just do' state. She said she'd seen it coming for a while. We kissed again, with less restraint; I hadn't imagined her lips would be so soft. Feeling a bit exposed on the quay, we got up and began walking in a direction away from the boat, frequently stopping to kiss. A floodgate had opened and it was difficult to maintain the flow. I tried to will myself into a world outside the one I was in, one where I wasn't making out with my best friend's wife. For moments I was successful, and wrapped in bliss, but in others the feelings of my betrayal prevented me from gaining much pleasure from the situation. Despite the remorse, I was still hostage to my desire for Carly, and the kissing continued.

The sour note of dawn glared down on us, muting the dull sense of anonymity that the darkness had afforded, and we started back to the boat. We came around a corner, grinning at our indulgence and mutual flattery, and there was Pat, looking completely haggard. While Carly and I were indulging our base desires, Pat had clearly been in agony. Fortunately we weren't holding hands or kissing. "We'll see you back at the boat Mike," Pat said, doing his best to contain his pain and disappointment. That is the last time I saw his face and the memory of his tortured visage still burns in my mind's eye.

I made my way back to the boat, titillated by the taste of the forbidden fruit on my mouth and heavy with the weight of my perfidy. Mostly I was exhausted, and all of my feeling came through the filter of extreme fatigue. I crawled into the womb and passed out.

Pat and Carly were nowhere to be seen when I awoke the following day, though their stuff was still on the boat. I didn't know exactly what would happen but I had trouble imagining Pat and Carly sailing off to the next port with us.

I spent the day with Brandoni, Chris, and the two American chicks, going for a hike. The exertion was a nice distraction from the new universe I'd created the night before but a tangle of emotion was never far from my mind.

The following day I woke up to a pleasantly deserted boat and got to work on some projects I'd been putting off. Working on the boat was always a good tonic for a distracted mind. I found engine work in particular extremely meditative.

The exertion of force against a wrench translated into leveraged torque could drain my mental stress and leave my brain floating, once again, in a purified bath of amniotic fluid.

Carly stopped by the boat as I torqued away at the engine, wearing a new red dress. Clearly she had her own tonic. She said that they were leaving but wanted to talk. Pat was on the dock. I only saw his legs. I was taking a bus to the other side of the island to meet up with my mom and the team later that day. She said she'd come by and see me before I left.

I waited and waited but she never came so I took off toward the bus station only to find her waiting around a corner. Apparently she hadn't wanted to see Brandoni and Chris. I had waited so long however, that we didn't have more than a few moments together before I had to leave to catch the bus. It didn't really matter, there wasn't too much to say anyhow. "I'll miss yous," were exchanged, I kissed her on the forehead and sprinted to catch my bus.

When I returned after a night on the southern coast, Pat and Carly were gone. Their stuff was absent from the boat aside from a few forgotten items; an emptiness enveloped their deserted area and my chest.

I wrote an e-mail to Pat and Carly, saying that I wished them the best and hoped they could work things out. Despite feeling extremely bad, the gravity of my actions hadn't truly sunk in. I was still vexed by the night I'd shared with Carly so when I received a response from her, including a question, I eagerly replied and thus perpetuated the mistakes I'd already committed. I failed to put myself in Pat's shoes in more than a cursory sense and to try and empathize with how he must have been feeling. I was way more wrapped up in my own interests than his. I even decided that, had Pat been in my shoes, he would have tried something with Carly years before I did. A former girlfriend of mine had said that he'd made some sort of pass at her, the details of which she was too embarrassed to relay. At the time I excused him. "I'm sure he was just drunk and didn't know what he was saying," I defended. She argued otherwise. He'd also almost broken up another relationship of mine because he had a thing for my girlfriend, and he even had a girlfriend of his own at the time. I was looking for justification, but ultimately there was none other than my own selfishness. What Pat would or would not have done in my shoes was irrelevant.

After several exchanges with Carly, I saw a message from Pat in my inbox and felt a sinking feeling in the pit of my stomach. I'd been carrying on with Carly almost as though Pat didn't exist, deluding myself into believing that he and Carly had probably reached some amicable understanding; that things just weren't working out for them and that he wouldn't mind if I simply corresponded with his wife, my old friend. I discovered that I was way off base with my assessment which, if I'd taken the time to honestly look at the situation, I knew already.

Pat reminded me that there were 3 billion other women in the world and told me in no uncertain terms to "stay the fuck away from his wife." The e-mail was rattling. I naturally shouldn't have been surprised but I'd never encountered such words from Pat and having the new parameters of our relationship defined so harshly was sobering and pulled me out of the fantasy world I'd begun to build around Carly. I sent one final e-mail to Carly, not mentioning Pat's e-mail, stating that I'd been awakened to the realities of what I was doing and could no longer interact with her.

Russian Chicks Part Duex

About 30 minutes after the American chicks packed up their shit and headed for the ferry terminal, I saw the Russian chicks walking towards the boat. We were tied up on the main quay not more than five minutes walk from the heart of town. It was only a matter of time before they happened upon us. Brandoni dove down the companionway and hid below deck. "Mike, what should I do? What should I do?" he pleaded. Chris had his back to the quay and just froze with an inaudible, "oh fuck," on his tongue, pretending not to see them; perhaps with the thought that if he sat still enough, they wouldn't be able to see him. "Tell them you're an asshole and beg for forgiveness," I offered to Brandoni.

The Russian chicks seemed almost equally caught off guard and, after exchanging confused expressions with each other, just kept on walking. They didn't walk for quite as long as Brandoni and Chris would have hoped. On their next pass they stopped right by the stern and looked down on us; Chris' chick with her hands on her hips, Brandoni's with her arms crossed.

"You're going to have to go up there Brandoni. They've already seen you. They know you're here," I stated, barely able to contain my excitement to see how things would unfold. "I know, I know, I'm just trying to figure out what to say." "I'm an asshole. I'm an asshole," he murmured as he climbed the ladder into the cockpit. Chris was doling out his Aussie charm with a big smile, hoping that perhaps they hadn't noticed that he and Brandoni had totally blown them off. "Hiya laydies, it's great to see ya." They weren't having it. Chris' chick in particular seemed thoroughly pissed off. "Why you not e-mail us?" she demanded. I watched, delighted, from the cockpit as Chris and Brandoni climbed onto the quay and began trying to explain themselves. "I'm as ass…" began Brandoni, but Chris interrupted him, "We just got here ladies. We were just about to e-mail you." It was a fine start but it required him to explain how it took us a week to sail down from Santorini. The girls were wise to this and Brandoni cut back in, "I'm an asshole."

At some point the Russian chicks decided that Chris and Brandoni were worth forgiving and it wasn't but a couple of hours before there were again four spasmodic legs protruding from Chris' bunk.

The next day however, Chris showed up at the boat looking utterly down trodden. "What's up?" I inquired. "It's all over. Over Red Rover." "Red Rover?" I inquired, having yet to be introduced to that particular Aussie euphemism. "Russian chick says she's pregnant." "Seriously?" "No way," cackled Brandoni, unable to contain a 'tough times' laugh. "That fuckin' sucks man," he added, hoping to take some of the sting out of his snicker.

Shortly after joining the crew, Chris had told us how, when he'd worked in the mines as a surveyor, the miners insisted that whenever you get hit by a rock or something pain inflicting, which, as one might imagine, happens fairly frequently in a mine, the proper response was, "I love it." Chris brought this with him. So whenever someone got their hand stuck under the anchor chain, spilled hot water on their crotch, chipped a tooth on a beer bottle, got a leech stuck in their eye, or puked in rough weather or rough drinking, the proper response was, "I love it."

"Do you love it Chris," I asked. Chris lifted his blank gaze from a spot between his feet. "I fucking love it," he replied in monotone. "What… what happened. What did she say?" begged Brandoni, still unable to conceal the grin on his face, hungry for details. "She said she doesn't want anything from me. Says she's keepin' it but that I don't have to do anything… I'm not totally convinced she's actually pregnant though." Chris livened up a little with the last thought. "She seems like she could be capable of something along those lines," I said, nodding. "Let's go get a pregnancy test and make her take it mate," Chris stated with determination.

We tracked down a pregnancy test but that night when Chris tried to get her to employ it, she balked at the idea. "No, I have been to doctor. I am pregnant," stated the Russian chick with finality. Chris continued to push, but she was firm on the point. The night progressed as many did and we all became intoxicated. All of us but Chris' Russian chick of course, because she was pregnant. I ended up passing out on deck and getting severely chiefed. I was covered in Russian writing the following day, which I found kind of exciting. I was just happy that my shorts were still on and my eyebrows intact.

Despite the situation, Chris still managed to find himself in the throngs of lovemaking with his Russian chick late that night. Having learned his lesson, he was in the process of trying to put on a condom when the Russian chick interrupted. "No, you don't need that," she cooed in his ear. Fortunately, Chris was aware enough to put things together and insisted on using the condom.

After a few days the Russian chicks left. The consensus was that Chris' chick probably wasn't pregnant, though the test was never used.

Chris and Brandoni's antics had been a pleasant distraction from my own fucked up situation but I realized that in truth, their folly was minor compared to the wrongs I'd perpetrated. I'd managed to convince myself that Pat and Carly's relationship was doomed before I interfered. But in the quiet solemn moments of future passages, with a clear headedness that only clean salt air can produce, I was reawakened to the complexly of romantic relationships; the most challenging of all social interactions. Clearly Pat and Carly had their issues that didn't involve me, but playing the easy role of a charming friend who possessed so many qualities that Pat did not, made all of the flaws in their relationship glare. In so many other situations, with a different paradigm of pressures, Pat and Carly may have worked through their issues and grown closer. Being committed to someone is infinitely more challenging than being a casual interloper delivering fleeting happiness in a dynamic reality. It was easy for Carly and I to blind ourselves; not distinguishing the line between love and lust.

Malta

The voyage came to an end in Crete for Chris as well. He'd been on board almost six months and had plans to rendez-vous with his mum, and a half of his family that he'd never met, in England. Brandoni and I weren't alone for long how-ever. We met a Canadian chick in a convenience store and before long she and her Australian friend were scrubbing the hull in preparation for our journey to Malta. Fortunately, they turned out to be agreeable shipmates and, more importantly, prevented Brandoni and I from spending 12 hours a day on watch. They also provided some entertainment.

The Aussie guy had a curious obsession with tanning his ass and cock. He would hang out on the foredeck on all fours (doggy style) with his shorts around his ankles and his ass pointed toward the sun. "Tell me when fifteen minutes are up so I can rotate and tan my cock and balls," he requested in a matter of fact tone. "Alternatively, we could jam a spit up your ass and put your on a rotisserie," I offered. "That would be weird," he pondered. "Oh yeah, that, would be weird," I replied casually. "Not nearly so normal as being down on all fours pointing your corn hole at the sun," I murmured to Brandoni.

He also admitted to shaving and even waxing his scrotum. Brandoni winced, "what, you wax your scrotum?" Brandoni and I looked at the Canadian chick to see how she was reacting. She shrugged, "it's actually more common than you might think…in non-pirate society of course." "Of course." The Aussie eventually returned to the cockpit after a few rotations, leaving a fairy large slick of sunscreen on the foredeck. I was fairly revolted after identifying a few hairs that probably came from his ass, since he presumably, though I never inspected, had no hair on his cock and balls. I had to resist the gag reflex. "Let's put a towel down when we tan our asses in the future," I suggested. "Yeah, no worries."

After several days at sea we pulled into Malta. In a nutshell, Malta was kind-of like Rhodes, only not nearly as cool. Had we gone to Malta first, it would have been much more impressive.

Elton John was giving a concert, affording us a good excuse to drink a lot of red wine; as if we ever needed one. Tickets naturally weren't in the budget, or the prerogative, so we all climbed up onto a seven foot pillar where we could see a little speck that was presumably Sir John. The top of the pillar consisted of a four square foot surface to stand on and there were about five or six of us crammed on top dancing, or at least bobbing. All was going well until one corner of the pillar, probably a couple thousand year old artifact, gave way, almost taking down one of the bobbers with it.

With the fall of the pillar and the consumption of enough wine we decided it was time to crash the concert. The plan, if you could call it that, was to climb the fence all at once and scatter, hoping that at least some of us would be able to elude security.

Brandoni with a Shortbilled Spearfish in the Mediterranean

For me, the plan went pear shaped early on. Having an open cask of wine in one hand and a bag with a couple of backups in the other, didn't leave me with anything more than a few fingers to devote to the climbing. Going up the fence went fine but then I tried to flourish the descent with a little head first flip. The fence refused to let go of me however. Both my shirt and the plastic bag of wine got caught on the wire, tearing open the bag of wine as I mostly slid down the fence. In doing so I managed to tear down an advertising banner in which became ensnared. There was nothing discrete about my entry, though I did manage not to spill my open cask of wine. I think Elton looked up from the piano for a second.

After gathering my wine, and pushing the torn advert back against the fence, I did my best to achieve a casual demeanor and trotted off towards the crowd. I failed to make it more than five steps before I was approached by a large dude in a tight black T-shirt. He didn't say anything, just looked at me cradling my three boxes of wine and pointed towards the door. Apparently I'd already done a good enough job roughing myself up. Brandoni had managed to get about five feet past me but was apprehended by the same tight T-shirt. "Cumon' man, we came all the way from California to see Elton man!" Brandoni pleaded with a red toothed smile. "No."

I handed Brandoni the open cask of wine as we stood looking back at the door we'd just been escorted out of. "At least we tried." "Yeah, and it could have gone a lot worse. We're not in jail." "Not yet." As we stood staring at the door with wine dripping from our chins, reminiscing about our 60 seconds of glory, we saw the Canadian chick being shoved out the door. Brandoni extended the cask her way. "Thanks."

Tunisia

The Aussie and the Canadian departed in Malta and Brandoni and I set sail for Tunisia. The 175 mile passage took us about five days to cover; owing to extremely light winds. It was tiring only having the two of us to alternate watches, but calm and pleasant enough. We drank a large cup of wine every night. "Hey captain, what time is it?" "I'd say it's about wine thirty."

Tunisia was hot and dry. We decided we wanted to check out the Sahara so we embarked on a 13 hour bus/van ride south. We rode camels in the desert for an hour and then took the 13 hour bus ride back to the boat. Apparently, most people go to the desert in the winter. Now we know.

Brandoni and Mike riding camels in the Sahara Desert

Mallorca

The wind was more constant for our sail up to Mallorca, Spain, but consistently from the direction that we wanted to go and, frequently, quite strong. One mighty gust shredded the jib. Fortunately, I had a back up. I didn't care for the cut of it but it was in good condition.

After six days at sea, Brandoni and I pulled into Palma de Mallorca of the Balearic Islands. We eventually found our way into the crystal clear water of Illetes Bay, which would become my home for the next several months.

Having felt we'd exhausted our ability to party, and our finances (I hadn't worked in over a year) we decided to spend our time exploring the island via bike. Brandoni rented a bike and I spent half a day removing all the rust from mine that, coincidentally, Brandoni had given me before I left California. We spent the better part of a week devouring a small portion of the island, which turned out to be perfect for biking.

Brandoni was scheduled to fly out of Palma at 11:25 pm. As a fare well to the summer in the Med, we planned to go big.

I've since discovered that I typically go at least one level past what I plan, so planning on going big, often equated to going huge. Hell, 'having a couple of beers,' often led to going huge.

The morning was spent casually packing up Brandoni's belongings and cleaning the boat. We finished off the previous night's cask of wine, smoked a little of the hash that we'd procured since arriving, just to get warmed up, and paddled to land, sipping on the water bottle we'd filled with wine. We returned Brandoni's bike and walked the couple of miles into town.

Just as we dusted the plastic bottle of wine, we headed into the Consum Supermarket. We B-lined it to the warm beer section and stashed a couple of 22 ouncers under the frozen vegetables. We'd discovered that they only sold cold beer at the smaller convenience stores, where the beer cost double what it did in the markets. Hence we arrived at the stashing the beer under the vegetables solution; arguably one of Brandoni's most brilliant ideas. With the beers in place, we took our time perusing the market for lunch supplies. Brandoni also decided he was going to bring home some Spanish wine. The one litter casts were only 49 Euro cents, making them one of the best deals on alcohol worldwide; as a bonus it actually tasted pretty good. It also traveled well. Brandoni loaded up the cart with 19 casks, all that they had, and we got in the checkout line. I scrambled back to get the two beers stashed in the vegetables just as the last cask was being scanned, to maximize coldness.

Loaded up, we found ourselves a good 'people watching bench,' made a couple of sandwiches, and sucked down our beers. Feeling full but not quite content, we headed down to McDonald's for a back to back session of soft serve ice cream. I was done after the first one but we'd planned on doubling down the previous day, when we arrived at McDonald's post closing, and I didn't want to spoil the fun. Buzzed and bloated, we planted ourselves on our favorite tree lined promenade and let it all sink in.

Temporarily satiated, we made for the internet café so that Brandoni could check on his flight and burn a couple of my CDs. The burning process took awhile and we utilized the time by opening another cast of wine. We chatted up a Polish chick who shared our box of wine.

I received an e-mail from a Dutch couple sailing on a tri-maran who we'd met in Greece, saying that they'd just arrived in Mallorca and were tied up close by. We decided to meet up with them and invited the Polish chick along. She was inter-ested but wanted to get her friend first and gave us her phone number in case we left before she got back. We did end up leaving before she returned. She was quite cute but I was get-ting the same vibe from her that I'd gotten from Chris' Russian chick so I wasn't too disappointed when the CD burning fin-ished up and she hadn't returned.

The next section of the evening is almost a total blank. I recall fashioning a hash pipe out of a Coke can. I don't recall actually using it but what happened after makes me inclined to think that we did.

I woke up under some sort of a hedge. After establish-ing the basics, that I was on land, on Mallorca, I tried to get more specific bearings. I noticed a half eaten sandwich on the ground next to me, picked it up, brush off some of the juniper needles, and resumed, I assumed, eating it. I looked around for any sign of Brandoni but only located my back-pack jammed a bit further under the bushes. I stood up and recognized my general location. I still didn't see Brandoni, but feeling rather sober, figured I must have been out for awhile, and since it must surely be past 11:25, he was on his flight back home.

As I rounded the hedge back onto a bike path, I saw Brandoni. He was laying face down, half in the bike path and half on the island that separated the two directions of the path. "Brandoni!" He rolled over in a state of stupification. "Shit…

what happened?" he moaned. "No idea, but I'm guessing you missed your plane." "Shit, where's my backpack?" "Must be around here somewhere," I estimated, offering Brandoni a bite of my sandwich. We searched around, trying to piece things together, but no pieces came; nor did the backpack, which contained his passport, his plane tickets, all his personal shit, and 14 or 15 boxes of wine. He still had his sleeping bag stuff sack that he'd been using as a pillow and planned on using as a carry on. It contained his driver's license, bank card, and a hand painted porcelain plate he'd purchased in Tunisia as a gift. He opened the sack and took out the plate, now in two pieces. "Shiiiiit!" "You might be able to glu…" he chucked the plate in trash breaking it into several more pieces and we started walking. "Sandwich?" I asked, offering him what was left of my surprisingly tasty morsel. "Thanks." We eventually determined that it was 3:30 am. We'd left the internet café at around 9:30 pm, which explained why we felt relatively sober.

We wondered aimlessly around town trying to figure out what had happened, hoping his backpack might magically appear. "What are you going to do?" I asked, unable to hold back a chuckle. Brandoni, looking a bit haggard, like he'd just spent the night in a bike path, responded, "catch a cab to the airport and try and sort shit out there…I guess. There's a 7:30 am flight to Barcelona. If I can catch that, I can meet up with the rest of my flight back to the States." "I guess you'll be needing some cash for cab fare." I gave him about 13 Euros and he was off. "I wonder if that Polish chick slipped us a mickey," I thought to myself as Brandoni's cab sped towards the airport.

Mallorca II

Making money was a necessity. I was down to a couple hundred US. I met up with my Dutch friends and brainstormed ways to make some dough. There were a number of street performers in Palma, so painting my body gold and juggling was on the table for awhile, but didn't stick. There was probably some sort of street performer's guild and I barely had enough money for the gold body paint.

The second option was to sell beer on the beach. I already had a decent sized cooler and beer in the super market was very cheap. It seemed I could make a fortune selling beer for two or three Euros a pop. There were some logistical problems however. The beaches were a few miles away from the boat and I would have to get the cooler, ice and beer down to the beach using just my backpack and bike. There were also numerous bike cops patrolling the beach and I was sure that if selling beer on the beach was legal, someone would have already have been doing it. There were also bars next to the beach selling beer at five Euros a pop that wouldn't likely be too fond of my undercutting them. I eventually put the 'beer on the beach' idea to rest.

The most plausible and time tested idea seemed to be to 'pound the docks.' Every morning I got at the butt crack of dawn and made my way into town and down to the marinas. Once on the dock I went from boat to boat, "any day work?" Or, "*necesita trabaja para el dia*?" if they looked to be Spanish speaking. It was a demoralizing process; over 99% of the attempts ended in failure. I generally wasn't too disappointed, however, if on any given day I didn't find work.

An early start on the day put me in a position for a good long bike ride. A bonus to the ride was that I could pick food along the way. The first stop was the fig tree. Figs were just starting to ripen but I could usually find four or five that were edible. After the figs, I climbed into the hills and fed on black berries until my fingers were purple. Depending on which way I went, I might also happen upon pears or apples. Around lunchtime I found myself in some quaint little town where I could buy a baguette, a tomato, and cheese and ham by the slice; putting together a sandwich for less than two Euros. I fell in love with Mallorca.

On one occasion I did find work on the docks. I'd become so accustomed to being rejected that I was actually taken aback when a German guy responded with a, "yes, we have a very dirty boat." I'd determined that the going rate for day work was 12 Euros an hour and made about 450 over the course of three days; I was stoked. Unfortunately at the end of the three days, stem to stern was completely buffed, polished and scrubbed and I was once again pounding the docks.

"Hanuman…Hanuman…," poured down the companionway early one morning in an accented voice. I crawled on deck to find Olf, the German single hander, doing circles around me. It was good to see someone from the Red Sea. It reminded me of a time when life was more elemental. We spent the evening drinking beer on Hanuman and then rowed over to a German boat who's owner Olf had met the in the marina he had just skipped out of paying from, explaining his early arrival, for a few more beers. Tom was a general manager in large tourism company that managed rental cars and cruise liners. Olf thought he might be able to hook me up with a job; the main purpose of our visit. Tom respected Olf's and my sailing prowess, affording us a little respect and clout. We eventually alluded to the fact that I was looking for work and he slowly agreed to see what he could do.

Olf left the following day but a couple of days later Tom took me to work with him. His English wasn't stellar so I was a little confused as to what was going on. He said that I wasn't technically allowed to work, "perhaps you can take a Spanish wife, hee, hee, hee." I shrugged, "give me a couple of days." I thought he was just showing me around, and that I might be working at some point in the future if things could be worked out, but then came the, "okay, bye," and he was off.

He dropped me off at one of the companies' rental car garages. It wasn't a typical garage, and I wasn't quite sure precisely what went on there, but it turned out to be my new place of work. The place was run by Klaus, a German guy in his late 40ties wearing flip flops with socks and overalls, who spoke only German and some Spanish. It was actually advantageous that his Spanish was limited, it kept conversations simple. Once I learned a few more curse words, communication was no problem at all. Gerhard, another German in his early 20ties, was in the process of becoming a licensed mechanic and was Klaus' understudy.

I worked most closely with Wofa from Ghana. He'd immigrated to Spain about five years prior. He spoke Akan, the native language of Ghana, English, which was taught in school in Ghana, and Spanish, which he'd picked up, though not too well, since moving to Spain. We conversed mostly in English. "I no really like talking Spanish," he stated. We got along well. We were responsible for moving supplies from the old garage into the current one. The garages were several miles apart and I drove Wofa and myself back and forth in a van, transferring car parts.

Wofa had never driven before. There was a large parking lot at the garage where we picked stuff up, and we were completely unsupervised, so I though it my obligation to teach him how to drive. Wofa wasn't a natural driver and the van was a stick shift which didn't make things any easier. I persisted with the instruction, though we never got to a place where I felt comfortable taking him out on an actual road. Wofa never fully grasped the clutch to gas ratio and frequently panicked and got all of the pedals confused. I wore my seat belt and kept one hand on the emergency break.

Over time I pieced together Wofa's story. He'd left his wife and four children in Ghana and headed north through the Sahara Desert. It took him and the two friends he'd left with over a year to get to Morocco. I'd initially pictured him crawling through the sand to get to there but after getting to know Wofa better, I gathered he'd taken buses and just stopped along the way for periods of time to make money. He had a shoe repair kit and set up 'shop' on the street in various towns. "Is it difficult to make money doing that?" I asked. "No, everybody have shoe." His friends were tailors and made money in the same fashion. "Everybody have clothes," I thought to myself.

He eventually arrived at a Spanish refugee camp where he spent four months waiting for papers to get into Spain. He ultimately got the papers and, after working as a night watchman for awhile on the mainland, made his way to Mallorca where he got a job in the garage. "Is it hard to find work in here," I asked. Wofa shrugged, "one man's luck is not like another's. One man can walk down the street one day and find no work and the next day another man can walk down the same street and find a job." Wofa had the tendency to answer yes or no question with a complex answer and complex questions with a yes or no answer. "How did your family feel about you leaving? Were they okay with it?" "Yes."

I discovered that Wofa had left his family previously, when he took a three year trek to inland Africa. He didn't contact them the whole time he was gone and only came home because he "had a little problem with one man's wife." "I hear that," I thought. "How did they feel when you returned?" "They were happy."

Wofa came to Spain to make money. His father had owned a building supplies shop but after he died, the shop fell apart and he needed money. After working with Wofa for a couple of weeks I wasn't particularly surprised to learn that the shop had failed. He seemed to have some serious short comings in the 'building things' department. "Mike, this one very tight," he commented in reference to a bolt he was trying to undo. It wasn't the first time I'd seen him in such a conundrum. "Righty tighty, lefty loosey" clearly didn't translate well in Akan because he was tightening the bolt he was trying to get off.

His business sense didn't seem spot on either. He confided that he had a plan to load up a shipping container full of stuff in Spain, have it shipped down to Ghana, and sell it at a profit. Given the relative economies of Spain versus Ghana, it seemed to me a much better idea to fill a container with things from Ghana and sell them in Spain. But then what did I know about business, my first business idea involved covering myself in gold paint.

With the advent of a job my life became rather routine. I would get up when I saw the silver glow of dawn peeking through the main hatch, down some water, and climb on deck for a piss. Relieved, I would turn on the radio, listen to the BBC, and scrounge around for something to eat. Stale bread and half fermented jam was the norm. After brushing my teeth I'd pack up my dry bag with shoes and a shirt and jump in the water. The floor of the dinghy had completely given out the night Olf and I rowed over to Tom's so it was on deck for repairs.

In the cool water I'd take a crap, tie the dry bag to my ankle, and swim for shore. Walking up the pebbly beach, I'd shake like a dog, get out my shoes and shirt, and hop on the bike for a 45 minute ride to work. Work lasted until six and then I'd head back to the boat via SYP Consum market for some bread and, if I was treating myself, some fruit and vegetables. The drudgery was eventually broken up when I met Roccio.

A few bikini clad girls in a power boat that had anchored nearby Hanuman caused me to alter my gaze from Sputnik, who I was trying to glue back together.

Giles, who worked for a restaurant in the next bay over, ferried people to and from boats in my bay to the restaurant in a large dinghy. I'd gotten to know him during his frequent visits to 'my bay.' He was English but had been living in Spain for several years. If he had the time he would come on board, have some cask wine and shoot the shit. After dropping a couple more people off on the boat with the bikinis he swung by and climbed on deck.

Giles had delivered a boat up the Red Sea and had a measure of swarthiness to him but still held onto a certain amount of the English sense of diction. He managed a dynamic equilibrium. When I mentioned that I didn't own any pants, he felt inclined to inform me that if I wasn't wearing pants then I'd be in my knickers, as shorts were in fact just short pants. "Well in that case I'd actually just be naked since I've deemed knickers superfluous," I chuckled. "Right-O."

"What's with that boat over there with all the young flesh?" I inquired. "Just some rich stuck-up fuckers from Madrid," responded Giles' saltier side. I handed him a mug and poured some wine. A couple of roaches came out with the pour.

346

"They won't have drunk much," I offered. Giles eyed the two roaches bobbing around in his mug dubiously. "The problem with the 49 cent casks is the pull tab opener. You can get into the snap top cap for 75 cents but I personally would rather invest those 25 cents in the wine itself," I explained. "How long has this box been open?" queried Giles. I could see his English sense of order invading his mind once again. "Give me that you pussy," I demanded, jerking the mug out of his hand. I opened a fresh cask, poured him another mug, and took the roach garnished mug for myself. I normally would have fingered out the roaches, but left them in to prove a point. Mildly disgusted Giles downed his wine and jumped back in his company dinghy, he was working after all.

One of the dudes from the bikini boat, Albacore, swam over and asked me where I'd come from and other details relating to my vagabond lifestyle. Still intrigued he invited me over to Albacore for some coffee. Coffee turned out to be code for gin and tonic; all the better.

I was introduced to the rest of the group; five girls and one guy, my kind of ratio. They were all Spanish and mostly lived in Madrid. Albacore belonged to the family of one of the girls; Roccio. She flew to Mallorca almost every weekend during the summer and sunned herself on the boat, movie star style. After a few drinks Roccio yelled down to the captain for some nuts and fruits and, shazam, nuts and fruits appeared.

The sun dipped and the captain said he wanted to head back before it got dark. Roccio claimed he was lazy but said that he'd saved her father's life at some point, ensuring his tenure as captain. I thanked them for the drinks, dove in the water and started swimming back to Hanuman. As I was swimming, Roccio called to me and asked if I wanted to come to the boat for dinner back in port. Naturally I accepted.

We dined on rich foods that my stomach hadn't experienced in recent memory. I had to hold back to avoid making a pig of myself. The night eventually wound down and Roccio and I found ourselves alone.

Roccio and I commenced a borderline relationship that took place on the weekends. A weekend or two later the rest of her family was came to Mallorca. They had a house in Mallorca as well as Madrid and possibly a couple of other houses.

I arrived at the dock and found Roccio's mom, dad, younger brother and younger brother's friend hanging out in the stern of the boat. It happened to be beard day and despite not having any crew around to join in on the festivities I deemed it obligatory to participate; consequently I arrived sporting a pretty nifty little facial motif. They must have thought I was some sort of a quack; an estimation probably not too far off the mark.

I wasn't sure which language to go with but decided on Spanish and asked the mom if Roccio was available. She said that she would be up in a moment but ventured no further conversation. The dad didn't even look at me, at least not directly, but I could see that he was studying me out of the corner of his eye. He may as well have been holding his newspaper upside down for all his discretion. The brother had his back to me and never turned around. In his father's vein of counter intelligence his friend was clearly relaying the details of my appearance. The friend only thinly veiled his laughter. I could see his chest convulsing as he stared wide eyed and tight lipped at a point exactly two feet to my right.

I hung out in the comically awkward situation for a few prolonged minutes. I considered just leaving but eventually Roccio emerged and we walked off, no introductions or anything. I tried to imagine any of my family interacting in such a manner. The dad was clearly way too full of himself to ever stoop to the level of introducing himself to some ruffian that his daughter had dug up.

"Great, now I have to explain 'beard day' to them," Roccio whined. After a few other such incidents, where Roccio came to question my socialization, talk quickly changed from, "I think I want to sail to the Canary's with you (though I'd never actually invited her) and maybe fly and meet you in the Caribbean" to "I think I'm busy this weekend." Ultimately she broke it off with an e-mail. I saw it coming and my ego considered doing a preemptive breakup but I was still hoping to get at least a little more prosciutto out off the deal. I was a little upset initially, especially since a Roccio sponsored weekend on the other side of the island was in the books, but also a little relieved since I was starting to get the 'I might be stuck with her' feeling. Ultimately I summed the relationship up with a, "that was nice," and moved on.

To my surprise I received an e-mail from Nicole saying that she wanted to sail across the Atlantic. After the trip up the Red Sea I thought that she might be done with sailing forever. It turned out that she'd developed a love hate relationship with the sea, common to anyone who's spent a significant time off-shore. While she may have been miserable for a good portion of our last voyage, life on land didn't seem quite as fulfilling as it had before and the Siren's call was too pervasive to ignore.

I quit my job several weeks before departure so that I could work full time getting the boat ready. Since leaving San Francisco, the mast had been slowly sinking into the mast step; the chunk of wood that supported it. I'd been gradually tightening the turnbuckles that kept the mast in place but they were maxed out. Something had to be done.

I had the mast pulled at the marina that charged the least. It seemed that the crane operator had never performed such a task however. I actually had to climb up the mast and put on the hoisting sling. The crane operator had no idea where it should be attached. I'd had the mast pulled once before but had no hand in the operation so I wasn't super confident. I figured just above halfway seemed like a logical place to put the sling; allowing the mast to be pulled up vertically and set down horizontally without catastrophe. To my surprise everything went according to plan.

With the mast removed, I dug out the rotten mast step and, consequently, all surrounding floor. Using mostly hand tools, and making extended trips to the lumber yard on my bike, over the course of a couple weeks I constructed new step and several new floor supports. I cut a couple of inches off the bottom of the mast because the aluminum had corroded severely. To compensate I raised the wooden step. "Maybe problem with all this changing things," Gerhard commented between gulps of beer. "Nah, it'll all be fine. I've measured everything," I replied, pointing to scrape of mangled paper covered with my chicken scratches. Eventually I had the mast step epoxied in place and covered with several layers of fiberglass, complete with proper drainage channels to ensure no future rotting. "Looks pretty good actually," Gerhard commented, as he pounded on it with his free hand. "Hopefully it lines up with the hole in the deck." "Hopefully."

Nicole and I motored Hanuman back to the marina for the reinstallation. It was a big day. If things didn't go well, there was major potential for a serious wrench in my works.

The guy operating the crane had equally large gaps in his knowledge of mast installation as he did of mast removal. His foresight wasn't spectacular either, and on the first go he failed to realize that the mast would be backwards when it got to the boat. Nicole and I turned the boat around and we proceeded with the install. To our amazement the re-step, if not entirely smooth, was as success. The hole in the deck lined up with the new step and the rigging went into place. I'd been without a mast for a month and felt whole again with it back in place.

Gibraltar

Two weeks after celebrating my 30th birthday, we'd transformed Hanuman from a floating party platform back into a sailing vessel. We pulled anchor, mostly ready to go. A trial run day had been scheduled to test the new mast placement and see if any adjustments needed to be made. I'd also switched out the thoroughly chewed up main I'd been using, for another, less used, main that had come with the boat. I'd never actually taken it out of its bag but inspection of the cloth revealed it to be in good condition and constructed by a reputable sailmaker. The sail didn't quite make it to the end of the boom but I figured… "Perfect." The day scheduled for the test run turned out to be overcast and drizzly; a day more suited to drinking and socializing than sailing.

"What about that whole test run thing," Nicole asked as we hoisted the anchor, bound for Gibraltar. I'd previously informed her that a test run was absolutely necessary because the rigging was likely to stretch a little once we loaded it up. I didn't frequently totally contradict myself and I could sense that Nicole might be wondering if the Med had softened my brain. "Well, I figure that the first half of today will be the test run and if things don't go well we can just turn around and come back. "Hmmm, turn around aye?" "Yeah, turn around." Turning around wasn't one of my strong points, and Nicole sensed the disingenuousness of my offering, but did me the courtesy of not pushing the point; she too, was ready to be on our way.

A gentle tailwind escorted us out of my home of three months. I began hoisting the 'new' main for the first time. Since the sail didn't make it all the way to the end of the boom, I expected it not to make it to the top of the mast. I was quite surprised when it topped out and I still had and few folds at the bottom. "It would appear that it's too tall," I casually informed Nicole. "What's that mean?" "I guess we'll have to cross the Atlantic with a reef in the main." "Hmmm."

Nicole had spent enough time on board Hanuman to know that less sail area meant less speed and a longer passage. I was also using the 'new' jib which was considerably smaller than the one that had been shredded on the way to Mallorca. "It's gonna take us forever to cross the Atlantic isn't it Fellasio?" "You have to think of it as more crossing for your money." Ultimately getting paid eight Euros and 35 cents an hour at the garage hadn't translated into huge saving. I had considerably more flexibility in my time line than I did in my budget.

Despite the lack of sail area, I was pleased with the shape of the new main. The old one had become so 'bellied out' that its performance to windward had been severely compromised. The fact that I anticipated a mostly downwind run across the Atlantic, where a bellied out main was ideal, had to be ignored.

By late October the Med had turned cold and angry; if not angry than certainly a little peeved. The second day out Nicole and I found ourselves in Polar-tech and full rain gear. Our tailwind swung around, heading us with 25 knots and putting the new main to the test. The sail performed well but

Nicole and I were less than stoked with the wintery conditions. "This kind of sucks," I observed. "Yeah it does. And the fact that it's raining just sort of seems like a slap in the face." As a consolation we saw our first moonbow.

We decided to pull into an anchorage prior to Gibraltar and wait for better weather. It was actually a loading area for huge ships transporting coal, and certainly not the prettiest place I'd ever anchored, but it was well protected and no one told us to leave.

Arnout, the Dutch guy on the trimaran I'd met earlier in the summer, was to meet us in Gibraltar and join us for the sail to the Canaries and the across the Atlantic. He ended up bussing it to our location along the Gold Coast, which was anything but gold. Arnout had grown up sailing but had never crossed an ocean and was excited to do so.

The second day in route to Gibraltar, Arnout was in the galley eating an apple and making dough for bread. The wind had mellowed but the rain increased. It was a crappy day. I had no motivation for such activities as bread making but admired Arnout's energy and was excited to eat fresh bread, though I thought it unlikely that the dough would rise in such frigid conditions. I was taken aback when Arnout came flying up the stairs. Such weather didn't generally instigate sudden anything. The motivation for the flight was soon evident when Arnout bent over the rail and started blowing chunks into the sea. "I love…it," he grunted between heaves. It wasn't just a little spit up either. Legitimate chunks were chumming the water. "Good form, good form," I applauded. I ended up with a half an apple out of the deal and was impressed when he resumed kneading the dough. The Rock of Gibraltar rose out of the mist and we motored into a well lit port in the early evening.

Gibraltar was cold. In my recollection the sun never came out. I imagined that the British brought their weather with them. We were pinned down for a week and half waiting for a reasonable weather window. The Strait of Gibraltar accelerated the Westerly's into hellasious winds. There were two days during which we couldn't even leave the boat and the threat of dragging anchor and ending up on the rocks was tangible. Hanuman was hobby horsing so badly that I practically had to crawl to go forward and check the anchor chain. Waves crashed over me as I did so. I found the bow roller broken and lashed it up with multiple lines. Crawling back to the cockpit, soaked, I looked across the water, streaked white by the wind, at a boat whose dinghy was flying behind it like a kite. The catamaran behind us had a roller furling head sail that the wind managed to get a little piece of. Once a small portion was exposed, the wind sunk its claws into it, unraveling it completely. Once unravel, it didn't stand a chance. The sail did one big whomp up, one down, and the whole mess of sail and rigging came crashing down on deck, leaving the mast shuttering from the strain. The whole process took less the than three seconds. It was the most wind I'd experienced on Hanuman; probably the most I'd experienced in my life.

Still bloated from our second 'all you can eat' session at Pizza Hut, we pulled up the anchor and left Gibraltar with the tide, anxious to capitalize on a good weather window. Lashing the anchor in place, I noticed the gate of the large shackle attaching the anchor to the anchor chain was drastically bent. I had to cut it off to replace it. Never skimp on ground tackle.

Atlas, deeming us worthy, let us pass the gates of Gibraltar without further delay, and our first sunrise of the passage was in the Atlantic. The air was warm, we were followed by a school of Bonito that could be caught as soon as the lure hit the water, and the heavy cold that had enveloped us for the previous month was just a memory; albeit a goose-bump inducing one.

New challenges awaited me in the Atlantic however, namely Arnout. He was a great guy in general and I was sure he wouldn't have bothered me on land but the pace of the ocean is unique and his idea of how things should go was different that mine. He was way too much of a 'Type A' for my liking. He was constantly tugging on lines that didn't need tugging on. He jerked the wheel back and forth when he steered, and generally just moved around in an overbearing manner. His presence began to feel like an invasion of my boat, my home, my temple. He even jerked the wheel out of my hand when I was steering once. I let him know as calmly as I could, but in no uncertain terms, that that was completely unacceptable. But what I really wanted to do was bitch-slap him.

He also lacked the patients that I though necessary for passage making. He cursed the wind, or lack thereof, on calm days and paced around on deck. He called the fish stupid for biting the lure. Insulting the intelligence of an animal seemed the height of narrow mindedness to me. "Sit down, be calm," I wanted to say to him. But telling someone to be calm can have just the opposite effect, so I ended up spending more time in my bunk so I wouldn't have to share space with him. I was sure I was annoying him as well. An overly tranquil person can be just as annoying as a restless one from the opposite prospective. But for the most part we all got along and pulled into Gran Canaria after just over a week at sea.

Some boats where hanging out in the Canaries, waiting for the trades to fill in, hoping for a fast passage. My mom had bought me a plane ticket home for Thanksgiving from the US Virgin Islands and I was anxious to get underway so I that wouldn't miss it. The thought of sitting on the couch watching TV with a beer in one hand and the remote in the other was a strong motivating factor.

The Atlantic

The passage from Gran Canaria to St. Martin was slated to be the longest passage, mileage wise, of the trip. We started off heading south, hoping to pick up the Trades and make a faster passage.

I'd spent plenty of time planning and preparing Hanuman for the passage but I failed to anticipate the excessive amount of time I'd have for introspection. As the passage progressed, the image I'd created of my 'vacation' at my mom's, chillin' in a world free of dog watches and midnight sail changes, was replaced by the thought of encounters with all those who'd become aware of my antics in Crete. I imagined being confronted by a combination of angry faces, blank puzzled stares, and pitying eyes. Beyond that, there would be the general onslaught of repetitive questions that I would be continually trying to answer with few and fewer words. "Have you been in any storms?" I decided I'd just answer that one with a simple, "No." Then there were the questions that would be simply impossible to really answer. "What's it like?" I couldn't help but think of Aussie Chris' favorite modification of a common Thai response, "same, same, totally fuckin' different." The thought of leaving the boat went from exciting to unsettling. I felt the boat and the sea had become an extension of me. Things happened on my terms and harmonized with an inherent logic I felt in the stem of my brain. Interacting with land people seemed a grating task.

The night became my favorite time. I'd begun the around the world journey with a distrust of the night. My senses cloaked, I felt exposed. The boat's erratic motion had induced a feeling of vertigo. The breaking of dawn was always a relief from the mild tension that had made camp in the pit of my stomach.

In the mid-Atlantic, the night comforted me with a cool blanket of stars. The quiet alone of the cockpit tapped the tension of the day, draining it to a bottemless sink of emptiness.

Asleep in my bunk, dreaming that I could see the stars through the ceiling above me, as I often did, I got two gentle knocks from Nicole, who was on watch. On the overcast moonless night, we slowly headed south in search of the Trades. "I heard breathing," Nicole whispered as I ascended the ladder. I soon heard it as well. It was the long deep breath of a giant, and close enough to smell. "It's as dark as the inside of a cow, I can't see anything." Nicole had just been introduced to the new metaphor and was giddy with the excuse to use it. The night was dead quiet, save the breathing of the whale.

We tried to roust Arnout but he was an extremely heavy sleeper and a bitch to get up. I'd consciously put his watch after Nicole's so that I wouldn't have to deal with waking him. In addition to being slightly evil, I figured I had enough other responsibilities without adding waking Arnout to the mix.

The breathing stopped. Nicole and I waited silently for something to happen. Arnout had come to and was thrashing around looking for his glasses. A large shape emerged from the blackness just below the surface of the water not ten feet off the port side. It wasn't the whale itself that we could see but the phosphorescence excited around it, form-ing a perfectly illuminated ghost-like negative extending the length of Hanuman. In the darkness, it was hard to tell where the sky ended and the sea began. The whale, perfectly motionless, appeared to hover in mid air.

Arnout clamored up the companionway, adjusting his glasses as he did so, but just as he made it in to the cockpit shouting, "where is it, where is it?" the whale, with a single beat of his tail, submerged into the depths leaving a comet streak of light in his wake. "Damn it!" Arnout lamented. Having never seen a whale, he was bummed to have missed out on the experience. It was on his checklist of things to do while crossing the Atlantic. "Why didn't you guys wake me up sooner?" "We tried," we responded with a shrug. Nicole and I had to wait until Arnout went back to bed before rehashing the magic of the experience.

Despite the ethereal visit from the whale, my mental con-dition continued to degrade. Something about my mental chemistry wasn't right. Darkness overtook my thoughts and mood. The feeling of love and compassion I sought to main-tain was overtaken by indifference and a devious enjoyment of the suffering of others. The frequently overcast skies and squalls didn't help. I partially attributed my condition to lack of exercise and frequent over eating.

In an attempt to rectify my feeling of well being I decided that a day of fasting was in order. With the fast, I hoped to reset my metabolism and other chemical factors and also cleanse my spirit through deprivation. My ideas of metabo-lism and chemistry had no grounding in any actual science, having come purely from observation and speculation. But, since I was ultimately just trying to change my perception, I figured it didn't really mater. I also had to admit that part of me decided to fast just for something to do, and for the sensa-tion of hunger, to feel something.

After my turn to the dark side I had trouble feeling anything aside from a dull hateful feeling. Listening to music on my night watches didn't give me as much pleasure as it had previously. I couldn't find a CD I enjoyed. Conversation was empty and often annoying and aggravating. I got no real satisfaction from eating but over ate anyhow, longing to fill the void.

I considered cutting myself, just for the sensation, for the first time ever. I didn't seriously consider it, but the thought entered my mind. I imagined carving an anchor into my arm but was still concerned enough with societal acceptance to think that people would see it and say, "Yup, he's gone over the deep end… too much time at sea… should have gotten a regular job while he could still function in society." I began to realize the importance that my fast be intended to increase my well being, instead of just an act of masochistic desperation.

I started to feel hungry around 10:23 am and considered what a great act of weakness it would be to give in so early, after investing so much thought into the effort. Upon further contemplation, I began to feel that recently my life had become a string of acts of weakness, and that failing at my fasting endeavor might be right on par with how I'd been living my life.

I managed to make it through my day of fasting without too much difficulty. I asked myself if it had been all that I was hoping for. I wasn't really under the illusion that after a day without food all of my problems would vanish, and I would suddenly gaze upon the world as if awakened form a trance and weep for the beauty of the sunrise, but it had been nice to feel the hunger. It was satisfying to resist eating. I considered that in resisting the temptation to eat, perhaps I was trying to fortify myself to resist other temptations I'd given into in the past…or perhaps not.

In reality, complete abstinence wasn't really a problem for me. It was moderation that was one of my biggest hurdles. The 'stop eating' signal often didn't flash in my brain until I was stuffed like a Thanksgiving Turkey; hence my love-hate relationship with 'all you can eat' buffets.

My outlook did marginally improve after the fast, though that may have come from changes in Arnout's. While he still occasionally annoyed me, he had become more settled into the rhythm of the boat. He could sit for hours at a time reading, completely absorbed in his book, without the need to move around excessively. A pleasant calmness came over him. We'd also managed to find our way into more consistent winds after a week at sea, which had a settling affect on everyone.

After a week in the Trades we found ourselves halfway to St. Martin and well settled into the passage. Making good mileage was always a sure cure for over analyzing ones' life. Conversation turned to stimulating subjects, like defecation.

We spent a great deal of time talking about shitting. Nicole's shitting specifically. She seemed to have a real problem with constipation. Of course, one person's problem can be another's comedy and Arnout, who had been renamed 'R-2,' and I thought the situation pure hilarity.

We decided that Nicole's chief problem was that she didn't know how long it took for a given food item to pass through her system. We tried to devise ways to measure the passage of a given food item. "What you need is a 'shit meter,'" I declared. "A shit meter?" "Yes, the devise would consist of a stainless steel probe with a sensor at one end and a liquid crystal display at the other. Simply insert the sensor into the shit and the LCD gives you a read out of the shit's contents. Cross reference your 'eating log' and you've got passage time." "How much do you think something like that would cost me," she asked. Nicole had become accustomed to her intestinal maladies being fodder for my amusement and so dismissed what on land, in a more public forum, she might consider irritating and degrading. Plus, she welcomed any topic of conversation that was a distraction from the monotony of the passage. "I could probably get it to you for $49.99" "$29.99 seems more reasonable," she countered. "Are you kidding me? It's got a liquid crystal display, a small micro-processing unit, and a stainless steel probe." "I guess $49.99 isn't such a bad deal," she agreed. "Of course with shipping and handling it comes out to more like a hundred bucks, but I might be willing to throw in a set of Gin-Su knives."

"Perhaps a device that monitors not only what comes out but also what goes in might be better," I offered, unable to let the subject die. "One micro-chip sensor could be inserted under the skin near your ass and one in your lip. The remote sensors would download all of the in and out data to a small MPU worn on the wrist. The MPU would also tell time, store addresses, and have five alarms, a stopwatch, countdown timer, barometer, and a GPS. Of course its main function would be to record elapsed passage times of individual food items in addition to quantity of food in and shit out." I had long argued that Nicole had five to ten kilos of shit scattered around her digestive tract that had probably been there for years, if not decades.

R-2 came up with the idea of using radioactive die, added to different foods, which could be measured on the way out. "R-2, now that's just silly," I joked. "I suppose you could just eat some corn and see when it comes out."

We also offered some methods for simply getting the shit out. "Can't beat a boa constrictor around the mid-section to just squeeze the shit out of you." "I bet I could beat it, and I'd be a little nervous the snake would try and eat me," Nicole retorted. "I'd offer a money back guarantee on the boa... naturally."

"You could drink a cup of olive oil and the shit might just slide right out of you," offered R-2. "Whoa there buddy. We don't have all that much olive oil. Howzabout a cup of bilge water? That's got plenty of oil in it." Nicole made an audible wrenching noise.

We continued on that vein until it was thoroughly played out and then an alternate line of reasoning occurred to me, "Nicole, perhaps you don't really want to shit." "I assure you, I do." "Perhaps you had a bad shitting experience as a child which you've subsequently suppressed. On the surface you want to shit, but some deeper part of your psyche is afraid to. One part of you is squeezing out while the other is contracting in." "Is that even physically possible?"

While we all sat, silently contemplating the inner-workings of Nicole's digestive track, a longish flying insect flew into the cockpit, through the companionway, and into the cabin. It looked like a cross between a dragonfly and a grasshopper. "Where the hell did that guy come from? It doesn't look like it belongs in the middle of the ocean," Nicole asked. "It's probably looking to lay eggs and colonize the boat. It would be nice to have some flying bugs for a change," I stated. Nicole gave me a sidelong glance and went down after the winged beast. Thrashing ensued and shortly after, the creature flew out the hatch and back to sea. Such an event could punctuate an entire day.

On any given passage, 'Hanuman time' always remained in the time zone of the country we departed from. During a westward passage, as most tended to be, the changing of longitude was noticeable. The effect was that, with our set watch system, the actual period of day that one performed their watches changed a few minutes every day. Fifteen degrees of longitude traveled equaled a one hour difference; or something like that.

On day seventeen of the passage I held the sunrise watch. It was a prime watch. The sky changed by the moment, making it considerably more interesting than the average mid day or mid night shift, where things were often pretty much the same at the end of the shift as they were at the beginning.

I sat in the cockpit, with a light scrap of blanket thrown over my legs to ward off the slight chill, while watching the silhouette of the Aires wind vane making subtle constant adjustments against the pastel blue, gray, orange predawn sky. Evenly spaced small cumulus, frosted with muted silver, blue, gray tones, looked stable and non-threatening. We'd been frequently visited by rain clouds on the passage and a stable sky was never completely taken for granted. The promise of continued dryness, along with the steady fifteen knot wind, gave me a feeling of serenity as colors intensified on the sun kissed horizon. I basked in mindless appreciation as the sun crested the horizon, giving its full spectrum to the firmament, bluing the sky and blinding me. A school of flying fish took flight between my eyes and the sun, pulling the shimmer of the sea into the air. Sadly, the rustling of crew below pulled me out of my bliss and as I peered up at the freshly patched main I was reminded of the previous night.

The sky faded to black, as it always did, and after a few cups of box wine and few rounds of 20 questions, I retired to the embrace of my bunk, leaving Nicole at the helm. I fell asleep effortlessly, as I always did at sea, but was eventually awoken by the nudging of my bladder wanting to be let out. I crawled up the ladder, worn smooth and bare of varnish after years at sea, and emerged into the cool night. Nicole was nested in the cockpit with a cup of wine in one hand and the wheel in the other, her head bobbing to the tinny music emanating from her headphones.

Seeing me coming, she craned her neck to the red light of the compass to see if she was on course. The wine was thick in her brain and she was giggling like a fool. The boat didn't feel right and I looked up at the sails to see what was going on. The main was back winded. Only the preventer kept the boom from flying across the boat. Nicole saw me looking up at the sail and sensed something wasn't right. "I'm on course. I'm on course," she babbled, still unable to hold back a snicker. I tried to explain that the main was back winded but she just stared up at it mumbling, "I'm on course." I looked up at the main and noticed a tear. I pointed it out to her. "Whaaaat?.... ohhhhh." I furled the main, rolled out the jib, and took piss before returning to my bunk, utterly disgusted.

Just after I returned to my bunk, Arnout came on watch and she explained the reason for the sail change. "That's no good," Arnout sighed. "Nothing to worry about boy. Nothing that can't be fixed," Nicole pronounced with all of her conde-scending wisdom.

I should have seen that Nicole's proclamation came from her confidence in my ability to fix anything that broke and that her condescension came from the annoyance with Arnout that I often wasn't able to conceal from her, and taken it as flattery, but that eye was closed and I was just annoyed. I had to bury my head in the pillow to keep from hearing any more of her bullshit on the quite night. I could have easily dis-missed her foolish antics if not for the tear in the sail. Knowing that I had to sew it up, while she threw out a few, "no prob-lemos," and passed out, awoke the hateful demon I'd put to sleep when we'd entered the Trades.

I wanted to put off the sail repair until the morning, but conditions were calm and good for sewing so, knowing change could come quickly, I decided it a good idea to get it out of the way. Also Hanuman went slower under the jib than the main in light conditions and my contempt for waste extended to the wind. Two and a quarter hours after starting, I put in my last stitch, raised the main, and furled the jib as it luft in the main's wind shadow. I was happy with the repair and relieved to be done, but my annoyance was rekindled with the recollection that I had hoped to sell the sail in the Caribbean and put the money towards repairing the old main and getting a new (used) jib. The large patch wouldn't do anything for its resale value.

The sharp bitterness awoken by Nicole's morning rustling milked my brain for hatred, like a separate entity looking for a place of feed.

Not long before the boxed wine that led to the tearing of the main, Nicole complained because she and R-2 were a bit ill. She had the runs and R-2 was experiencing some gut rot. Her tone was accusatory. "It sucks that you don't feel well but don't blame me," I replied defensively. Nicole often shot from the hip, not taking time to contemplate what she was about to say. She rarely measured her words. "It's probably from your cooking. You're always scratching your balls and your prick and that wart on your foot and then cooking our food. And I've never, ever, seen you wash your hands." Normally I didn't allow any particular word to arouse emotion in me but Nicole's use of 'prick,' especially literally, boiled my ire. "First of all, the notion that my wart, which I rarely pick at, gave you're the runs is absurd. Secondly, it's not as if I'm scratching my balls all of the time or shoving the spatula down my shorts when I'm cooking. Furthermore, the meal that R-2 cooked last night had those raisins in it that gave us all problems in the past." I wanted to mention the fact that I cooked 90 percent of the meals and that she could cook her own damn food… ungrateful wench, but I measured my words and decided against bringing the argument to the next level. Instead I added, "With your constipation issues, you should be happy with some runs for a change." "My ass is bleeding from all of the wiping." "Perhaps a tampon would help." "I don't use tampons, I use pads, we've been over this." "Perhaps a pad would help." "Why don't you just open us a box of wine." "Sounds good," I replied, giving my left testicle a quick scratch. "You get it, I'll open it," added Nicole hastily. I sniffed my finger. "No worries, the balls are clean," I said as I pushed my finger towards her nose. "Go get the wine you filthy mongrel." Fortunately the Trades were quick to cleave any negativity I attached myself to and I didn't cling to the poisonous thoughts evoked by the food issue.

In good Trade Wind conditions, rain is infrequent. But on our Atlantic passage the pleasant little white cumulus clouds I lovingly associated with the Trades, frequently grew into large cumulus or thunderheads. I constantly scanned the horizon, hoping to avoid getting wet. Getting wet wasn't 'that bad' but it was enough to change ones mindset and posture from a comfortable, "this is nice and relaxing," to a hunched over enduring, "sure will be nice when this cloud passes." On a long passage such subtle changes in perspective can, over time, translate to huge changes in attitude.

Days passed with little punctuation. I sat reading and absorbing all that was around me, mostly with ambivalence. R-2's behavior fluctuated with the wind. When the wind died so did his calm. I found his behavior as intriguing as annoying. Many of his actions seemed contradictory. On the one hand he was obsessive compulsive. He just couldn't stop touching the wheel when the Aries was steering the boat; frequently jerking the wheel one way or the other. "If you want to hand steer go for it, but stop fighting the Aries," I said, unable to relax with Hanuman getting jerked around in such a fashion. He responded with the sort of "why" I would expect out of a four year old. The sort of "why" that would be followed by another and another. I answered regardless of the feeling of futility. "…puts too much strain on the servo rudder." I left out, "it bugs the hell out of me," the more important factor. He did his best to stop but he was like a child next to a candy bowl and continued to occasionally paw at the wheel, mostly without any effect or even intent.

On occasion he would even jerk the wheel in the opposite of our desired direction.

I'd previously associated compulsive behavior with tidiness. R-2 had no sense of tidiness what-so-ever. He left shit lying around constantly. He couldn't boil a pot of water without making a huge mess. On land, disorder is a luxury that one can afford. On the boat, leaving a fish hook on the floor of the cockpit or a knife where it can go flying across the cabin in a moderate swell can be dangerous. The worst of it was his tendency to leave his beverage resting wherever he happened to thoughtlessly set it. There were only two ceramic mugs on board when we left the Canaries. One was mine and Nicole claimed the other, leaving R-2 with a crappy, mildly rusty, tin cup. Despite the fact that it was so well suited to his lifestyle, he coveted our ceramic mugs. For his birthday I gave him a ceramic one I'd picked up for him in the Canaries. He broke it the following day. While he cursed, Nicole and I gave each other a little grin. "Saw that coming," we thought in unison. The only thing that really bothered me about his mindlessness was the amount of alcohol he wasted. It got to where I would make a point of watching where he set his cup down to mitigate the losses to our grog supply.

"Do you miss people when they leave the boat?" Nicole asked me one lazy day as we hung out in the cockpit, wondering if a passing cloud would grant us clemency. It was a rare question that didn't involve ingestion or defecation so I had to take a second to think about it. "Time together on the boat tends to be full on. A certain group consciousness inevitable evolves where I'm forced to meld with the energy of the crew. It's often rejuvenating to re-center after they leave. I can't say that I really miss anyone." "Do you miss people?" I asked. "I miss all of my friends when I'm not with them. Even if I don't always get along with them I still miss them. I guess your circumstances are different with the boat and all though," she finished. Her last statement sounded as though she where trying to justify my position, as if my response was heartless and cold. I felt a little heartless and tried to justify myself, "I do get lonely from time to time when I'm by myself, and long for some companionship, but I can't say that I actually miss anyone." As I finished my statement I realized that I still sounded heartless. "I'm always very excited to meet up with old friends…and look forward to it," I stated, in an attempt to humanize myself.

Upon further evaluation I decided missing people had few redeeming qualities. Missing was just a form of sadness. How could sadness be good? And if one was fully engaged in their surroundings, it was almost impossible to miss others.

Nicole maintained relationships much differently than I did. In the time that we'd sailed across the Indian Ocean and up the Red Sea, she'd met about ten people who she was still in close contact with. She wrote post cards, e-mailed, talked on the phone, and even wrote actual letters for Christ sake. I hadn't kept in contact with anyone from that period. The only reason I was still in contact with Nicole was that she e-mailed me so often and said she wanted to cross the Atlantic.

The days at sea gathered and pressed on us. I started having 'it would be nice to get there soon' thoughts. We made up holidays to pass the time and for the sake of something to look forward to.

I thought of the ticket home for Christmas I had waiting for me. I was looking forward to indulging in all of the luxuries that home had to offer. I still had some mixed emotions about the trip however. I managed to mostly put Pat and Carly out of my mind, but the thought of going to a place where they might be, rekindled all of the memories from the Med and left me feeling heavy.

On the night of our 29th day at sea we pulled into St Martin and anchored under sail in the outer bay. After being in motion for a month, the fixedness of our position felt awkward yet calming. It was 3:30 in the morning and there were no "hurray's," just a feeling somewhere between deep satisfaction and relief. I drank a small celebratory mug of wine and watched the moon rise over the island.

St. Martin

My flight out of St. Thomas was in less than a week so Nicole and I only stayed in St. Martin, where we left R-2, for a couple of days. Time was spent in a surprisingly sober fashion. It felt a little wrong not to have a blow out but my mindset wasn't there. Plus, I had a little diarrhea so my body wasn't all that into it either. I went running and noticed my whole mental condition improved dramatically.

I made my way to an inter-net café and found two new messages in my in-box; one from Pat and one from Carly. My pulse quickened with the site of them and I felt new chemicals flowing through my blood stream. I was back in the 'real world.' I opened the one from Pat first. It was very short, just a few fragmented sentences, "…hope you are well," "…too confused for words." The e-mail was a great relief. The fact that he wished me well was elating. My former concern was that he was stewing with hate and contempt for me. I feared that, not only because I didn't want to be hated, but also because I didn't want him to be filled with bitterness and anger for his own sake.

The 'confused' part also seemed positive. It seemed better to accept confusion than to simply feel wronged and angry, though of course he had been wronged. I feared a thick anger could lead to hate and, while justified, that hate could be difficult to recover from. Confusion and sadness seemed like a healthier avenue to recovery as long as it didn't lead to self-pity and depression. Also, the confusion, and the admitting to it, suggested a desire for understanding and change and could lead to healing and rebirth which seemed necessary for recovery.

Contemplating Pat's situation in such a way seemed wrong. Not unlike contemplating the fate of a fly whose wings you've just pulled off. To have not considered him, however, seemed even worse.

The emotion I felt seeing Carly's e-mail in my in-box was of a whole different vane. I was excited to see it but the excitement came from a different place. One that reminded me that my will to forget about Carly might not be all that strong, or that honest.

She explained that she and Pat where separated and that she was living in Davis, our hometown, but made no indication of where Pat was living. Her e-mail was long. She gave me insights into her mental state. She said she was "soaring." She didn't mention anything about the intimate night we'd shared, nor express any feelings towards me. But she told me about her life as one would a confidant and I felt a desire for her I knew no good would come of. I didn't e-mail either of them. Such a reply demanded contemplation.

Nicole and I still had to sail to St. Thomas, 90 miles away, so St Martin didn't have quite the 'yee haw, we made it' feeling it might otherwise have had.

Aside from a few hours of almost windless conditions, we made the passage in an easy overnight and anchored in Charlotte Amalie Bay. I didn't fall in love with the place but it was nice to 'be there' and there was a certain novelty in being back, more or less, in America.

I decided to e-mail Pat. "I just finished crossing the Atlantic but was even more excited to get your e-mail. Heading home for Christmas hope we can hang out. I also got an email from Carly and figured it couldn't hurt to reply to her." It had been over six months since Crete, which seemed like forever to me. I figured that whatever they had needed to work out had been worked out one way or another and had become ancient history. Objectively, it's difficult to imagine how I arrived at that conclusion. I believe I saw things as I wanted them to be rather than as they were. I didn't receive a reply from Pat and took it as a go ahead to correspond with his wife.

I sent Carly a brief e-mail telling her about the trip and that I was coming home for Christmas but didn't indicate a desire to meet. With the e-mail, I felt some impure thoughts enter my head, forcing me to take stock in my position. I knew that I didn't consider her in a purely plutonic manner but just figured I would just have to watch myself. It wasn't a matter I dwelled on long, for fear I would have to look deeper into myself and my motivations than I was prepared to.

Christmas Vacation

Nicole was kind enough to stay and watch Hanuman before she returned to Canada, while I flew to California for a couple of weeks. The flight, including the 12 hour layover in Chicago, was a welcome transitional time between worlds.

I soon learned through the grapevine that Pat was back in Alaska. I considered it unfortunate but also a relief. I wasn't fully prepared to face him.

It wasn't long before the novelty of remote controlled television and the proximity of refrigerator filled with food and beer wore off, or at least was diminished, and I began to consider calling Carly. She'd given me her new phone number in the e-mail that she's sent me. The idea of calling her had been floating around in my sub-conscious since I'd received the number and before I'd even given it much thought I found my thumb navigating the digits of the key pad on my mom's phone. The conversation was brief. She was in Tahoe for a long weekend but wanted to meet up and chat when she got back.

We went out for a mid-day beer and a slice of pizza and discussed what had unfolded since she'd left Greece. We summed up events in an academic fashion, evaluating emotion, primarily Matt's, with the outward expression of lab coat wearing scientists monitoring a Petri dish. Yet, while the discussion was superficial, it was clear that we both hungered for the emotion behind the facade. Words trailed off into extended eye contact that faded into thin coy smiles. Sitting, drinking beer, and chatting felt like, with exception of Matt's absence of course, just an extension of what had existed before Crete, the relationship we'd always had. To take the discussion further seemed somehow taboo, despite the fact that we'd already crossed bolder lines. I managed to mentally alter the truth that our very meeting was exceedingly taboo in itself.

Carly's cell phone rang. She looked at the monitor to see who it was, silenced the ringer, and returned it to her pocket. I didn't ask who it was but gave her, as subtly as I could muster, an 'I'm curious who's calling, but it's not my business' look. "It was Pat." I nodded my head, convincing myself that I was just a friend of Carly's who happened to be having a slice of pizza with her. "Besides," I thought, "he's probably just calling to chat and isn't feeling castoff and impotent, thousands of miles away."

Lunch ended and Carly and I parted with an extended hug and an "I'll talk to you soon." Things didn't end there however. The following day was overcast and seemed to merit a movie rental and some couch time. Carly agreed and we headed to Block Buster. A couple of Pat's younger sisters also had the same idea and Carly and I were spotted. I didn't think too much of it other than that I ought to e-mail Pat to let him know that Carly and I were simply renting a movie together, not starting some sort of relationship. In my naiveté I still believed Carly and I were simply living an extension of the friendship that had begun a decade and a half prior.

I placed the DVD in my mom's new DVD player. In my absence from land life the DVD had taken over as the dominate technology. I was using one for the first time. It seemed fairly strait forward. I pushed in the disc, the movie started playing and I rescued my beer from the floor, and approached the couch. "You have to press play Mike," commented Carly, seemingly amused by my performance. "Clearly it's playing," I responded gesturing toward the screen. "No, it just does that when you put it in…" Carly responded in a tone that she suggested she thought I was joking. My head swiveled between Carly and the TV, "it sure looks like it's playing," I responded suspiciously. "You've been gone awhile. I assure, you it's not playing." "It certainly appears to be playing," I mumbled setting my beer back down and kneeling before the machine. After a bit of hunting I found the play button and pressed it. "Ahh," I expelled, and chuckled at myself as the movie began to play. "Like I said Carly, you have to press play." Carly shook her head, grinning at my foolishness.

About halfway through the movie Carly started massaging my foot. Metaphorically, my eyes rolled back in my head and any vestige of clarity I had was buried below the lustfulness that took over. Carly and I spent the following week in an embrace that shut out all light except that which we created. My notion of e-mailing Pat that our time together had just been as two old friends in passing, became absurd and out of the question. The time we'd spent in public seemed utterly foolish now that we were guilty of what others suspected. I had a distinct longing to be back on Hanuman, in the Caribbean. In a world I hadn't totally fucked up. Simultaneously, I was like a moth mesmerized by the flame that Carly and I had ignited.

Pat's sisters reported back to the family of their sighting at Block Buster and Pat's dad felt it necessary to report the news to Pat. I maintained the notion that Pat had moved on and was just trying to live his life in peace. I felt that Pat's dad was only serving to torture him. Later I would realize that Pat was still hoping Carly's absents from his life was just a temporary condition which would be remedied in time. With that realization I came to understand that Pat's dad was just doing his best to keep Pat abreast of the reality of the situation.

Pat didn't receive the news of our being seen together well. He called Carly, mercifully when I wasn't around, and asked her if she and I'd gotten together in physical sense. Carly responded that it was none of his business. Her treatment of him seemed rather harsh to me, but of course she had a totally different relationship with him than I did. It would be easy to presume that I caused the downfall of their relationship but it wasn't that simple. They'd had their own problems before Crete that were still fresh in Carly's mind. I just happened to be the tipping point. To be fair however, I have to concede that I have no idea whether, without my interference, they may have eventually worked through their difficulties and lived happily ever after. Or at least Pat may have been happier.

Pat's conversation with Carly obviously did nothing to quell his concerns. In fact, I'm sure it tortured him to the point of madness and desperation. In his state, he sent e-mails to all of the high school friends we had in common, plus my mom, pleading with them to somehow come to his aid and get me away from Carly. He also e-mailed me, saying that he wished for my death. The e-mail gave me insight into the hell he was living, but calling for my demise didn't exactly melt my heart. I replied to his e-mail, doing my best to assure him that I was leaving in two days and not planning any meetings with Carly in the future. I didn't go into the details of Carly's and my relationship but attempted to convey, without lying, that whatever image that he'd gotten about Carly and I was inaccurate. "We are not a couple. We will not be meeting up anywhere on my journey. I am leaving in two days and will not be returning anytime soon." I finished by recommending he do some yoga or meditate to contain his anger. It once again elicited the image of the fly, only now that I'd torn off its wings and its legs I was encouraging it to move on with its life.

The whole scenario unfolded in the worst possible manner. Our high school friends, who'd all been groomsmen at Pat's and Carly's wedding, received the news with a "whoa!" Pat hadn't previously been especially engaged in their lives and I believe Pat's torrent of emotion shockingly awoke them to his mental state. It was a jolt to our union and tasted of Jerry Springer. I had frank conversations with our high school friends that made me feel guiltier with the depth of their concern but didn't really affect the already sorry truth of the situation. The following day I was on a plane back to the Caribbean.

St. Thomas

Two days after my return to St. Thomas, Nicole left for Canada, or Canadia as I called it, and I was alone on Hanuman. I felt greatly relieved to be in a condition of social solitude again. Anchored in Charlotte Amalie Bay, I was once again in command of my sphere of reality.

I got the lay of the land and determined what my new home had to offer. Since the decapitation of POS (piece of shit; the outboard) during a storm in Mallorca where another boat had dragged anchor past Hanuman's rail, where POS had been hanging, I'd been kneeling on the front of the dinghy, paddling with one mangled oar to and from land. I was sick of the production and started looking for a new outboard. I eventually came upon a used four horse that one of the charter companies was trying to off load.

I carried the 'new' outboard the two miles back to the dinghy dock and strapped it on Sputnik's transom. Miraculously it started on the first pull and I putted gingerly back to the boat. After a torturous 30 seconds of minimal throttle I decided it seemed secure enough and I opened her up, full bunny. The engine made a lot of noise but I actually slowed down. "Fuuuck!" I went back to my slow pace, imagining what the liver of the guy who sold me the engine was going to taste like when I ripped it out and ate it in front of him. I was thoroughly annoyed but familiar with such a scenario from the POS days and decided that I'd have a look at it before I chucked the whole thing through the asshole's window. I figured it might just have a broken shear pine, an easy fix.

Whilst hoisting the new outboard on deck, however, I realized that I was dealing with a new configuration. There was no shear pin. Instead, the mechanism was governed by a rubber friction thing-a-magigger that was part of the prop. I decided to stop taking things apart before I had the whole outboard spread out on deck. Needless to say I was having serious misgivings about the outboard. It seemed as though I had just purchased something to fix, the last thing I wanted.

I ran back to the dude. He was fat as hell. Probably from stealing from people, I decided. "Sounds like you've got a spun prop," he oozed. "I've got a spun prop? I've got a spun…? You just sold me this piece of shit, mother fucker!" That's what I was thinking but I remained silent and just stared at him with my best 'this is totally unacceptable…you asshole' look. He handed me new (used) prop. "That's all I can do." "All you can do? All you can do? You just sold me something that doesn't work you fat fuck!" Once again that's what I was thinking but I just grunted, snatched the prop out of his hand, and stormed out the front door.

With the new prop in place, I opened her up. The prop held and Sputnik's bow shot skyward. I moved forward, centered myself, and one of the great joys of physics kicked in, we were planing. I'd been longing to plane ever since I'd bought Sputnik but the 2.5 had never been able to quite get me there. Once on the plane I just kept going and shortly found myself on the down town quay, where there was some sort of celebration with music and much fan fare.

I trotted around town, still grinning from my planing experience, and quickly realized there was free booze. Rum is cheap in the Caribbean and it wasn't unusual to see it being given away. I promptly got myself in line. When I got to the front of the line however, I was offered, "iced tea or water." I was certainly disappointed with the selection but, never one to thumb my nose at free anything, responded, "Iced tea please," and found my way into the proper line. I downed my tea before making my way to the front so I had an empty cup to hand the teenage boy with the bottle of rum. "Punch or rum punch?" the kid asked as he took my cup, which I realized was bigger than the cups he had, serendipity! "Rum punch," I, of course, replied. I was delighted to see he had a heavy hand with the rum. He handed me the beverage and, making eye contact for the first time, said, "You look like a heavy drinker." "Thank you," I nodded, thinking the comment odd yet insightful.

Having spent my last dollars on an outboard, I was forced to look for work. The restaurant industry was as an easy go to so, after some scouting, I narrowed it down to the two that seemed the busiest, the Hard Rock Café and the Green House. I was offered a job at both as long as I could pass the shit test. The shit test consisted of shitting in a small cup and getting it tested for worms. Thankfully I passed and was rewarded with a health card.

I didn't consciously choose the Hard Rock. Somehow I got sucked into it and before I knew it I was wearing the ridiculous outfit, complete with the minimum three pieces of flare, and watching a corporate video on sexual harassment. "Of course, you've all worked in a restaurant and know how it is…just use your better judgment," chuckled the manager at the end of the video. I would later find out that his better judgment included having sex with several of the female servers. He ended up getting fired a week after I was hired. "Bureaucratic bull shit. Fuckin' corporate jackasses. They just needed a fall guy," was his response.

Since hitting land in St. Martin, I'd committed myself to vanquishing the lethargy that had made camp in my gut and after few weeks of running in the hills, found myself in decent shape. I hadn't made too many friends and was living a fairly monkish existence and began to feel glowingly strong and healthy.

My plan had been to work for about four or five months and then take off for the Panama Canal before hurricane season. Over the course of my first couple of months in St Thomas, however, I had a change of heart about my journey in general. I'd been feeling a dull sense of urgency about completing the trip but it faded and I was left with a "what's the rush" feeling. It was a sentiment amplified by the fact that my last 'back home' experience had been a disaster. The thought of not moving towards all of the havoc I'd created had considerable appeal. I decided that instead of proceeding forward with my circumnavigation ambition, I would take a year off and sail south of the hurricane zone for the season and return to the Virgins, or perhaps Puerto Rico, to work again the following season before heading through the canal. With the acceptance of my new plan, any residual stress I'd been feeling about my personal 'manifest destiny' dissolved, leaving me free to just enjoy where I was.

Months passed and I became more entrenched in St. Thomian life. I made a number of friends and one in particular, Karl, became a solid partner in mayhem. My monkish existence of early to bed, early to rise, slowly morphed into waking up mid-day on Karl's' couch with the TV blaring and a mess of half eaten buffalo wings spread out on the coffee table before me; my fingers and face stained red with sauce.

Carly and I had been keeping up a slowing fading correspondence since my trip home for Christmas and not long before the end of my stay in St. Thomas I got an e-mail from her saying that she had started seeing someone. I received the news with a dull mixture of sadness and relief. I'd come to associate many attachments with pain and stress. Losing the connection to Carly felt freeing and partially fulfilling of an inkling of a desire to have no attachments what-so-ever.

More shocking, was the news I received from my ex-girlfriend from the Pacific, Amanda. Apparently Pat had visited her in Alaska and stayed with her for a week. Pat and Amanda had only met briefly on one occasion during which Pat hadn't made a particularly favorable impression on Amanda. "I'm sure he was just drunk and joking," I defended. Amanda gave me a firm, "it wasn't joking like I'm familiar with," look but the subject was discussed no further.

The idea of Pat electing to visit Amanda blew my mind. I was glad I was only told about it after the fact. Otherwise I may have thought that Pat had really gone off the deep end and feared for Amanda's safety. I tried to imagine what train of thought led Pat to the conclusion that it was a good idea to visit Amanda, but had difficulty doing so. Was he trying to get together with Amanda as a means of getting back at me? Was it a desperate attempt to gain some sense of control in a world he perceived as having taken everything from him? I was baffled.

The visit left Amanda fairly distraught. Amanda concluded the e-mail with, "I must try and simply forget the experience and do my best to excuse Pat, given his condition."

I'd always sensed that there was a part of Pat that was closed off. Certain conversations I had with many less close friends, I didn't have with Pat. I felt there were some things that for some reason he was just not comfortable talking about. There was a little part of him that he kept closely guarded. I wondered if traumatic events had opened his Pandora's Box of inner turmoil and plunged him into a psychosis that I couldn't begin to imagine.

Grenada

After loading Hanuman down with as much rum and pasta as she could hold, Karl and I, still dazed from the previous night's umpteenth bon voyage celebration, shoved off, bound for Grenada. With the sails set, the Aries happily steering, and St. Thomas moving towards the horizon, I experienced the slow swells sliding beneath us bring me back to an awareness I'd been dulling over the previous weeks of excess. I felt like I was in recovery, or rehab, lying on a hospital bed which was the ocean. My mind slowly awakening as my body recovered, awkward and itchy.

The first three days were a dream. I didn't have to touch the Aries. Winds stayed between 10 and 15 knots. We caught a large Dorado, though probably over estimated its expiration date. "How's your stomach treatin' ya Karl," I asked after the third day of gnawing on the large fish. "Not so well…yours?" "Stomach's alright but let's just say I'm not too confident farting. We should definitely make sure we cook that last little chunk of Dorado really well." "Hmmm…yeah, I might actually be done with the Dorado. You can have my portion."

On the fourth day our heading shifted more to the south than I was excited about, pointing us towards Venezuela rather than Grenada. I hadn't touched the Aries for three days however, and with a potential record at stake, I decided to go with it, hoping the wind would give us a lift before long and bring us back on course.

The next four days just sucked. The wind didn't shift back. It simply increased in strength. I noticed the water change from a cool Caribbean blue to a menacing Amazonian green and feared we'd entered a west bound current. I tacked and reefed, but making any eastward progress toward Grenada seemed impossible.

I'd had the original main sail repaired in St. Thomas but hadn't gotten around to putting the third reefing line back in place, figuring we wouldn't need it. I cursed myself for my laziness. I hadn't pictured beating into 25 to 30 knot winds.

On the morning of the seventh day out we spotted Grenada, who's even existence we'd come to question, on the horizon. We arrived at sunset and dropped anchor in The Lagoon on Grenada's eastern side. After a few vodka and juices, the trials of the passage were forgotten.

Karl and I spent a week wrestling with the island, trying to wrench her secrets from her. We took busses all over, climbed peaks, and attempted to get to the top of Mt. Elizabeth, but ended up mainly stumbling around in the jungle, pretty exciting in itself. At the end of the week Karl flew back to St Thomas and I was left alone.

Hanuman was showing signs of neglect so I got to work sanding the toe rails, which hadn't a speck of varnish left. It took me several days to sand them down but I enjoyed the work. I found the simplicity of the repetitive physical task rewarding. I liked seeing the old grey wood turn golden brown. I liked the sandpaper heating up in my hand from the friction. I liked the accumulation of wood dust laying on deck, a testament to my progress. I liked the fatigue and the sudden twinges of pain from the unfamiliar exertion.

My plan was to haul Hanuman out in Trinidad and paint the bottom, but Grenada was treating me well and the rates at the new boat yard were reasonable so I decided to pull Hanuman out there and give her a nice new coat of much needed bottom paint.

I thrived in my alone time, as I always seemed to. I started a book on meditation and began the process which I quickly learned was a long and challenging one. I spent a significant amount of time with my eyes closed but never reached first stage, called Samadhi, where one's mind is completely free of thought, for more than second. My mind actually felt most clear while I was sanding the rails, possibly explaining why I enjoyed it so much.

Grenada was considered to be south of the hurricane zone so I hadn't been listening to any of the cruisers' nets on the VHF radio or paying attention to the weather forecasts. As such I was caught off guard by Tropical Storm Earl.

I poked my head out of the companionway one morning. "Windy," I thought… "and dark." The palms were swaying back and forth with gusto. I checked the anchor. It seemed secure. The dinghy was secure but I gave it more slack so it could bounce over the passing waves without jerking. I couldn't locate the blue nylon BBQ cover but it seemed like an acceptable loss. I eyed the darkening clouds and turned on the radio to discover that we were in the middle of a tropical storm. I went back to bed. I wasn't in the most protected anchorage but I had ample room to drag and not too many boats close by. Fortunately neither the winds nor the swell ever reached critical levels and the loss of the BBQ cover was the extent of the damage.

It occurred to me that if a tropical storm could hit Grenada then it stood to reason that I wasn't entirely safe from a hurricane. I started monitoring the weather.

Trinidad

After spending a month in Grenada I felt I'd pretty much gotten the gist of it and decided it was time to move on. I took off solo for the relatively short passage to Tobago but hadn't made much headway when the sun rose the next day so I decided to make way for the easier to get to Trinidad and save Tobago for later.

I dropped anchor in the murky water of Chagauramas Bay. "Kind of a shit hole," I thought. I wasn't particularly excited about hanging out in Chagauramas but I found a reputable local sail maker who could sew me a new jib at a reasonable price. The whole job would take five to six weeks. I decided it was worth it and did my best to entertain myself but found it challenging.

I went for a long run on my second day but was disappointed with the running prospects. There was only one road to run down and I could see myself getting bored of it quickly. I was also disappointed to find out that it was only 10:30 in the morning when I finished the run. It was the only activity I had planned for the day. I delved in to various boat projects but was unable to dispel a lingering boredom. I felt boredom a weakness of the mind and was disappointed with myself for having succumbed to it but forced myself to face it. I tried to meditate through it but found meditation to be more boring than anything else.

Exploration seemed like my most useful weapon against boredom but my bike, my most valued ally in Mallorca, had been stolen in St. Thomas. After I decided to buy a new bike, the size of my world expanded tenfold. I had to replace the brake pads three weeks after the purchase from so much riding on the hilly island.

Despite the freedom and excitement I felt with the addition of the bike, I still found myself going through dramatic mood swings. One moment I felt extremely engaged in every nuance of existence and the next I couldn't find a single thing in the world that could hold my interest. I was drinking a lot of Coke, and the sugar and caffeine blasts may have had a significant effect.

After my experience with tropical storm Earl, I began listening to the cruisers net on the VHF almost daily to get the weather reports and also for the amusement of listening to people rant. News of tropical storms, forming somewhere and heading somewhere, were almost constant in the middle of the hurricane season. Much of the news was simply academic since most of the activity was well to the north of us but Hurricane Ivan perked up my ears. Its projected path was much further south than the norm. It wasn't head straight for Trinidad but seemed likely to brush by. Additionally, the dynamics of a hurricane's heading are complex and it wasn't out of the question for Ivan to turn south and tear us in half.

I decided to pull up my anchor and move to a mooring. Normally I would trust my anchor over a mooring but the anchorage was notoriously hazardous, having been a dumping ground for sailor's trash for centuries. It was hard to be sure ones anchor was well set in the mud and not just hooked around an old cable that would break under the strain of 20 knots winds. I attached myself to the mooring ball with three lines.

I poked my head out of the companionway on the morning of the day Ivan was predicted to arrive. The sky was grey and menacing. Small wavelet's rolled through the cloudy water. It wasn't a nice day by any means but it didn't say, "Hurricane coming" to me either.

I planned to remain on Hanuman all day to monitor the lines and make sure everything was okay. I made some oatmeal and sat in the cockpit, waiting for Ivan. The usually morning crapola on the cruisers net was suspended for a special hurricane net. Someone on land who was connected to a weather service announced frequent updates on Ivan's position. Its eye was predicted to be a hundred miles to the north but significant winds were still in our forecast. The height of the storm was expected in the early afternoon.

The winds continued to increase throughout the morning as Ivan began to put a strain across the anchorage. I watched as an awning on land beet itself to shreds. The waves built and threw themselves high on the beach, drawing down anything that hadn't been properly secured.

Hanuman started hobby horsing on the waves, but for the most part things were well within tolerances. Hanuman was a clean boat on deck and the wind had little to play with. I read my book in the cockpit and monitored my surroundings.

At the peak of the storm it became clear that one boat in the anchorage wasn't faring so well. It was a working boat of some sort and was apparently unmanned. It had both a bow and a stern anchor which prevented it from rotating and keeping its bow into the wind. With its full breadth exposed to windward the wind had a lot of area to bite into. The boat was slowing dragging toward the center of the anchorage.

It didn't appear as though it was headed for Hanuman but seemed bound to hit someone.

The first in line was little French boat. The boat was powered only by an outboard. I heard some nondescript cursing over the VHF. The French couple on board were running around on deck frantically as the 80 foot steel workboat dragged down on their 23 foot fiberglass sloop.

I'd seen fliers posted for the sailboat. It was for sale. The French woman on board spent a lot of time on the morning net with a number of complaints about various things. They all seemed like legitimate complaints but given the number of them, I had a hard time taking her too seriously. When it came down to it, I imagined what she really wanted was not to be on a boat in Trinidad at all. Her dude never talked on the radio. I was glad not to be him. The scenario of the male wanting to go on a sailing adventure and the female begrudgingly following along was common. The hurricane, and the steel boat about to collide with her, couldn't have improved her outlook.

Everyone else in the anchorage and I watched with mortified fascination as the couple fruitlessly tried to get their outboard started. I could see the curses on their lips from a hundred yards away. Eventually they gave up on the engine and readied their sails. When a collision course was inevitable, they released their anchor and hoisted the main just clearing the stern of the oncoming vessel. It was a nice bit of sailing and I couldn't help nodding my head in admiration. A few tacks and they were free and clear. Once the work boat dragged by, they were able to rescue the anchor chain they'd attached to a buoy.

After tracking the path of the workboat I was forced to reassess my assumption of safety. It seemed as though there was a pretty good chance I was right in the big piece of crap's, as I came to call the work boat, path. I decided it was time to fire up Big Red, just to be on the safe side. The big piece of crap continued toward me and I released all of my mooring lines, save one, so that I could be out of the way in a flash. I also placed a serrated knife next to the line… just in case.

Another boat close to me, and on line to get hit, was also making ready for the worst. He was anchored instead of moored, and having some sort of trouble with his anchor windlass. I was close enough to see the look of panic on his face as the big piece of crap closed in on him. He banged away at the windlass but clearly it was jammed. There was a whining noise and a puff of smoke rose up from it.

The way the big piece of crap was moving, it was due to collide with both of us at about the same time. The dude next to me continued to bang away at his windlass with increasing desperation. I'd uncleated my mooring line and held it, ready to let go. I was still hoping that the boat might just miss us. I didn't want to let go until impact was inevitable. I wasn't excited about having to motor around in the hurricane. I looked over at the dude to my left. The big piece of shit was about 30 feet from him and about 35 from me. "Yeah, he's fucked," I thought. Just before the dude was about to get hit I released my mooring line, quickly pulled in the slack, and ran back to the helm. I put her in gear and got the hell out of the way.

The dude was standing limp with submission on the bow of his boat when out of nowhere a tugboat appeared. It swooped in, put its bow to the starboard side of the big piece of crap, and gave it throttle. The tugboat, come angel, pushed the steel beast slowly but surely back into the heart of the bay.

I motored around for awhile, allowing the tug to clear out my area. I was actually pleasantly surprised; having thought the motoring would have been difficult. I decided that the wind and the tide, which can be fairly strong in Chagauramas, where probably working against each other, making my life a little easier.

Once things cleared out, I headed back to my mooring. Grabbing a mooring solo can be tricky in the best of conditions. I wasn't excited about the added challenge of the storm. There's always a little guesswork involved. When you get up close to the mooring you can no longer see it because the bow of the boat blocks vision. Once it's out of sight you just have to estimate where it is. You can't have too much momentum, a 24,000 pound boat doesn't stop just because you're in neutral, and it's easy to just go right over the thing.

With the mooring in what I figured was about the right place, I ran forward to grab it. Grabbing it wasn't all that straight forward either. There's a special hook for grabbing, but I'd never purchased one. I didn't attach to moorings all that often and figured, "I don't need no fuckin' boatswains hook." Plus I had a gaff for gaffing fish which, though not as long, did the job, albeit poorly.

All that was academic however, since this mooring was of a variety that didn't allow for grabbing with a hook. It was a huge ball with a steel loop on top. The ball couldn't be lifted out of the water. I had to lay on the foredeck and reach down for it.

The first attempt was a failure. I had too much momentum and went past the ball. I managed to get a line through the ball but didn't have enough slack to work with so I had to let go and start over. I wasn't discouraged. I hadn't really expected to get it done the first time.

The guy next to me, who'd just been saved by the tugboat, clearly feeling grateful to the world, decided he'd get in his dinghy and help me on my next attempt. I was appreciative yet skeptical. Another boat and person in the mix, I feared, could simply complicate matters.

The dude, not exactly a spring chicken, was waiting on the mooring ball for me on my next attempt. The idea was, I assumed, to hand him the line and have him put it though the mooring ball eye and hand it back to me. I would then cleat it off on deck, safe and secure.

Everything started off well. I handed the dude the line and he started putting it through the mooring eye. In the process the wind gusted and pushed Hanuman's bow off to port. The slack line I had on deck, uncoiled and slid off the rail as we drifted away from the mooring ball. The dude handed me the end of the line but got turned around backwards in the process, loosening his grip on Hanuman's rail and unseating him from his dinghy. As he clung to Hanuman, trying to pull himself back along side, his ass slid off his dinghy. I had the end of the line he'd handed me in one hand, and was trying to temporarily secure it to any fixed point, while trying to grab the dude with the other so he wouldn't fall in. The dude managed to get both hands fixed firmly on Hanuman's rail but was only attached to his dinghy by his desperately clinging calf's and ankles. His ass was in the water and as he tried to pull his dinghy toward him, he accidentally kicked the throttle lever with one of his feet. His outboard whined at full bunny. Fortunately, it was positioned so that it caused his dinghy to ram into the side of Hanuman instead of flying away, which surely would have left him in the drink with his dinghy buzzing towards shore. With the hand I'd been using to support him, I quickly reached down and hit his kill switch, silencing the motor. The dude got his bearing and scrambled back onto his dinghy while I secured the mooring line.

Having Hanuman somewhat secure I was feeling fairly good about the situation until I looked over at the dude who was pulling madly at his starter rope but to no effect. In the high wind he was drifting towards a wave beaten jetty at a disturbing rate. Then I heard the comforting growl of his outboard and he motored safely back to his boat. We exchanged stoic waves. "Piece of cake," I thought, and went back to reading my book.

The rest of the day passed without drama and by bedtime the storm had lost its' ire and I slumbered easily.

Many of the boats in the marinas had received minor damage from rubbing against the docks but on the morning net I learned that Ivan had destroyed Grenada. Over the next few weeks boats filtered down in various states of disrepair and relayed stories of total destruction and looting. It sounded like Mad Max.

On a selfish note, the storm delayed the sailcloth that was on order for my new jib, thus expending my stay in Trinidad. After Grenada got totaled, however, I wasn't too anxious to be heading anywhere to the north.

Tobago

Several uneventful weeks passed in Ivan's wake during which time my new jib was completed. It was a thing of beauty. I hoisted it and was off for Tobago with the tide.

The sail from Trinidad to Tobago is typically challenging. Tobago is up wind and up current of Trinidad. But I timed the tide well and the wind wasn't too strong, making it fairly easy.

I arrived on the second night out. I'd hoped to make it in before sunset but it wasn't in the cards. I gingerly entered the wide opening of Store Bay and dropped anchor as soon as depth meter read 35 feet. I rolled out my mat and dragged my ratty blanket into the cockpit and passed out under the stars listening to the waves caress the beach. In Trinidad I'd become accustomed to the incessant hum of the oil refinery and the blare of the halogen lights. The cleansing peace of Store Bay dissolved the subtle tension I'd accumulated in Trinidad.

I spent the following day scrubbing Hanuman. I hadn't realized how dirty she'd become in Trinidad. The deck had such an even layer of scum I'd forgotten its' true color. As I watched brown water drain through scuppers into the ocean I felt I was cleansing mayself as well as the boat.

I made my way along the coast to Mt. St. Irving Bay, another beautiful clear water anchorage where I would end up spending several weeks. I celebrated four years since sailing under the Golden Gate Bridge. It was a good place to do so, embodying the beauty and serenity that I'd envisioned waiting for me in exotic locales when I began the journey. I rehashed the events of the previous four years trying to categorize and quantify the experience. I asked myself what I'd gained and what I'd lost. I figured I was probably just breaking even.

I watched my mind float away like a helium balloon, reminiscing of the past, and into an imaginary lala land. My mind had a way of doing that. Formerly I'd considered it a nice escape from the tedium of day to day existence but I came to realize that there was little benefit to tuning out the world. I found that my most rewarding moments were those where I was completely submersed in what was around me. The realization was only the first phase however. Once aware of it I quickly realized how hard it really was to stay completely focused on what was actually around me. My brain had formed patterns and preferred to live in its own manifestation of the world it had created, one that required little actual thinking or concentration. I was faced with the challenge of transforming my mind from an implement of obstruction, into a tool for my benefit. It was a battle of opposites that I would loss nine times out of ten.

I quickly realized that Mt. St. Irving Bay was a popular surfing spot. When I arrived the seas had been totally flat. I'd actually snorkeled around the area that I came to realize was where the waves typically broke. There was even a little surf camp on the beach. Before long the waves returned and I dusted off my surfboard for the first time since Fiji.

The conditions were perfect for me. I really didn't care how big the waves were. I was okay with getting dragged over the reef by the large ones and perfectly happy to get less inspiring rides on the smaller ones. My main criterion for a good wave was that there weren't too many other surfers on it. A certain attitude seemed present whenever there were more surfers than waves. Ultimately I needed room to flail. The fact that the waves weren't all that big kept most of the surfers away and me happy. I spent several weeks honing my skills and by the end of it felt I at least resembled someone who wasn't out for the first time. The fun ended when the big waves arrived however. Surfers flew over from Barbados and Trinidad on a good surf report. The morning that I pulled anchor there were fifteen guys bobbing up and down on their boards waiting, or jockeying, for their turn on the next good wave.

I moved my way up the coast and spent a few days in Man-O-War Bay before checking out of Tobago and heading to Union Island.

Union Island

I pulled away from Tobago in a decent breeze but as the sun fell so did the wind. In light air, especially down wind, the Aries did a poor job of steering. When alone, I relied on the electric auto pilot to do the steering while I slept in such conditions. I attached its belt to the wheel and pressed the engage button. It started off doing its usual thing, steering without complaint, but before long the off course alarm started beeping angrily. "That's strange," I thought. Normally the unit only got upset in heavy winds when it was forced to work hard. I got Hanuman back on course but it was less than a minute before it was beeping again. I was lying in the cockpit enjoying the stars, about to doze off and not at all too excited about having to deal with malfunctioning equipment. I reset it several more times before giving up and succumbing to the fact that unless the wind picked up I was stuck hand steering for the night. I was forced to regress to the steer and sleep at the same time method I'd employed back in the South China Sea when I didn't have enough power to run the electric auto-pilot. I neither slept nor steered very well but made it through the night and pulled into Union Island the following day.

There wasn't much to do on Union Island. After spending half a day walking around and sweating, I set up camp at a funky little artsy looking bar owned by an alcoholic German lady. There was only one other person in the bar, an older white guy with a red nose who owned a small marine paint and epoxy supply shop next store. I sensed he spent a lot of time there.

"What do you think the verdict is on Scott Peterson?" he asked. I racked my brain over who Scott Peterson could be but came up with nothing. "Who's Scott Peterson?" I ventured gingerly.

I was half expecting him to tell me he'd just landed on Mars or something of the like. The BBC was the only news I'd been picking up on my short wave radio and I was quite removed from popular American culture.

"He's been on trail for a couple of years for murdering his pregnant wife. They're announcing the verdict here in an hour," he said, gesturing at the TV with his beer. "His dead wife was actually pretty attractive," he added. "Yeah, it's always more tragic when the good looking ones die," I responded, unable to resist throwing in the tactless comment. "His girl-friend was even better looking though." "I guess that explains things."

The Grenadines

Everybody seemed to think the Grenadines were something special, so I decided I'd check them out. The first thing I noticed was the high volume of charter boats. I did my best defy my 'magnetic anchor' theory, where people can't seem to avoid anchoring right on top of each other, and found my spot a little ways off from the horde. The water was shallow and clear, making anchoring easy.

With the anchor set I donned my snorkeling gear to have a look at the aquatic life that was supposed to be so fabulous. The water was turbid and I had difficulty seeing what all of the fuss was about. I imagined the Grenadines had gained popularity for the above water view of the numerous small islets and turquoise water, but I wasn't too impressed.

Bequia

I left for Bequia the next day. Bequia was nice enough but all of the islands had begun to look alike and I found myself a bit bored of island hopping. I checked my e-mail and discovered that my uncle/godfather had been diagnosed with fairly advanced cancer. My initial thought was, "how will this affect me?" The coldly pragmatic, sea tempered reaction was followed by guilt over my own self absorption.

My uncle Bill had been supremely supportive when I announced my desire to sail around the world one Thanksgiving. The fact that I'd never even been sailing didn't faze him. "Do it. Do it now," he responded with earnest enthusiasm. I nodded with appreciation, having been a little reticent about even announcing such a grand scheme.

Thanksgiving was eight days away but I deemed it important to try and make it home. The problem was that I was on some random little island in the middle of the Caribbean. My mom suggested that I leave Hanuman in St. Vincent and fly out of there. The idea didn't appeal to me. I didn't know where I'd leave the boat in St. Vincent and I wasn't too excited about coming back after a land stint and having to sail back up to St. John, my next work stop. I decided I'd try and sail up to St. John and fly out of St. Thomas. The problem was that St. John was 379 nautical miles away. I'd spent more than eight day sailing 379 miles in the past but was excited for the challenge; after months of more or less just hanging out, finally something to do.

After making some repairs to the Aries rudder, I put to sea. The first half day out the winds were light and I started doing the always dangerous calculation, "at this rate I should get there…way too late." Fortunately the winds picked up and I found myself beating into a gale. I had no complaints. I got Hanuman balanced perfectly with a double reefed main, full stay sail, and heavily reefed jib. I'd paid a little extra to have a foam luff inserted into new jib which gave it better shaped when it was heavily furled. I adjusted the sheeting angle to perfect the shape. The wind angle was such that I could just barely keep the bow pointed at St. John, meaning, with any luck, I wouldn't have to tack back and forth to get there.

I pulled into Great Cruz Bay, St. John, on my third night out, quite pleased with myself for my sub three day passage. I was back in California a few days later for Thanksgiving with my uncle. Bill was weak but in good spirits, sneaking shrimp cocktail, which he wasn't supposed to be eating, when his wife, my aunt, wasn't looking.

St John

My arrival in St. John heralded a new work stint. Without difficulty I found two bartending jobs. One was at a bar that ended up being rather slow, but air-conditioned, and the other as a banquette bartender at a large resort. The banquette position was a thoroughly amusing gig. I got to drive a golf cart, a constant source of amusement for the mischief minded. By the end of the night, being in control of the bar, I usually had a couple of drinks in me, and one in my hand, making the golf cart even more entertaining. Everything was done at full speed in the cart. If something didn't fall off the back in route, you weren't pushing the envelope.

I drank freely, but managed to prevent things from digressing to the level they had on St Thomas the previous season. Ultimately St. John suited me much better than St Thomas. St. John is about 70 percent national park and I spent most of my free daylight hours running on the myriad of trails that traversed the park. The addition of a girlfriend also probably helped to keep me out of the bars.

I strolled into the resort staff Christmas party after finishing up at my air-conditioned gig. I grabbed a drink and quickly chased it with another. In tropical climates the first drink serves only to moisten the palette, getting mostly absorbed in the mouth and throat. I strolled through the place scouting the scene, wondering if there might be some food left over. I wasn't really hungry but there's always room for free. I stepped quietly into a side room that appeared to have been the buffet area and my eyes halted on a blond in the back corner carefully wrapping desserts in paper napkins and stuffing them into her satchel. Emitting a pinkish, yellowish glow, she immediately captivated me with her radiance...*coup de foudre*. She didn't see me at first so I stood quietly observing her. She appeared to possess the combination of mystical luminosity and down to earth pragmatism that mirrored all that the sea had shown me over the past four years.

Eventually she felt my eyes and looked up with a 'deer in the headlights' look on her face as she was licking a morsel of chocolate from her finger. "How long have you been standing there?" "Long enough," I replied, shaking my head as if disappointed by her behavior but with a conspiratory smile. "This isn't what it looks like. I have some friends coming in on the late fairy and they just called and said they were really hungry," she replied, smiling. "Hey, I'm not the dessert police. You don't have to answer to me."

Amber and I had an extended conversation and I knew I'd met someone who would become a compelling element in my life.

Passage to Panama

The hurricane season had a nice way of preventing stagnation, forcing me to leave St John before I got sick of it. Some people kept their boats in St. John for the hurricane season but they were gambling. I figured they either had no choice but to stay or didn't really care all that much about their boats.

Karl hadn't quite gotten enough on his first passage and, looking for an excuse to quit his job, decided to return for some more punishment. Derek, a friend of ours who we'd met in St. Thomas, sent me an e-mail saying was up for anything and wanted to join the adventure. He flew in with Karl and I had my crew.

Amber was making good money as a massage therapist at the resort and not quite ready to leave St. John but planned to meet us in the Marquesas several months later. She got a few days off work to sail with us to Puerto Rico however.

Derek was puking on the first passage. In typical sailor fashion he'd had a few drinks the night, and probably into the morning, before leaving, which didn't quite agree with the motion of the ocean. Thus he was baptized. Amber was curled up in the fetal position for the majority of the passage.

I hoped she wasn't having second thoughts about coming to the Marquesas. Short passages can be the worst, not allowing one to move past the seasickness and become the accustomed to the motion. Fortunately, Amber was resilient and committed to future passages.

Karl, Derek and I departed San Juan and hopped along the Puerto Rico's northern coast. Going over the top, I hoped to find some surf and more consistent wind than on the bottom. The wind was consistent but the water was mostly just cloudy, turbid, and confused so surfing never happened.

We left the Puerto Rico not especially impressed, aside from our stop at Mona Island, promoted as 'the Galapagos of the Caribbean,' and headed for the San Blas Islands off the coast of Panama.

We'd been boarded by the US Coast Guard before leaving Mona Island and they'd recommended that we return to the Puerto Rican mainland because some of my flares were expired. We nodded in a, "yeah we'll probably do that" manner and then pointed the bow at Panama. The crew wasn't too concerned with the expired flare situation but I threw in a, "we'll get some more flares in Panama," just to make everyone feel safe.

We had perfect conditions for the first day and half but after that things turned nasty. I'd been told the winds could get testy in that stretch of ocean but didn't think we'd be running down wind under bare poles and still making four and a half knots.

For three days the seas built and we raced down the faces of ever growing breakers. Fortunately, down wind was where we wanted to go. The difference between being able to head where you want to and not being able to makes a world of difference in rough conditions. Getting your ass kicked is one thing. Getting your ass kicked and being pushed away from your destination is a real morale thrasher. Never the less, the conditions were still shity and the 20 foot waves that we surfed down seemed to want to engulf us as they swept across Hanuman's decks, leaving an angry, foaming mass of water struggling to return to the sea, unconcerned with whether or not it took Hanuman with it.

"Are the waves this big in the Pacific," Derek asked, ducking into the companionway to avoid the wrath of a breaking wave, concerned that this would become the norm. "Sure hope not," I responded. I got a quizzical, "weren't you there" look from Karl and Derek but just nodded my head. I decided to leave my sanity in question, feeling it created a richer experience for the crew, giving them some, "and that crazy captain…" stories.

All cooking ceased during the blow and we resorted to eating canned corn, or "canned carn" as Karl, with his Wisconsin accent, said. "Carn? What the hell is carn?" asked Derek. "Canned carn damn it! Open a can of canned carn!" responded Karl from behind the wheel. "I have no idea what you're talking about. What the hell do you want?" Derek and I occasionally regressed to the humor level of second graders, spending hours heckling Karl about the way he said corn or warm (rhymes with farm). "Shut up and get me some coooorn damn it." The fact that Karl was so into canned corn made it all the more humorous. "This sweet carn is just so fuckin' good!"

On the third day of the blow the storm dropped off almost all at once. I could actually see a visible vertical plane ahead, where our wind ended. We sailed into the new weather system as if pushing threw a curtain. The wind direction changed almost 180 degrees. The sails thwacked about for a minute before we were able to adjust to the new paradigm. Our new wind deserted us almost as quickly as it came on. Before long, we found ourselves becalmed but still experiencing the large swells that the storm had created, as absolutely deplorable condition.

The seas eventually calmed but our wind never returned and we oscillated between sailing very slowly and not moving at all. The calms have an interesting numbing effect on the mind. One looks for any sort of mental stimuli one can find. Usually it's reading, but occasionally it's something a little less traditional, like 'carn fetch.'

Karl swam around in the ocean as Derek did 360's, trying to get Hanuman back on course, or at least pointing in the right direction. A task that can be surprisingly difficult when there is little or no wind. I threw an empty can of corn in front of Karl as he snorkeled, face down, contemplating the depth of the blue. He watched mesmerized, as the silver can, glinting in the sun, descended to infinity. "Again, throw in another one," Karl exclaimed like a child on a roller coaster. I grabbed the empty can of tuna fish that, combined with the corn and half a box of Triskets, had constituted our lunch (known as cold POF, cold pot of food) and chucked it in front of him. It landed face up and floated, which Karl seemed to find just as fascinating as the sinking. He splashed water at it until filled up and sank. Instead of letting it sink however, he dove after it. He repeated the process of floating it and sinking it with the obsession of a springer spaniel playing fetch. Only after an hour of 'carn fetch' did he return to the boat.

The days quickly ran together. Hey Karl, "did we see those whales yesterday?" "No that was today." You'd think it would be easy to at least remember what happened on the day that I was living in, but throw in a good nap, and the segmentation of the days could really go awry. "Well what happened yesterday?" "That was the day we ran out of beer." "Ahhh yes, the day we ran out of beer. Good thing for all that rum aye?" "Aye!"

The day we got rammed by the whale shark was a difficult one to forget. We'd just settled into our evening cocktails and were enjoying the fact that we had the potential to reach the San Blas Islands on the following day when, "…thud." The 'thud' wasn't enough to spill our drinks but, accompanied by a thrashing noise, was enough to get us out of our seats. Looking to port, we saw the huge trashing sickle shaped tail of a 30 foot whale shark, half out of the water, plowing into the side of Hanuman. Its movements were sluggish however, and since whale sharks are toothless filter feeder, it didn't seem all that threatening. It was hard to tell if it was intentionally ramming us or if it was just stubborn and refusing to go around. I jumped down below to get my camera but by the time I returned it was gone. "Well…that's not something you see every day," I offered. "No it isn't." "Need a freshening of those cocktails gentlemen?" Karl asked. "Please," Derek and I sounded in unison as we downed what was left in our cups and thrust them towards Karl.

San Blas

We pulled into Poviener, of the San Blas islands, in the late afternoon. Three dug-out canoes filled with women and children clinging to Hanuman's rail were trying to sell us *molas*, the local tapestry, before we even had the anchor set. I ducked below to log our arrival time and engine hours. When I came back up, the women had Hanuman's starboard deck covered with their *molas*. They smiled, looked up at us, and just waited. Their children played and bailed the dug outs. It was obvious that not buying a *mola* or two wasn't an option. Before long Karl was wearing a *mola* head-band type thing and Derek owned a square foot of fabric with various animals hand sewn into it. Despite our purchases, they weren't totally convinced we were done buying and just sort of rested on our rail, occasionally holding up a random *mola*, shaking it, and nodding. It wasn't until it got dark and we were completely ignoring them that they decided it was time to shove off. Karl kept on his new head-band for our amusement, looking half native, half cholo from the barrio, and all clown.

Derek buying Molas from the locals in the San Blas islands

The following day we took the beach and started checking out the island of Poviener. It was flat and small and took only about 20 minutes to explore. Half that time was spent amusing ourselves with the island's one bathroom which was just a toilet seat on the end of a pier that emptied directly into the ocean. "Probably has to be the best view from a toilet I've ever seen." "I don't really have to go but I'm tempted to try… for the experience." "Might wanna wait for an ebbing tide." "Well…if no one's' shittin', I guess it's time for some cold beers." A couple nods of agreement and, "*tres cervesas por favor.*"

Before the sun went down we'd repeated the "*tres cervesas*" mantra several more times and decided we needed some food. We were on our way to a small restaurant, or at least a little place that could make us some food, when we were stopped by a counselor of a Christian group that was having a retreat on Poviener. He said that they had some left-overs that were just going to be thrown in the ocean and that we were welcome to them.

We'd been observing the young Christians for a good part of the day and were surprised by the offer. We'd invited one of the young Christian girls to play horseshoes with us and were rebuffed, a bit angrily, by one of the counselors, for "interfering." Not ones to hold a grudge when it came to free food, we accepted the offer of scraps readily.

Three tortillas remained which we topped and scarfed down quickly. But they served only to stir our appetites. The campers seemed to have their own personal plates, leaving none for us, but we had no intention of letting the mere lack of a vessel of delivery stand in our way. Derek and I cupped our hand while Karl scooped in rice, ground beef, onions, and a couple of tomato chunks. "Hot sauce?" "Please." Had we a third hand, we could have ingested the food in a remotely civilized fashion. As it stood, the only solution was to go at it face first, pig style, "oink, oink." After consuming what was left, we did some dishes to express our gratitude and loaded up in the dinghy. We weren't ready to call it an evening however so we swung by Jack's boat.

We'd met Jack, a fellow sailor, during the day and he'd invited us over to his boat for a drink. He gave us cold beers and we settled into the cockpit to spin some yarns. He had a drunk, local guy on board who we speculated might be acting as a cabin boy. We inquired about weed and in seconds he'd called a friend on another boat, who came over with a joint. I'd met the friend several times in Trinidad but he didn't remember me. I occasionally had that effect on people. It was like we occupied different dimensions that didn't quite line up. Plus, he was always pretty fucked up when I met him. Despite that, he was a nice guy and extremely generous. He, Jack, and another guy had been cruising together for awhile.

It didn't take long to see what they all had in common. They were the partying womanizing types. We were titillated by their exploits but also left with a slight feeling of repugnance. They definitely seemed at the opposite end of the spectrum from Christians, but I mused that perhaps they just occupied two sides of the same coin. One group obsessed with getting into heaven in the next life, the other trying to create it in this one. Both, like most of us, participating in the same ego pageantry.

It would be difficult to say whose conduct was outwardly more christianly of the two groups. Take out the specifics of what was being offered and Jack seemed more outwardly more Christian than the actually Christians. The Christians, to varying degrees, seemed guarded and not overly friendly. One of them was downright hostile.

I learned that the Jack was just letting the local guy hang out on his boat because he was from another island and didn't really have a place to stay. He'd clearly had a few drinks and got up from the cockpit, declaring he was going to find a place to sleep. "Here take this pad," Jack offered. "I'm indigenous. I don't need a pad," he responded with feigned drama. With that, he grabbed the pad and went to the foredeck to sleep.

In the end, I found that both groups made me feel slightly uncomfortable. I sensed they both hoped for me to perform in a particular way, their way, that I wouldn't be entirely comfortable with. It made me wonder if I ever had the same effect on others. Did I accepted people as they were, with the hope of learning something from them, or did I simply desire to mold people into to some form which resembled my own?

I was 'over' pathetic used outboards and had purchased a brand new Yamaha 15 horsepower outboard before leaving St John, strapping it onto the 'maximum eight horsepower' dinghy. It was a life changer. I could get the dinghy on fast plane with four people. When I rode solo, the ride was beyond loose. It seemed as though only the outboard was actually touching the water. Full throttle pushed the limits of control. I wondered how easy it would be to flip.

The new outboard also opened up a whole new sport, 'scurfing.' I started off at the helm of the dinghy, with Derek spotting, and Karl, who was on the surfboard, hanging onto the end of a rope that was attached to the back of the dinghy. I idled forward to take the slack out of the rope. "You ready," I hollered back to Karl. Karl was lying on his belly and shifted his weight, not knowing quite what to expect. "I guess."

Getting from the stomach to the feet proved a challenge that none of us managed on our first attempt. We honed our technique however, made a few adjustments to the rope, and after a few goes we all managed to achieve standing postures. Once standing, it became even more fun. Throw in some long swells from the northeast and it was hard imagine any activity being more entertaining.

The Panama Canal

Despite having discovered our new favorite sport, after a week in the San Blas we felt that unless we were going to move in with the locals, we'd experienced the place and it was time to take on the Panama Canal.

A short passage found us in Colon, Panama. "Wait, how do you spell colon, as in the lower digestive track," I queried. "C-O-L-O-N," Derek responded. "Hmmm... how fitting," I replied, as we walked the streets of Colon, breathing the fetid morning air. It was my kind of shit hole though. It had charm. And by charm I mean 25 cent ice-cream cones. An ice-cream cone became a permanent fixture in my right hand.

There was also a lively market. On our first visit we found fresh pig faces for sale. Karl and I were on the verge of buying one. "What the hell are you guys going to do with a pig face," Derek coughed. "Just because you already have one Derek, don't be trying to deny us." We decided to forego the pig face, but with a touch of melancholy thinking of all entertaining scenarios that could have unfolded had we possessed them.

Brandoni had apparently made his way back to the States after we parted ways in Mallorca. He and his new girlfriend, Noel, met us in Colon with the intent of sailing to the Galapagos. In addition to the return of a friend, we also gained two additional line handlers for the transit of the canal, giving us a total of four; the required amount.

We went through the canal transit formalities more fluidly that I'd expected. The specifics of the transit regulations changed from year to year so we got the low down from recent transitees. Apparently, it was crucial to say that you could make eight and a half knots under power, a number that was unachievable by all but a few large, high powered sailboats. One sailor that we met didn't claim the eight knots and was forced to pay double what we did.

The transit was a two day affair. Our transit pilot was dropped off in the late afternoon and we pulled anchor and headed up to the first lock. Being reliant on Big Red always made me nervous but she'd been running well ever since I'd installed the new lift pump in the Med. Our pilot was friendly and easy going and we made our way through the locks up into Lake Gatun without major incident. We attached ourselves to a large mooring where our pilot was retrieved and we were left by ourselves for the night.

Monkeys, which I decided were Howler Monkeys due to their predawn alarm, got me up well before our new pilot arrived the following day. Their screeching was unearthly. I decided that they sounded like the Ring Wraths from *Lord of the Rings*. They imbued me with an uneasy feeling until the golden orb breached the horizon.

Our new pilot said he'd been under the weather. He clearly wasn't too excited about being at work. He set up camp in his collapsible chair on the side deck, raised his sun umbrella, and didn't say much the whole passage.

Making our way to the Pacific required 60 miles of motoring across Lake Gatun. Big Red hadn't done a full day of motoring since the Suez Canal and I didn't have supreme confidence in her. The consequence of engine failure was a very expensive tow across the lake, one which I didn't have the money for. I wanted to keep our speed below four and half knot so that Big Red wouldn't have to work too hard. I wanted to avoid overheating. I still hadn't installed engine gauges and continued to rely on my 'sniff and listen' method.

Brandoni and Karl working the bow lines as we transit the Panama Canal

"How fast you going," the unhappy looking pilot yelled back to me. Brandoni looked at the GPS and whispered up to me, "four knots." "Four and a half knots," I shouted back to the pilot. He said nothing and returned his glazed gaze to the horizon.

The day proceeded in a pleasantly uneventful manner as we made our way across the lake to the locks on the other side. We pulled up to a dock where we had to wait an hour before proceeding which gave me an opportunity to check the fluids. The engine oil was fine but the transmission, whose seals had been on their way out for a couple of years, required almost a quart. Adding transmission fluid was par for the course however, and I was content with Big Red's condition.

After passing around sardines and crackers, and sweating profusely for an hour, our pilot returned from his air-conditioned office and we were off. We proceeded down a couple more sets of locks and across Miraflores Lake and Hanuman was in the Pacific. I breathed a deep sigh of relief. Back in the Pacific! I'd given Big Red a "just get us through the Canal" pep talk, prior to the transit (an offer I'd later be taken up on) and, being in my ocean of origin and return, felt freed from reliance on the engine, reunited with the wind, and despite still having 8000 miles of sailing ahead of me, relatively close to home.

We rented a car for a couple of days to go surfing. Splitting the bill five ways made it cheap. Having transited the Canal, we were also in celebration mode, meaning we had to drink a lot. I woke up one morning after a good night of partying and climbed up into the cockpit flooded with light. The reflection off the white paint was brutal. I put on some shades and tried to finish a letter I'd started to write to Amber. But both the hangover and the blistering rash that had developed above my left eye the day before, festered in the sun and blew my concentration. I wasn't sure of the rash's origin, but during the previous couple of days, in a marijuana induced munchies fit, I'd devoured over 50 mangos. The park next to where Hanuman was moored contained an unlimited supply of ripe mangos. Between the munchies and mangos being my favorite fruit, I went to town. I came out of the experience yellow. I ate the mangos not only with my mouth but with my face, hands, arms, and, so it appeared, even my hair. A yellow slick extended from my nose to mid way down my chest.

It also occurred to me that the rash might have originated in my crotch, where I'd been harboring a case of jock itch for the past week. I couldn't decide whether I was more disturbed by the fact that I might be allergic to mangos, my favorite fruit, or that I had a dick rash on my face.

Las Perlas

Karl, Derek, Noel, Brandoni, my rash and I loaded Hanuman up with provisions, including a couple of bags of mangos, I still wasn't convinced the mangos had actually caused my rash, and headed for Las Perlas islands, not far off the Panamanian coast.

My rash continued to take over until my whole body itched. It was the worst around the eyes. It didn't totally disfigure me, like a poison oak rash, but it definitely irritated the shit out of me. It got to the point where I stopped eating mangos, just to be on the safe side. I also took a fist full of Benadryl, but I found that being in the water and drinking large amounts of alcohol were the most effective treatments. Fortunately, we found a little resort with a poolside bar. After four or five cocktails, I stopped noticing the rash and was almost ready for a mango.

To the Galapagos

Noel eventually decided that hanging out with four foul smelling guys on a small boat all the way to the Galapagos wasn't exactly what she had in mind for a vacation. She and Brandoni were expunged from the crew list, leaving Karl, Derek and I back on our own. It was probably for the best. The passage crossed a broad band of the Inter Tropical Convergence Zone, which normally would make for inconsistent, shifty winds interspersed with squalls, but we experienced a whole different scenario.

In case my rash wasn't bad enough I came down with some sort of stomach flu a day or two out. I started off thinking I was just seasick but I soon realized that it was something else. I spent several watches wrenching over the rail.

The wind picked up from the direction we wanted to go and before long we were tacking under reefed sails. The heavy wind meant the Aries was steering like a champ so fortunately, when I was on watch I could mostly just curl up in a ball, when I wasn't retching up bile.

As a consolation, my rash eased up during the worst of my sickness. I suspected that after a couple of days without food my body was just too weak to generate an allergic reaction. I fell into a state of delirium. I guess I managed to navigate but was surprised to find out after the fact that Karl and Derek had covered a watch for me during the worst of it.

I spent my off watch time in my bunk trying to find the least painful position. My whole body ached. I thought of all the places I'd rather be, which amounted to anywhere but where I was. Slowly, I became weaker and began to let go of comforting fantasy thoughts and contemplate mortality. My uncle Bill had died two months prior, after the cancer had thoroughly revenged his body. I felt closer to his suffering, though he'd endured it for six months, and I, only for a couple of days.

I was pretty glad to have crew at this point but after three days day without food I was getting a little annoyed that they'd just been eating cans of sardines and crackers and not cooked an actual meal. I simply wanted something to puke up. I also felt that they could do a better job keeping the communal cockpit water bottle filled. There's nothing like puking up a mouth full of bile, reaching for a gulp of water to dampen the after wretch, finding the bottle bone dry, and having to choke down the bile flavor. At the end of the third day I felt well enough to do some cooking and made up some simple POF.

The whole experience affected me. It left me with a sense of the closeness to death, a greater appreciation for the fragility of life and a desire to treat it, especially in myself, with greater reverence. I didn't drink or smoke any weed for the remainder of the fifteen days it took us to get to San Cristobal, Galapagos. The passage was less than 800 miles but the wind never let us take the first reef out of the main. And, due to the wind direction, we had to tack back and forth the whole way. It was a brutish passage.

San Cristobal, Galapagos

Pain is easily forgotten and despite having contemplated not drinking until reaching the Marquesas, I had a beer in my hand before the sun was down on the day we dropped anchor in San Cristobal. Of course one led to another, and before I knew it we were smoking joints at three in the morning.

Despite a night of 'rock staring,' I managed to maintain a level of temperance, avoiding hangovers and that 'I hope I didn't do anything stupid last night' feeling. We also achieved a good level of physical activity, sending energy back to the muscles after the passage.

The image I'd formed of Galapagos was shattered on arrival. I'd pictured mostly deserted islands, crawling with finches and enormous tortoises. We saw considerably more people than tortoises. The only tortoises we saw were in captivity and people were everywhere. There were even entire towns.

Quick to adapt, we made a number of friends and soon became known as the three wise men. We hadn't shaved in many months and in our tattered clothes took on a biblical appearance. Once people got to know us a bit better the nickname was amended and we became the three wise guys.

The visit wasn't totally without wildlife interaction. The sea lions didn't seem fazed by the fact that humans had tried to take over the bay where Hanuman was anchored. I'd read that they were inclined to crawl onto any floating objects, including dinghies, and I was anxious to see it. One night when we arrived back on Hanuman by water taxi we were delighted to find one in our dinghy. We took pictures. We were less delighted in the morning when the sea lion was gone and in its place was a huge sea lion turd. "Ah man… that's not cool." We were still amused however, and the aqueous turd was easily flushed out the drain hole. The humor was gone the following day when the lion not only shat in the dinghy but bit a hole in it, completely deflating its port side. "God damn it!" The dinghy, whose floor boards where slowing sliding into the water, had to be hauled on deck and repaired. We hadn't even used it. We'd quickly discovered that there were reasonably priced water taxis and that there was no safe place to dock the dinghy. We'd pretty much kept it in the water just for the sea lions. Stupid!

Isabella

Of the many people we met in San Cristobal, an American girl named Kimie somehow got wrapped up in our antics and found herself onboard for the overnight passage to Isabella.

When we first saw her, she spoke to us as though we'd already met, like she was just picking up on a conversation left unfinished. I could almost hear the slow turning of sea rusted gears as Karl, Derek and I tried to recall if we'd met her some evening after a few too many drinks. "No..." our sea synced thoughts emitted into the ether, "she's kinda' cute, we probably would have remembered her." We hadn't met her. She was just outgoing and confident. I considered her prime sexual fodder for my two sex starved shipmates. "What do you think of that tattoo behind her left ear?" I asked. "Sexy... and a little frightening...making it even sexier."

Kimie, pronounced kim-yay, started puking not long after dinner. She'd brought supplies to make a meal for us but after a few minutes down below, found she was feeling sick. She stubbornly wanted to continue cooking. "Don't be stupid... let Karl do it," I insisted. She felt a little better once on deck, but after eating, was bracing herself against the downwind

433

rail. "Don't listen," she insisted, feeling self conscience about her retching noises. "We're not," I lied. "At least you have something to barf up. It's the dry heaving that's a real bitch."

Kimie's puking was unfortunate. It was a beautiful night and conditions were ideal. Whales were plentiful and made rings of bubbles illuminated by phosphorescence to confuse and capture fish. At least that's how I chose to explain the phenomena. When stated confidently, there was no room for doubt. And it seemed a reasonable explanation.

We drifted into the anchorage the following morning under light winds. Kimie recovered in the light of day with a stable horizon to focus on and though dazed from lack of sleep was in good spirits.

Both Derek and Karl were interested in Kimie. Derek was interested like a stud sniffing around bitch. While he genuinely liked her, he was probably moved more by his libido than his heart. Karl on the other hand was not only intoxicated by her sensual mixture of Asian and Caucasian features but also very attracted to who she was. She got his Star Wars references, a clincher for anyone with nerdy tendencies. Karl's position of captivation was unfortunate however, as it became evident over time that Kimie had taken an interest in me; nothing more alluring than someone who's not available.

Though I'd made it clear that I had a girlfriend, I could've perhaps done a better job of distancing myself from Kimie, allowing Karl more of a chance. Kimie and I established a mutual affinity however, and as closeness ensued. Fortunately, the relationship ended where I should have ended it with Carly. I decided no good could come from the next step unless I could do it with heart; to be able to do it knowing that I wouldn't be hurting someone else, and ultimately myself. And though Amber was an ocean away and I hadn't seen her in months, we had forged a bond that I still cherished. I knew that if I crossed a line with Kimie I would be severing something that could not be fully restored, even if I kept the offense in the deepest caverns of my mind. I began to feel a deeper connection between those I might wrong and myself. As if it was impossible to do something to someone else that I wasn't doing to myself.

A running joke had begun about instant karma. I threw a berry at someone and instantly I stubbed my toe. "Ha ha... instant karma." As I thought about it, I realized that all karma was instant. We bear the weight of our wrongs.

Galapagos to Marquesas

We had a large chunk of ocean between ourselves and the Marquesas, our next destination. Providentially, it was a stretch known for its benevolence. We looked forward to some high mileage days and pleasant conditions.

The passage didn't start off entirely well. It began with a large POF involving massive quantities of rapidly degrading cheese we'd procured on Isabella. The cheese may have passed its prime. Derek emerged on deck during one of my night shifts looking like death. "What's up?" I asked. "Puking, pissing out my ass, chills," he stated mater-of-factly. "That sucks." "Yeah."

A day and a half later, Karl and I still weren't showing any signs of illness and thought that perhaps we'd dodged a bullet. No sooner did we vocalize the thought, than Karl approached rail and went down on all fours. "Need me to hold back your beard?" I offered. I'm sure that some part of his psyche was laughing at my witty remark but the rest of him was retching violently. "How ya' feelin'?" I queried rhetorically. "Awesome."

The following day I was in the same position. The nausea, achiness, and all over body pain passed in 24 hours but we all continued to piss out our asses for the next week. A firm shit became the illusive white whale we all hunted. We'd give a play by play as we hung our asses off the leeward rail. "Piss." "Mayonnaise." "Marinara." "Just like last night's POF. Like it wasn't digested at all; only with consistency of peanut butter." "Peanut butter? That's not bad." "Actually it just started off like peanut butter and then regressed to marinara." "Still, marinara's better than piss." "True." Karl got fed up with wiping his ass to the point of bleeding and decided to all but give up eating, in hopes of regrowing the skin on his anus. His method was effective and his shitting ceased all together. Derek and I felt that eating, being one of the chief sources of pleasure on passage, was non-negotiable and decided pissing out our asses wasn't all that bad.

During my time hanging out in the Caribbean I'd resolved to remedy Hanuman's poor downwind sailing performance. The problem was that on a downwind run it was impossible to have both the main and the jib up at the same time because the main blocked the jib's wind, leaving it just fluttering about. The solution was to build a whisker pole so that I could fly the jib on the opposite side as the main.

I ordered a couple of gizmos online that I could attach to either end of a pole. One end would attach to an eye I'd bolted onto the front of the mast and the other would attach to the jib sheet, holding it opposite the main.

I elected to make a pole out of PVC pipe and fiberglass; the least expensive solution. The initial trial, off the coast of Puerto Rico, went well but in rolly conditions the pole tended to bend to a rather dramatic degree. The problem was quickly remedied at the next stop by inserting a square metal tube down the center of the pole. The modified pole performed perfectly and a few days out of Isabella the wind shifted and we went from a beam reach to a broad reach. We threw up the pole, along with a whole mess of new rigging to keep it in place, and we moved along with a whole new sense of speed.

Long swells filled in, along with cheery small cumulous and I really started to feel like I was back in the Pacific. The rhythm of a long passage set in. Our shit eventually firmed. We read a lot. We did crossword puzzles. I was once again drawn into excessive introspection resulting in a confrontation of the unresolved history I felt I had with Pat. Despite having tried to convince myself that, in wronging Pat, I was suffering just as he was, I caught a whiff of bullshit in my conclusions and thought I still owed Pat something. I decided to write him letter.

Dear Pat,

Time has passed, perhaps too much. I should've written a year ago. I should've called. I know it's not time that heals all wounds but word and actions. Perhaps, I too whole heartedly accepted your 'leave me be' e-mail because I really didn't know what to say to you. I still don't. "I'm an asshole, a jerk, I'm sorry," would probably have been a good place to start.

I'm sure you must still ask the question "Why?" "How could my so-called best friend have fucked me over so hard?" Don't think about it too long. I didn't. That's why it happened. I guess that on that night in Crete I felt as though I was in some sort of bubble, separated from real time and real consequences. Of course part of me knew that that wasn't the case, but that part of me was weaker and was over ruled.

Coming home the following Christmas began my next mistake. Somehow I had the image in my head of the three of us sitting around a pizza, gulping down litters of Martzen, rehashing the folly of our youth. I was clearly way off base. I imagine 'insensitive, selfish, and thoughtless' would be a more accurate assessment of my state of mind. Somehow I convinced myself that hanging out with Carly wouldn't be that big of a deal. Clearly I missed the mark but I had no idea of the steam of events that would follow. I apologize for all of the pain caused you.

I know this must seem like way too little way too late and perhaps you're wondering why I even bothered. I had a dream last night. We were hanging out, just like old times. I know that will never be the case. I don't expect to be forgiven but I thought that perhaps it might make you feel a little better to know that I'm sorry and that I'm not walking around with a smug self contented grin on my face. The experience hasn't left me any better off. It's left me wiser to the darker side of the human condition, and my own, but it's dampened my childish enthusiasm for life. I wish you the best. Sorry, Mike

With August 30th came another beard day. We hadn't shaved since leaving St. John. We had a lot to work with. I'd contemplated it in years past but I finally committed to letting symmetry go. I really wanted to buck the social standard of facial hair. My original idea was to shave one side of my face completely, while leaving the other untouched. I was almost sold on the idea until I decided that it was just too simple. Beard day only came once a year and I wanted to go big. I decided to go with vertical stripes with the left and the right sides being mirror images of each other.

If looking ridiculous was the goal, I definitely succeeded. The message I was trying to convey got a little lost. It looked more like I had a case of facial mange than vertical stripes. Karl and Derek went with a more symmetrical guise but ended up looking almost equally absurd.

Derek developed a boil on his ass that eventually swelled to such a size as to require a name. Derek christened it Bobby Boil. Bobby created entertainment for Karl and me but caused a great deal of pain for Derek, as young ones tend to.

Eventually, Derek was caught off guard by a swell that sent him flying across the cabin. He landed, Bobby first, on the chart table rail. "Fuuuuck," screamed Derek several times, as Bobby exploded, sending a trickle of blood and puss down his ass.

All in all, the second longest passage, mileage wise, of the trip ended up going by fairly quickly. Aside from some light winds during the first couple of days, the breeze never left us and we made it to Fatu Hiva in 20 days.

Circumnavigation

The Bay of Penises marked the point at which I crossed my old path four years prior. Thus, I realized my goal of a circumnavigation. This time we anchored expertly under sail, avoiding wrapping a line around the prop shaft and breaking the engine mounts.

Fatu Hiva didn't seem to have changed at all; no K-Mart, no Wal-Mart, no McDonalds. In fact, the one tiny grocery store that had been there before seemed to have closed down.

We readied the dinghy and prepared to take the beach. "Are you really going to land like that," Karl asked, gesturing at my face. I paused for a moment to see if he was serious. "Of course," I stated, shaking my head, disappointed, if not disgusted, with the question. "Besides, when's the last time you had a look in the mirror Romeo?"

We wandered down 'the road' looking for some fruit to pick, but before long found ourselves heading back to the dinghy with just few limes to add to the 'rum and whatever's around' we'd be having to celebrate.

I busted out my final bottle of Hanumanuwine that Matt and I had crafted during the construction phase. Four and a half years of rolling around in the bowels of Hanuman had an interesting effect on it. If I hadn't personally made it, I might doubt that it had been made from grapes. I tasted like a mixture of brandy and sake. It was definitely potent and quite drinkable, after the first few sips inoculated the pallet. I was happy not to wake up blind the following morning.

After our brief visit to land we found ourselves content to spend the rest of the day playing scrabble and Jenga in the cockpit while sipping cocktails and looking at the scenery from the comfort of the boat. Derek was stupid drunk before the sun went down.

The next morning I crawled out of my bunk as Karl was tidying up. He grabbed the bottle of gin that we hadn't quite dusted the night before, gave it a little shake to get a better feel for the quantity, uncapped it, and downed what was left. I cringed and gave him a congratulatory, "niiiice." "Not enough left to bother saving," he responded, "but of course," and at that point I chimed in and we chorused, "Nothing gets wasted."

We spent the next few days surfing, hiking, and jumping off waterfalls before heading north to Hiva Oa, where Amber would be flying in to meet us.

Hiva Oa

There's no port authority of Fatu Hiva. It was one the features of the island that made it so endearing to me. Hiva Oa did have a port authority and we were required to check in. Technically, we weren't supposed to have even stopped at Fatu Hiva before checking in, but the last time I was there they were lax on such matters. Fatu Hiva is the most windward of the Marquesas so if one sails past it to check in at Hiva Oa then one has to sail back up wind to get to Fatu Hiva, which is just lame.

The problem with checking in is that the authorities require you to pay a bond (returned upon departure) amounting to around 600 hundred bucks. I was aware of the bond situation, and had paid it last time, but wasn't too excited about it. Karl and Derek were even less excited about it. None of us really had 600 bucks lying around. We decided to tell them we would just be checking out of Hiva Oa bound for Hawaii. Eventually we managed to weasel our way out of the bond but the port authorities weren't too thrilled with us since our plan involved us hanging around for a week unbonded.

BELOW THE HORIZON

A little ball of sunshine bounced out of the small plane and skipped across the tarmac into my arms. A sweet smell saturated my nostrils and melted the crusty, salt tempered exterior that had fused with my hide after four months with my briny mistress. Feeling her soft body pressed against me awoke an aspect I'd unconsciously resigned to Davey Jones Locker. We rented a room and spent several days rolling around in bed eating candy pumpkins and playing airplane.

Despite what we told the port authorities in Hiva Oa, we didn't head straight for Hawaii. I wanted to allow Amber time to acclimatize before taking off on a passage. In addition, I wanted to give the hurricane season in the northern Pacific a little more time to die out, ensuring that we wouldn't cross the equator into a tempest.

Cruising the Marquesas

We stuck to bays that were either completely uninhabited or that I was sure contained no authorities of any sort. Our first anchorage out of Hiva Oa was an uninhabited bay where we intended to just spend a night. I dusted off the spear poles and got to fishing. Food in the Marquesan stores was expensive and neither diverse nor plentiful. Having left the last town with a grocery store in Hiva Oa, it was important that we try to save our provisions for the passage. I found myself completely submersed in spear fishing. I dreamed of it at night.

In the evening, after a day of spear fishing, we would row to land with our catch and a few potatoes and cook over a fire. We squeezed fresh lime and poured coconut water over the fish and potatoes as they cooked. We also managed to find a few ripe bananas for dessert. We'd planned to move to the next bay after the first night of barbequing but ended up enjoyed it so much that we said, "one more night" several times before we left.

I found myself in a state Persians call 'yarak.' It is a term used in falconry to describe the condition the falconist wants their falcon in when hunting; hungry, yet strong; alert, ready to hunt.

On the third day of fishing, after spearing a couple of small groupers, I saw a shinny object glinting in the sun on the sea floor. Always with an eye out for treasure, I dove down to explore. As I approached, I could see that it was a bottle; not an uncommon or particularly exciting find. I grabbed it anyway. I noticed the cap was still on which is unusual for a bottle on the sea floor. Typically, capped bottles end up on the beach. As I grasped it, I noticed that it was almost full with a light amber liquid. My pessimistic side suspected it might be some sort of festering fluid. But it looked quite clear. Ascending to the surface, I made out the black Bacardi bat on the cap and hope flourished in the pit of my stomach. We'd exhausted our seemingly endless supply of booze in Hiva Oa and had been running next to dry for weeks. I breached the surface, bringing the bottle into the air. I grasped the cap. It was tight. "A good sign," I thought. I twisted harder and it came off cleanly. The aroma of Bacardi Gold quickly filled my nostrils and I brought the bottle to my lips, kicking hard with my feet to make sure a passing wave didn't breach the bottle's opening. "RUM!"

We'd often talked of finding a floating bale of money or weed at sea, but at the time the almost full bottle of Bacardi Gold seemed as grand a find as I could have hoped for. I had my picture taken with my fish in one hand and bottle of rum in the other. "All in days work," I stated with mirth.

On the beach, we machetteed the tops off of a few green coconuts, and added the rum and a squeeze of lime… paradise. After the rum and fish were consumed we used a tarp to build a tee-pee like structure under which we rolled glowing red rocks we'd heated in the fire. We crawled in with a couple coconuts filled with water and closed the flap behind us. Pouring the water over the rocks created a steamy seaside sauna. Once thoroughly sweaty we ran into the sea, hooting and hollering, capping the day of perfectly.

Amber and Mike drinking the sea floor rum out of coconuts on a remote beach in the Marquesas

Amber slowly adjusted to the new lifestyle, though she wasn't captivated by it in the same way I was. She wasn't really a water person. She sighed a lot and made bored flapping noises with her lips while I strapped on my flippers. She surely questioned trading in the companionship of the friends she'd left behind to come sailing with my two swarthy shipmates and me.

In my state of yarak, I was more focused on the water, the wind, and elements within those from which energy could be harvested. I expected Amber to enter my arena to rekindle our bond and didn't really make much of an effort to move into hers. I considered entities outside my immediate scope of tangibility to be, for the most part, irrelevant to the lives we had before us. Amber had just come from a different world and didn't automatically slide into mine. She couldn't really swim well, making forays into the water a different experience for her than for me. I spent a good portion of the day underwater. Amber spent that portion of the day thinking, "this is beautiful, but I didn't fly all the way down here to stare at the water my while boyfriend chases fish around."

Eventually we sailed to another island where we attempted to repeat our activities of the previous anchorage. The bay was rugged and instead of a nice soft beach, we were forced to land on a rocky shore after maneuvering the dinghy through a maze of reefs. Timing the waves was tricky, and we got pummeled by a few, but managed to avoid major injury and, more importantly, damage to the dinghy.

Becoming concerned about the upcoming passage and our dwindling supplies, we made a half days march to a town and bought all of their onions and potatoes and a few cans of tuna. Feeling the call of the passage, we didn't linger too long at the rocky shore anchorage and sailed north to Daniel's bay in Nuka Hiva. Since my last visit to Daniel's Bay, four years prior, a season of 'Survivor' had been filmed there. I was interested to see the condition of the place.

The bay was named after Daniel who, along with his wife Annetonnette, had been living there since the island was created.

It looked pretty much the same as it had the last time I'd been there. The bay had two arms. One occupied by Daniel and the other occupied by 14 of his various relations. Survivor had moved Daniel out of his arm and into his relation's arm so that they could produce their episode free of locals. "Survivor built you this?" I asked Daniel, gesturing towards a shack that consisted of a few pieces of plywood, muddy sticks, and some corrugated metal roofing. "Yes they built me this." Despite the shabbiness of his dwelling he seemed quite content with it. He hadn't exactly been living in a mansion before. After survivor, he'd chosen to stay where they'd put him and let some relatives live in his other place. He and his wife had amassed a respectable number of years between them and preferred the proximity to the main village.

We hiked up to the third highest waterfall in the world, where Lee had killed the goat four years prior. It hadn't changed. We didn't get to kill any goats however. I presented a photo of Lee, Amanda, the goat head, the family, and myself to the family we'd killed the goat with. They still didn't speak much English and I still didn't speak any French so things were a little awkward at first. I felt that they weren't getting the coolness on my presenting them with the photo, but things soon sunk in and we exchanged sandpaper and crappy tools for an abundance of fruit. We were given a lot of fruit but we hadn't obtained any pomplamoose, giant sour grape fruits, so we headed over to the other arm of the bay where Daniel told us we could find some.

No one was home at Daniel's old house when we arrived but pomplamoose were rotting on the ground so we figured it was safe to help ourselves. We ended up practically filling the dinghy with them. "No scurvy on this passage."

Passage to Hawaii

We rounded Nuka Hiva's west side, staying clear of its wind shadow, and headed north in lively Trades. We'd come a long way since St. John and were excited to be heading somewhere we could call home for awhile.

As we made our way further north, the wind shifted and blew more from the south. We crossed the Equator, wing on wing, using the new whisker pole. We were only making three knots in a light breeze but I knew we were approaching the Inter Tropical Convergence Zone and dared not complain about three knots in a region of extremely variable winds.

I grabbed a yellow banana from the half full rack hanging from the back stay and watched as Amber's head bobbed to the music being pumped in by her earphones. Her bug bites were healing up nicely and she was mostly over her seasickness. After a few tough days the rhythm of the passage had taken seed in her. She was still subject to occasional lows but that's all part of the rhythm. She could never fully embrace the fare on Hanuman, however. She found our heavy handedness with our economy size spice jugs unsettled her stomach. While she did find her sea legs, her stomach was never fully settled. The question of whether it was because of the POF or lingering sea sickness remained an unresolved subject. The fare had been better before she'd arrived but with the dwindling supplies and the lack of affordable provisions in the Marquesas, things took a turn for the worse. The only food we had that wasn't slop was prepared by Amber, who'd brought brownie mix for my birthday and discovered that she had a knack for baking corn bread. We were even little low on rice, a condition I'd never allowed to exist on the journey up until that point. To top it off, I discovered that one of the bags of rice was infested with bugs.

I'd finally rid Hanuman of roaches but I'd also taken on a new species of free loader. I never came up with an audible name for them, instead choosing to emulate how they moved. They had a long ant-eaterish looking nose and moved almost in slow motion, waving their head and nose from side to side. When referencing them I would simply move my head slowly back and forth. They weren't nearly as bothersome as the roaches. They liked flower and rice, didn't eat much, and mostly kept out of sight.

I decided not to mention the new infestation. I did a significant a portion of the dinner cooking and figured that perhaps no one would notice. I used the infected bag first, thinking that we had to get it down before the (visualize my head moving back and forth) finished it off.

I put whatever slop I'd lovingly concocted over the rice and served it up. "What do we have here, Michael," Karl inquired. I was in the habit of coming up with inventive names for my dishes to add interest to a meal that could easy have been described as 'gruel on rice' or simply POF. "Hot Halloween curry in the cool tropics," I replied. "Nice… what-a-ya got goin' on in there." "Pumpkin, bananas, curry, and a few secrete ingredients." After the first bite, Derek smiled and nodded his head in approval, revealing a little speck of something odd in his teeth. "What's that on Derek's tooth," asked Amber. "I dare say it's a bug," I replied. "I think we may have discovered one of your secrete ingredients," commented Karl. "There may have been a couple of bugs in rice." "You didn't think to remove them," Amber inserted. "I picked out a few…but it seemed hopeless." "So there are probably more than a couple of bugs in the rice then aye," Karl chimed in grinning. "Probably."

Karl and Derek stirred their food around, hoping not to see the bugs, and continued eating. Amber started picking the bugs out but gave up and after taking few more bites and threw the rest back in the pot. "Sorry," I whimpered. Ultimately, Amber lost a few pounds while on Hanuman.

After the sun set, Karl, Derek and I would generally start feeling a bit peckish and create what we called Phoenix POF. To the plain leftover rice or pasta, we would add whatever spices moved us and perhaps a little olive oil and soy sauce and from ashes of POF, Phoenix POF was born.

Luckily the sea gave us some reprieve from the monotony of our diet. We caught a large Bonito, bloated with life. It was good to see a creature thriving in its environment. Then we killed it.

We'd left Daniel's Bay with more lemons than we could conceivably use; especially since we were out of alcohol. The idea of making ceviche had been rolling around in my head for awhile. I'd even contemplated making onion ceviche by simply squeezing a lemon over an onion and calling it a meal. Adding fish to the ceviche was a no brainer.

I started with a small experimental test batch, knowing that it would have to be eaten however it came out. Nothing gets wasted. The Bonito flesh whitened almost immediately as I squeezed the fresh lemon juice over it. It was delicious. The experimental batch was followed by a large batch which we consumed until our teeth hurt from acidic lemon juice.

The simple meal ended up being one of my greatest culinary feats of the whole trip. Even Amber was impressed.

Our heading had brought us a little east of the course I'd plotted, but given the likely direction of the Northeast Trades in the Northern Hemisphere, I initially figured that being further east would mean an easier tack up to Hawaii. Another thought entered my mind as well however. Early October was still in the potential time range for a hurricane in the Northern Hemisphere. Remembering the difference the 60 miles between Grenada and Trinidad had made, I decided to alter our course to the west, an area less likely to be hit.

Several degrees past the Equator, we drifted into the Inter Tropical Convergence Zone and Hanuman slowed to a halt. The ITCZ was supposed to be narrow at our longitude. My guidebook said, "One often sails from the Southeast Trades to the Northeast Trades without even noticing." We definitely noticed. Amber made the mistake of recalculating our arrival time based on our daily averages in the ITCZ. "We might not even make it for Halloween," she fretted. I assured her that despite the a few slow days in the Doldrums we'd make up the miles we lost when we hit the NE Trades and still average 100 miles a day, getting us there in 21 days or less.

Four days after entering the ITCZ we were bream reaching at seven and a half knots in the NE trades with our bow pointed towards the Big Island. A week later, on day 21, we rounded Ka Lea Point and made our way up the Kona Coast to Honokohau Harbor.

The Big Island

After dragging my feet for a week, I got a job tending bar and waiting tables. Amber had to pass a test to be licensed for massage in Hawaii. Unfortunately the test wasn't being offered for six months so she ended up finding a job in a health food store. After her time on Hanuman, she'd gained an even deeper appreciation for a diverse diet that was well quenched by the market. The novelty of it faded however (as did the paltry financial compensation), and despite our desire to remain together, after a couple of months she left for a massage job in Big Sky, Montana. Tragically, after two weeks in Montana, she broke her knee skiing and was laid up recovering at her mom's in Idaho for months.

After six months on the island it was time to set my sights on the Golden Gate. Karl and Derek weren't quite ready to leave Hawaii and, with Amber's knee broken, I was forced to look for new crew.

Austin had approached Amber in the natural food store and declared that she was beautiful and that he had an irresistible urge to talk to her. Such declarations would turn out to be his MO. Amber got off the subject of his irresistible urges, interjecting that she and her boyfriend had sailed to Hawaii. Austin was adaptable and the idea of sailing back to the mainland had been floating around in his head already.

"I met some guy who seems very interested in sailing back to the mainland," Amber stated, relaying Austin's story. "Sounds like a bit of a wanker," I replied. "He might be a bit of a wanker but he seems like a pretty solid guy." I was still hoping that Karl and Derek would decide to join me so I put off calling him for several months until it became clear that they weren't.

I met up with Austin briefly while I was tending bar. A face to face can't be substituted for. He seemed relaxed, flexible on his time line, capable, and I figured him to have a good temperament for the sea. Most of all he seemed keen to go. I invited him and he was in.

Nicole decided that she wouldn't be able to live a satisfied life if she wasn't on Hanuman for the final passage, solidifying her position in my mind as 'the girl who keeps coming back.'

I was content with a crew of three but a week before departure Austin called and said he had a friend who wanted to go as well. I had mixed emotions about taking a fourth but decided it couldn't hurt to have a spare crew member and gave her a call. Plus, four people would ease the watch burden.

I got Sheala's voice mail the first time I called her. Something about "…aloha, peace and love." I could almost smell the patchouli over the phone. But I was down with earthy. I considered it simply an affectation of one's need for connection with something, and in my mind said little about who a person was. I did worry that she might be more enamored by the idea of sailing that the actuality. After talking on the phone I decided it a good idea to meet up before inviting her.

Sheala arrived on the dock with a guitar in her hand and a head full of partially formed, matted looking, dread locks.

She smiled a lot and began or ended most sentences with, "oh my goddess". Her head appeared huge with all of her hair which, upon closer inspection, had various herbs and shells mixed in with it. She had a large round face, framed on top by a conspicuous unibrow and wore what resembled a burlap sack. It looked like it had been a while since she'd been off the commune.

She navigated the plank, managing to get on the boat without falling in water. I took it as a good sign and decided she was in.

Kawaihae

We pulled out of Honokohau Harbor heavily laden with food. While provisioning I recalled our last, very lean passage and tried to convey the importance of not running out of food. Some people aren't able to fully fathom what a month's worth of food, plus extra, "in case we lose the mast and have to paddle," looks like. We left Costco mostly content but with the notion that we needed just a few more things…some tooth paste, maybe some more AA batteries.

Sheala was in charge of 'a few more things' but arrived the night before departure with a whole car full of mostly unrecognizable items. It looked like she'd just run through the commune with a machete and a sack. My cousin, Kelli, happened to be in Hawaii on vacation at the time and was a little perplexed by some of the items Sheala had brought. "What are you guys going to do with all of those flowers," Kelli asked, when we were out for pizza. "Are you sure they weren't just herbs." "No, they were full-on flowers." I shrugged, "eat um, I guess."

The first challenge was to pass through Alenuihaha Channel separating The Big Island and Maui. Winds are

461

funneled and accelerated between the mountainous islands, frequently making the channel treacherous.

The plan was to sail the 25 miles up to Kawaihea Harbor, which is only a few miles away from the channel, and leave from there early in the morning; passing through the channel when the winds were supposed to be the lightest.

The passage to Kawaihae wasn't particularly pleasant. The winds were mellow enough but the swell that wrapped around through the channel was enough to make Sheala puke and the rest of us feel ill. The channel actually looked fairly calm from our vantage point, pulling into Kawaihea, and it probably would have been a decent time to pass through it. But given the puking and the fact that I was sincerely looking forward to dropping anchor and having a good night's sleep after the previous night's over indulgence with my cousin, I decided to pull in. There were also a few small last minute items I wanted to attend to on Hanuman before putting to sea.

We spent a full day in Kawaihea, settling into Hanuman. We pulled anchor the following morning before sunrise and headed toward the pass. The forecast called for twenty knot winds but once we got into the channel it was blowing 30. After a gust buried Hanuman's port deck in the drink while sailing under a triple reefed main and stay sail, I decided to call it a day. "Not gonna happen today. But that was a good practice trip," I stated, throwing the helm over and releasing the preventer.

I'd hoped that perhaps the next day would be calling for better conditions but that wasn't the case. The forecasted winds were even elevated by the evening. We weren't going anywhere. We ended up pinned down in Kawaihae for two weeks.

Nicole's resolve waned and I overheard her talking to Sheala about leaving. I spoke to her, knowing that what I said could make or break the deal for her. She'd always been very wishy washy, almost getting off at every stop from Thailand to Egypt and almost not making it to Spain. She claimed to have a lot of bills due on the first of May that she had to take care of. I gave her a quizzical look, questioning such a statement as rather odd considering that she must have know about those bills before she'd left. "I'm not sure I can do it with four people on board," she stated. By four people she meant Sheala. Nicole was truck driver. Sheala walked around in the garden asking the flowers if they wanted to be in the flower essences she made. Sheala considered seaweed a vegetable. Nicole had irritable bowel syndrome. "How many cases of two minute noodles did we get captain?" Nicole asked. Two minute noodles had been a staple of past sailing ventures. They worked for Nicole. Sheala, Austin and I had done the shopping before Nicole arrived. "Well, actually, I don't think we got any." "What!?"

Sheala loved to cook but she didn't cook anything that Nicole had ever eaten. Most of her dished contain seaweed, (and we're not talking nori, sushi paper, we're talking straight up seaweed that looked like it had just been pulled out of a kelp forest and dried), various nuts, mystery whole grains, cacao nibs, coco butter, flax seed, spirulina, jicama, hemp oil, dried acai berries, and perhaps a few flowers. Nicole liked Sheala well enough but she wasn't into "all of the craziness."

Ultimately Nicole chose to stay. "You'll regret it forever if you go," I told her, matter of factly. She couldn't deny it.

The Final Leg

After invoking much patience, we had a weather window, or something close to it, and were off. I'd also discovered an anchorage that was actually in the channel. If things got bad we could stop there and still have a sense of progress.

We pulled anchor before sunrise and once again eased our way into the Alenuihaha Channel, hugging The Big Island's coast where winds were generally lighter.

We passed the bailout anchorage and I felt confident with our chances of success. Slowly the wind angle forced us away from the island and into the heart of the channel. I kept the motor running in hopes of transiting the channel quickly. It eventually became apparent that we were going to pass without get our asses kicked. I shut down Big Red, for the last time, and the passage had truly begun.

I considered the first phase of the passage, the Alenuihaha Channel, completed. It was freeing to be back in the open ocean. It was also nauseating. The Trades had been blowing with vigor for weeks and created some boat rocking swells.

In the strong winds the Aries steered like a champ, leaving the crew little to do. Sheala was mostly incapacitated and for the first couple of days, crawling up on deck only to puke. She managed a smile between vomiting sessions however and I was pleased to see that despite her obvious discomfort she didn't seem to be regretting she'd come.

Austin and Nicole were a little seasick but fell right into the watch routine without complaint. I was glad to have spare crew. There is a big difference between two hours on and four off, the watch schedule Austin, Nicole and I were married to, and the three hours on three hours off, Austin and I would have gone to had Nicole not been with us.

I broke the passage up into four parts in my head: The Alenuihaha Channel, the Trades, the Variables, and the Westerly's. The passage from Hawaii to the mainland isn't quite as straight forward as bouncing downwind from island to island in the Trades.

The Alenuihaha Channel was definitely the short-est section mileage wise but, with our two week layover in Kawaihae Harbor, turned out to demand the greatest amount of time.

Once through the channel we had about 700 nautical miles of Trade Winds. I figured the Trade Wind section would be the easiest.

The Variables to the north of the Trades are pretty much self explanatory. The winds tend to be variable: light and from all direction. The idea in the Variables was to head directly north, crossing the variable band at a right angle, until hitting the Westerlies. Most people motor through the Variables. Frequently, until they run out of fuel. We'd be substituting patients for fuel. We had tons of food and could stare down the calms.

The Westerlies, like the Variables, describe themselves if you remember that wind directions describe their origin, or where they're blowing from. The latitude of the Westerlies fluctuates, but I hoped to find them around the same latitude as San Francisco, 38N. Once in them, we'd make a right turn and head east for the final leg of the journey.

Sheala eventually found her sea legs and joined the watch rotation, giving us two hours on watch and six hours off watch, which I considered the perfect ratio.

I'd hoped 'the warm' would stay with us longer but both water and air quickly cooled. "At least all of the fruit and vegetables will keep longer," I said, trying to console mostly myself. It wasn't long before I had on all of my clothing which I removed only to empty my bowels.

The Trades we experienced had a lot of east, as opposed to the northeast I might have expected, in them and the temptation was to point the bow directly at San Francisco and take the most direct route. The odds of the Trades taking us all the way to San Francisco were slim to none, so we had to properly position ourselves for the next two sections.

After a week of 'roller coastering' north, the Trades eased, then died, and we drifted to a halt. Initially it was a relief to have Hanuman more stable for cooking, eating, and general lounging. But we soon wondered how far we would have to go to reach the Westerlies and wished the Trades had held out a tad longer. We still had several hundred miles north to go in the Variables before we could begin to hope to find the Westerlies.

Trying to busily myself with tasks that were easily accomplished in calm conditions, I decided to check the fluid levels in Big Red to make sure all would be ready when we needed her next. As the transmission's seals degraded, she tended to require frequent topping. And, after my experience in the Red Sea with the water pump, I took nothing for granted. I'd gotten close to taking the engine oil for granted however, so when I pulled the dipstick and found a creamy substance clinging to it well above the fill line, I had trouble believing what I was seeing. I wiped the dipstick on a dishtowel, shoved it back in and rechecked it; same result. "Fuuuck. That sucks." A few heads poked up to see what was disturbing the rhythm.

I wasn't too concerned with not having an engine for the passage, but I was planning on selling Hanuman when I returned and already had a long list of things to do to put Hanuman in a sellable condition without adding major engine work to it.

The fluid I pumped out of the oil pan had a greenish hue to it so I figured it was coolant rather than seawater. I estimated I'd probably blown the head gasket, which wasn't that big of a deal to replace when one was tucked away in some quite berth but next to impossible in my situation. I might have been able to fashion a temporary gasket out of some high temperature gasket sealant that I had around, but it was a procedure I'd never preformed. I wasn't anxious to give it a go in the middle of the Pacific on a pitching and rolling boat.

It occurred to me that I could also have had a crack in the engine block but that scenario seemed unlikely. In any case, all speculation was academic since all scenarios resulted in my not having a working engine for the passage home.

Recalling the engine seizing in Australia, I put a pipe wrench on the fly wheel nut and turned the engine over manually every day, hoping to prevent it from seizing. After a few days however, it became too difficult to rotate and I gave up. I hoped I could just sort it out when I got back, but the engine would never run again.

The Variables followed us as we struggled northward on what fleeting wind we could harness. Daily miles made good towards SF were minimal, especially since we were heading north and SF was to the northwest. And becoming more to the west as we slowly worked our way north.

The water and air continued to cool. The dampness that had taken seed at the foot of my bunk refused to dry in the overcast and rainy conditions.

We reached latitude 38 and still failed to feel so much as a slight breeze out of the west. We continued mostly north but I started to put a little more east in our heading; thinking we might never hit the Westerlies. I felt like we were sailing by San Francisco. We crept across 39N, 40N, and 41N, with our course becoming ever more easterly, but still without the aid of the so-called Westerlies.

Fortunately the crew was mostly fine with our slow pace. Nicole had come not to expect to motor in the light airs. The engine loss just solidified things. Though she, along with the rest of us, was definitely getting the, "it would be nice to get there," feeling.

Sheala, whose full name was Sheala Noella Rosemary Rainbow Child Gonzalas (a name she'd piece together from her given name and other names she'd decided she liked), started to wear on me a little. She dropped the lid of my pressure cooker, which I'd come to love, on the floor, breaking part of it. She grinned and shrugged her shoulders. Mistakes were easily forgiven but the stupid grin and shrug that followed really annoyed me. She dropped numerous things overboard during the course of the passage. She summed up all losses in the same manner. She was a disaster area. Her lack of body awareness countered all that I valued in seamanship. I began to think of her as an amoeba. She really didn't walk where she was going. She just fell in a direction and started crawling. While I respected keeping a low center of gravity and could forgive deficiency in coordination, I felt she made poor choices and wasn't present and conscious in her actions.

With the falling mercury, Sheala donned a pair of pants. "Yeah, I got these for fifty cents at the thrift store," she bragged. "Did you try them on," I wondered. The pants were so long that they came down past her feet by five inches, drastically hindering her ability to walk. She'd donned the pinstriped wool pants underneath her hemp burlap sack dress. The dress was ankle length with a very narrow aperture at the bottom which prevented her feet from ever being far from each other; not ideal for a wide, stable stance.

On the up side, Sheala did remain upbeat and amicable for the duration of the passage and when she wasn't breaking something I was happy to have her aboard. She also cooked almost constantly once she got over her sea sickness.

A small pod of Killer Whales broke us out of a ship wide state of oblivion that had taken root as we all stared off in separate directions. A deep whale's breath alerted us to their presents as they slowly coasted by. In their wake blew the wind that would pull us out of the variables and deliver us to the continent.

I didn't think much of the little breeze at first. It had a lot more north in it than I expected out of my Westerlies. Perhaps it had even a touch of east. The breeze built through the night and by the following morning had established itself as more than a fluke. A sense of time and distance that had been established in the Variables was shattered as we rocketed towards the mainland in a strong and frigid breeze.

"It's cold as hell. Look," I said, exhaling deeply, "you can see my breath." "Any colder than this and we'll be beating the ice off the rigging." I unearthed, and passed around, clothes I'd stowed deeply years before. They reeked of mildew and all the zippers were rusted in place but they were readily accepted. "Well…they don't smell any worse than you," Nicole noted, worming into another layer of aged fleece." "That's not saying much," I replied.

Homecoming

"Land Hoe!" Point Reyes emerged from the fog on May 18, our 27th day at sea. "I could swim from here," I thought, as I always did for some reason, once in swimming range.

Point Reyes was a little north of where I hoped to make landfall. But, with the heavy fog, I wanted to stay clear of the shipping lanes and the Farallon Islands; especially since we no longer had an engine. In addition we'd gotten pretty far north looking for the Westerlies so brushing by Point Reyes was almost inevitable.

Just past Point Reyes, as the sun burned off the fog, the wind died and we ghosted along in calm milky seas. We were stuck in a strange limbo, feeling like we were there, yet still having potentially another days worth of sailing before actually getting there.

Taking advantage of the calm conditions, Austin and I inflated the dinghy on the foredeck so that we could quickly winch it up with the stay sail halyard and drop it into the water if we needed use it to quickly tow Hanuman out of harm's way.

As the morning expired and the sun commenced its downward swing, the reliable sea breeze kicked in and we again found ourselves moving along at a respectable pace.

A shallow section of notoriously angry ocean called the Potato Patch lies just north of the Golden Gate Bridge. There is a deep channel between it and land that I thought might be tricky to navigate without a motor. The wind's direction favored the channel however, and going around would have made for a longer trip and potentially a pain in the ass. I decided to go for it.

We transited the channel flawlessly and saw the North Tower of the Golden Gate Bridge rising above the green, hilly shoreline. Rounding Point Bonita, the San Francisco Bay and the Golden Gate, in its full glory, came into view. "Better get that champagne ready. It looks like it's gonna' happen," I said to Nicole. Back in Hawaii I'd been ambivalent about the getting a bottle of champagne but Nicole had insisted. I was glad she had.

We sliced through the shipping lane to the southern half of the channel, tacked, and pointed the bow towards the bay. I wanted Hanuman sailed to perfection for the homecoming so we poled out the jib and sailed beneath the bridge wing on wing. The cork flew and the champagne was unleashed.

We dusted the bottle of champagne as the sun set behind Sausalito. "That was delicious. We should've gotten a couple of bottles," I mused. "You didn't even care about getting that one," Nicole added. "I know…foolish." The moment was intoxicating enough however.

The wind lighted as we passed Tiburon and Angel Island. Once we rounded Tiburon and darkness filled in, we were becalmed. The stars were out, it was a peaceful night, and we experienced a stillness and tranquility we hadn't felt since leaving Honokohau. Regardless of the magical serenity, I was ready to be tied to a dock. I was also a little apprehensive about how towing Hanuman down the mile or so long canal to the harbor would go.

I decided that it was time to launch the dinghy and practice towing in the forgiving openness of the bay. I motored the dinghy forward, getting the slack out of the line attached from its transom to Hanuman's bow. Once tensioned, I was surprised by how difficult it was to steer. I had to detention the line and get the dinghy properly aligned before I could apply the throttle. Despite some difficulty, I was eventually able to get things figured out and we moved along in the correct direction, if not quickly. I was happy I'd purchased the 15 horse power outboard.

After 20 minutes of towing, a breeze came up and I yelled back at the crew to unfurl the jib. Ten minutes later, the breezed stiffened and I felt Hanuman wanting to pass me. With some deft line handling we detached the dinghy while Hanuman threatened to start towing me backwards. I motored along Hanuman's port side, threw a line up to Austin, and jumped back on. I was surprised at how fast Hanuman moved. I'd never seen her from such a perspective and hadn't expected that I would need to have the dinghy on a plane to keep up.

With the dinghy tied off and skipping along behind, we spend toward the channel that led to the canal. The channel could be tricky in the best of circumstances. Two red lead lights on land had to be aligned to let us know we were in the channel. On one of a handful of practice sails Matt had drifted into the mud when we were returning to the harbor, forcing us to spend the night waiting for the tide to rescue us. It was a position I didn't want to be in so close to home.

Rounding into the channel, we were forced to harden up the sails and come to within a degree of Hanuman's windward capabilities. It was lucky that we were still able to sail. Trying to tow Hanuman upwind into the canal may have been impossible.

473

I transited the channel with my breath held, making constant micro adjustments to the sails and hoping the wind wouldn't shift to our disadvantage. Despite the tension, all went well and, after a quick transit through the channel, we found ourselves at the mouth of the canal, where the wind died completely. The wind's disappearance was welcome. It allowed me to get situated in the dinghy without Hanuman blowing into the nearby land.

The canal was tranquil and quiet, save the low grumble of Excalibur, the outboard. I enjoyed the slow tow through the familiar, yet somehow foreign, neighborhood. I experienced all that had become so pedestrian to me when I'd lived there, as somehow exotic. It was the first time I'd arrived somewhere I'd been before and the familiarity felt foreign.

Everyone had their roles, Nicole had earned her place at the helm, for the final two turns into the harbor, which they played to perfection, and Hanuman was lovingly and gently tied to the dock at 11 pm.

There were no streamers, no fireworks, no news teams. The dark harbor was wrapped in the soothing silence of the night. The sole movement came from the boardwalk above. A tangle of blonde hair fluttered in the glow of a solitary light as a silhouetted figure glided down the quay's weather worn ladder. Amber's bright embrace filled my salty bunk and I drifted into the subconscious with the long Pacific swell still rocking my mind gently to sleep in the stillness of the harbor.

Made in the USA
San Bernardino, CA
30 December 2013